Rebel Without a Cause

THE SUNY SERIES

HORIZONS OF CINEMA

MURRAY POMERANCE | EDITOR

Also in the series

William Rothman, *Cavell on Film*

Rebel Without a Cause

Approaches to a Maverick Masterwork

J. David Slocum, editor

State University of New York Press

Published by
State University of New York Press, Albany

Printed in the United States of America

Cover photo courtesy of Photofest.

For information, contact State University of New York Press, Albany, NY
www.sunypress.edu

Production by Marilyn P. Semerad
Marketing by Fran Keneston

Library of Congress Cataloging-in-Publication Data

Slocum, J. David (John David)
Rebel without a cause : approaches to a maverick masterwork / J. David Slocum.
p. cm. — (SUNY series, horizons of cinema)
Includes bibiographical references and index.
ISBN 0-7914-6645-0 (hardcopy : alk. paper) — ISBN 0-7914-6646-9 (pbk. : alk. paper)
1. Rebel without a cause (Motion picture) I. Title. II. Series.

PN1997.R365S66 2005
791.43'72—dc22 2005007110

10 9 8 7 6 5 4 3 2 1

It is, for some, a commonplace that scholars seek to study conflicts or anxieties in the world or in films that somehow correspond to those they have experienced in their own lives. No such imperative has motivated my editing here. With thanks for a lifetime of support and love, I am proud to dedicate this volume to my mother and father.

Contents

Acknowledgments

JUST AS THE ESSAYS COLLECTED here celebrate the continuing impact and legacies of a cinematic masterwork, the volume itself is a tribute to the commitment of a group of film scholars from around the world. Some of the authors here waited five full years to see their work in print. My heartfelt thanks to each of them for the analyses and insights they contributed and, even more, the collegial spirit they have sustained and intellectual excitement they have shared.

Other friends and colleagues have also been instrumental in shaping and realizing this project. Andy Horton was an early champion; Tom Doherty offered a ready ear and shrewd advice as the manuscript was being finalized; and, in between, individuals as diverse as Yvette Blanco, Wheeler Winston Dixon, Amy Loyd, Chris Sharrett, Jonathan Veitch, and Raeshma Razvi provided crucial forms of care and feeding. At New York University, Dean Catharine R. Stimpson was, as ever, unqualified in her support, as was the Chair of the Department of Cinema Studies, Chris Straayer, and colleagues like Cherone Slater, Israel Rodriguez, and, especially for her wonderful work on the index, Alice Fung. At State University of New York Press, James Peltz offered just the right mix of editorial encouragement and patience, and Marilyn Semerad coordinated the production process with graceful efficiency. This volume would not exist in its current form without Murray Pomerance, who, besides contributing his fine piece on performance, became a good and necessary shepherd for both the collection and its editor. My passion for *Rebel* and the films of Nicholas Ray, not to mention my more general zeal for the incisive and well-rounded cultural history of film, owes more than I can say to the exemplary scholarship and continuing personal generosity of Bob Sklar.

Thanks are due to the following for permission to include three essays in this volume: The British Film Institute for "Story into Script," by Nicholas Ray (*Sight and Sound*, Autumn 1956); The Johns Hopkins

University Press for "Nicholas Ray's *Rebel Without a Cause*," pp. 166–90 from *Narration in Light: Studies in Cinematic Point of View*, by George M. Wilson, © 1986; Media Studies Working Group for "*Heathers* and the *Rebel* Archetype," by James C. McKelly, pp. 107–14 from Murray Pomerance and John Sakeris, eds., *Pictures of a Generation on Hold: Selected Papers*, 1996.

Thanks also to Photofest, for permission to reprint 8 illustrations.

If I had one day when I didn't have to be all confused and I didn't have to feel that I was ashamed of everything. If I felt that I belonged someplace. You know?

James Dean as Jim Stark,
in *Rebel Without a Cause*

Director Nicholas Ray with Natalie Wood and James Dean on the set of *Rebel Without a Cause*. (*Courtesy of Photofest*)

Introduction

Rebel Without a Cause, Fifty Years Later

J. David Slocum

Five decades after its production and initial release, *Rebel Without a Cause* holds a singularly broad sway over the imagination of motion picture fans, critics, and scholars. An accepted cinematic masterwork, the movie retains an unusual cult status. A throwback to the studio era, it is also among the finest credits of a celebrated auteur director. A sprawling Cinemascope Technicolor feature, the action supports an intensive character study that takes place in almost theatrical terms, over roughly twenty-four hours. A breakthrough in its presentation of a social problem with specific historical roots, juvenile delinquency, the film has persistently retained its currency in succeeding years. A pointed commentary on the 1950s United States and, particularly, on the nuclear family and suburbanization, it has informed visions of adolescence and rebellion in far-flung societies. And while *Rebel* offers a potent and abstract reflection on the nature of rebellion in modern life, viewing the film released shortly after its star's untimely death at age twenty-four has always foregrounded the import of popular culture to our understanding of the world.

Rebel Without a Cause had its origins in—or, at least, took its title from—a 1944 case study of an imprisoned delinquent written by Robert Lindner in which the psychologist used hypnosis to probe his subject's proclivities toward antisocial behavior and criminality.[1] Ten years later, director Nicholas Ray produced a story outline about juvenile delinquency that Warner Bros. encouraged him to develop. Though the filmmaker claims explicitly not to have otherwise used Lindner's work, the title stuck. At least three screenwriters, with the advice of dozens of professionals who worked with troubled teenagers, as well as youthful offenders themselves, shaped the eventual production. The very tangle of voices involved in the film's preproduction enriched the eventual production but also reflected the complicated contemporary concerns over the causes and social significance of juvenile delinquency.

The "JD" problem was an uneasy one for Hollywood and the Production Code Administration charged with policing the content of its productions. It was at once of immediate interest to filmgoers, being, as the eventual trailer for *Rebel* would blare, "torn from today's headlines," and also alienating to some viewers or constituencies. While "social problem" films had arguably formed a coherent category of production since the 1930s, they characteristically relied on the careful reworking of sensitive topics such that the films presented actual social or political problems only to offer individually based moral resolutions.[2] Juvenile delinquency was made to fit this mold, in which the solution to widespread problems was constructed as local and moral, despite the anxiety-making potential of the subject's appearance on-screen and the emergent recognition of a discrete teenage audience for motion pictures.

During the 1950s, the emergence of teenage audience or market segments, and of teenage subculture, was both symptomatic of, and contributed to, sweeping changes taking place in Hollywood and U.S. society. In his standard study of the "juvenilization of the American movies in the 1950s," film historian Tom Doherty notes that the challenge for Hollywood was not only to produce stories *about* teenagers but to shift their operations so that their productions were more explicitly created *for* teenage markets increasingly understood as active and profitable.[3] Films like *The Wild One* (Laslo Benedek, 1953), *Blackboard Jungle* (Richard Brooks, 1955), and *Rock Around the Clock* (Fred Sears, 1956) not only featured stories of teenagers: they also challenged the conventional understanding that movies were to be viewed by the family—by Dad, Mom, and children together—by being marketed specifically to teenagers. That many of these films showed teenagers testing social boundaries and predominant standards for behavior (both on the motion picture screen and outside the theater) fit Hollywood's more general contemporary desire to be provocative, spectacular, and timely while also emphasizing the discrete social, emotional, and marketplace experiences of teenagers.

The concurrence of the juvenile delinquency problem and the emergence of the teenage market is indeed telling, particularly in light of popular cultural forms like movies that engaged issues of widespread social concern. It is necessary to keep in mind, though, what might be seen as the reflexive quality of these concerns. The controversies that erupted over *Rebel* and other teenpics at the time were often as much about the role of cinema as a social institution, and how it operated in representing experience to viewers, as about the specific, sociological subject of teenage delinquents. Hollywood during the year following World War II was forced to adjust to a changed society. Among the sweeping developments usually recounted in histories of the period are the breakup of Hollywood's integrated system of production, distribution, and exhibition ordered by the Supreme Court's *Paramount* antitrust case in 1949, the breakdown of the Production Code that had regulated the content of motion pictures for three decades, the proliferation of television, the suburbanization of America, and the broader consolidation of mass consumer society—with its delineated market segments and targeted advertising. Hollywood, as an industry that refracted social experience and told stories to viewers about themselves, was thus confronted by the need both to modify the stories it was creating and to resituate itself as a cultural institution. The teen market epitomized the changes occurring in society and in Hollywood itself, vexing to many, which appear more dramatically in the film's narrative of antisocial behavior and troubled families.

Premiering on October 3, 1955, *Rebel Without a Cause* appeared in the middle of a decade of profound social and economic consolidation for the twentieth-century United States and the motion picture industry that arguably provided its primary cultural expression. The film was well-received upon initial release, and would receive three Academy Award nominations (earning one for Ray for "original story"), though most critics wrestled more with the sociological issues of delinquency than with their cinematic presentation. Dean's acting was often singled out for comment, not always favorably, and particularly after his death, subsequent viewing would invite for many a fuller appreciation of both the specific social issues at play in contemporary debates about delinquents and the abstract reckoning of rebellion and marginalized individuals, notably adolescents, in modern society. That appreciation would also grow with the embrace by French writers and critics of Dean as American antihero and, especially, Ray as a maverick director and visual poet who dwelled on the nature of individuals facing hostile environments in a way that cut to the heart of life in contemporary society.

Historical Contexts

"The late James Dean, for one, was a hipster hero." That epigraph, from Caroline Bird,[4] opens Norman Mailer's seminal essay, "The White Negro," originally published in the Summer 1957 issue of *Dissent* magazine. Mailer argues that the white hipster is a "philosophical psychopath" derived from and akin to the earlier black hipster. Beyond its celebratory invocation of Dean, the essay speaks to broader concerns and, especially, anxieties about social deviance. It draws linkages between violence, criminality, and juvenile delinquency and looks to family relations and domesticity as the core of social experience.

Domesticity is a telling discourse for exploring the postwar years. The wartime home front, despite the threat of physical injury and death in distant battle, had been concerned with the emotional violence of mostly female communities. The return of men from the war, where they had enjoyed the simpler communities of the all-male combat unit, compelled changes in the gender relations that helped to constitute American society and to construct individual identities. A "crisis of masculinity" was not surprisingly a recurrent if inconsistently resolvable topic for postwar films, perhaps most recognizably in film noir but informing many other genres as well. The provocation of strong female identities was one way in which Hollywood films represented the new complexities of postwar society and, specifically, the threat and uncertainty facing returning and maturing males. Shifting discourses of masculinity and femininity alike combined to generate new narrative conflicts with ambiguous resolutions unthinkable in prewar productions.

Which is not to say that the 1950s simply represented a period of decay for conventional male and female domestic roles in society or its films. Elaine Tyler May has asserted "that postwar American society experienced a surge in family life and a reaffirmation of domesticity that rested on distinct roles for women and men."[5] One cause of the surge was the economic abundance and political stability that followed two decades of uncertainty; both the Depression and the Second World War "laid the foundation for a commitment to a stable home life, but they also opened the way for a radical restructuring of the family."[6] After the war, motivations for "restructuring" withered and the inscription of the domestic became pervasive. Hollywood films of the 1930s and 1940s had celebrated the strong and professional woman only as an alternative to the homemaker and mother. Independence for most female characters did not mix easily with depictions of home and family life. By the postwar period, representations of independent women were increasingly unsympathetic and often damning, marking a danger to the domestic society (and the authority of men).

Notwithstanding these frequent indictments of women and questions about the institutions associated with them, a more widespread anxiety had to do with the continuing plausibility of stable domestic roles determined by gender. It was unclear that many of the social norms represented by Hollywood since the mid-1930s—inequitable gender relations, the stability of the family and domestic home (especially as a core institution of the larger society), and the socially regenerative quality of violent actions—remained in a vastly changed postwar culture. The dangers of unconventional gender roles produced alienation and less clearly explicable acts of brutality that refused the resolution they had previously enjoyed. One group of Hollywood productions in particular, the melodrama, called attention to the uncertainty—and the potential for violence—of conventional gender relations.

Though graphic violence in film was not, per se, a consistently controversial issue during the immediate postwar period, its links to controversies over delinquency and sexuality are pronounced. On one level, film narratives inscribed by discourses of domesticity carried forth the emotional violence represented in wartime home front films. "The external violence in representations of the war front," to recall Dana Polan's words, "finds a parallel moral and emotional violence in narratives about the home front which read that front as a similar site for a similar story of a disruptive violence."[7] Though the war was over, narratives provided a continuation of homefront emotional violence by other means. Those eruptions of brutality, essentially connected as they were to contemporary questions of social relations, punctuate *Rebel* as well as many of Nicholas Ray's other films during the period.

As Elaine Tyler May notes, a pervasive cause of uncertainty was the "symbiotic connection" between the discourse of domesticity and Cold War culture. The emergence of the Soviet Union and, more generally, Communism as the basis for a pervasive culture of threat and fear took place rapidly during the late 1940s and early 1950s. From the activities of the House Un-American Activities Committee (HUAC) and the rabid pronouncements of Joseph McCarthy to the Korean War and the emergence of a national security state, the threat of communist subversion and conspiracy was seen as global but also quite personal, involving individual beliefs and relations. Hollywood, as an institution, was caught up in these fears when various filmmakers were targeted by the HUAC to defend their politics. On-screen, the air of paranoia is evident in both films explicitly about political beliefs, most memorably, *My Son John* (Leo McCarey, 1952), and others in which the core institutions of U.S. society and beliefs in such values as American individualism were questioned. In fact, anxieties about the Soviet Union and the atomic bomb are recognizable in productions that ostensibly focused on apolitical or at least domestic political concerns; in these terms, *Rebel* can be seen to demonstrate how discourses of domestic stability and national security were mutually reinforcing and even defining of the period.

1950s Hollywood and Melodrama

The far-reaching postwar question of reconciling changes in social standards of behavior appeared in Hollywood productions concerned with the social standing of teenagers, the gender roles of males, and the stability of the institution of the family. Every decade has its social transitions and shifting notions of deviance and normality: in the 1930s, for instance, the social emphasis refracted by Hollywood was on criminality and lawlessness as socially unacceptable behavior. Following World War II, with the consolidation of demographic and consumer trends and especially the emergence of the ideological conflict of the Cold War, U.S. society self-consciously focused on the links between the behavior of individuals as consumers, family members, or citizens and the larger integrity and security of U.S. society and way of life. Hollywood cinema was a cultural form that powerfully communicated patterns of behavior that were identifiable as "normal" or "deviant"; indeed, popular narratives often turned on the opposition between prevailing standards and individual actions and featured eventual conversions and reconciliations or final separations. "Rebellion," in this way, functioned dramatically to foreground social expectations and individuals' relations to them. Writing on the relations between the rebel and society in Nicholas Ray's films, film historian Thomas Elsaesser puts it well:

> Either they [Ray's rebels] attempt to escape from society altogether and retreat into a world of tranquility—in which they themselves are doomed, and their actions become suicidal. Or their revolt itself is an attempt to revalidate "degraded" ideals, of the social system itself, and then their reconciliation is bought at an exorbitant price. . . . These rebels try to live the explicit dreams of their society, while their very natures—or their alter egos—constantly belie any possibility of permanent reconciliation.[8]

Rather than a simplistic culture of consensus, in other words, the era and the films emerging from it participated in a complex and ongoing process of social relations in which individuals and the social standards themselves are tested and retested in postwar years. The newly populous demographic category of teenagers, for decades already a group of special concern for their vulnerability to inappropriate, immoral, or antisocial ideas, fit readily into broader sociological and popular cultural concerns about deviant behavior, its causes and remedies.

Through its entertainments, Hollywood had for decades played an important role in representing American society to itself. The film industry did so by employing various visual and storytelling approaches that had evolved over decades and could be adapted to engage various topics of concern or fascination. One of these approaches, the social problem film, sought to provide moral or personal—or, best of all, familial—resolutions to more wide-ranging social problems. In words resonant with our discussion of the 1950s, critic Michael Wood has observed that essential to this narrative process was the transmutation of contemporary concerns and the creation of a myth that "there is only one problem," namely of deviance from normalcy.[9] For teenagers, particularly delinquents, that deviance took the form of antisocial behavior. The roots of that deviance, moreover, were sought by society and especially Hollywood in carefully circumscribed places: the cause put forward, for Peter Biskind, was simply, "bad families, not bad neighborhoods."[10] The dysfunctions (to use a term popularized later) of the families in *Rebel* are thoroughgoing, allowing not only a displacement of responsibility from society to the family but also generating sympathy for the teenagers themselves. In the very structure of films about delinquency as social problem were tensions arising from how the problem being represented was constructed as social.

Shaping the tensions in social problem films and many other Hollywood productions was a mode of organizing experience and telling stories that emerged in the early nineteenth-century novel and popular theater and has remained central to popular cultural narratives in the twentieth.[11] This mode of melodrama emphasized clearly drawn conflicts built on loss, or threat of loss, of family, home, and community, a risk or threat readily transferable to the viewer's own life. Among the constitutive features often configured in different combinations in different works are pathos, emotionalism, moral polarization, and sensationalism. Pathos and emotionalism are closely linked, but also point to crucially distinct operations. "Pathos" turns on the Aristotelian notion of "pity": "a sort of pain at an evident evil of a destructive or painful kind in the case of somebody who does not deserve it, the evil being one which we might imagine to happen to ourselves."[12] It is the visceral discomfort experienced by the viewer of unjust suffering that also requires association between the two. This association emerges in part from filmmaking practices, notably the familiar format that positions a viewer as being familiar with the fictional world being represented and also as having an affinity with the suffering protagonist. Importantly, these emphases conduce to suppress the viewers' awareness of their own participation—indeed, sharing—in the production of meaning and emotion.

Yet the presentation of pathos and the resulting, often intense association between viewer and suffering protagonist are complicated in another way. It is bound up in the ideology of the experiences being represented. In fact, according to Jane Shattuc, the Hollywood melodrama involves a "dual hermeneutic" comprising both the emotional authenticity of the "good cry" and a complicity with the predominant white male ideology; the result is the production of a "bourgeois uplift story."[13] Shattuc's formulation is perhaps too schematic in its oppositional casting of positive and negative hermeneutics: when viewers cry and, especially, deem it "good," they do so both because of their humane values and culturally inscribed standards. Her insight, though, is that even the most visceral engagement with the perception of moral injustice or victimization remains closely linked to particular, ideologically inflected visions of individuals, families, and communities. Viewing Hollywood productions of the 1950s, this broader insight urges attention to the specifically American ideological underpinnings of the postwar worlds being constituted—worlds of stable domesticity, conventional family life, and tolerant community that were defined by the dramatic portrayals of individuals either being recuperated by these worlds or rebelling against them.

The critique of society evident in many productions of the 1950s is biting because it targets exactly those institutions of mass social or bourgeois life—family, home, school—meant to be uplifting, stable, and safe but that can turn out to be alienating and victimizing. Film theorist Laura Mulvey has written that, "the Hollywood narrative tends to resolve itself around marriage, as critics and theorists have frequently pointed out. . . . [T]his form of closure balances the stability of a story's opening, and both are frequently realised in the figuration of 'home' which the hero first leaves and then reconstitutes."[14] When melodramas address the institutions of home or family, in other words, they also engage Hollywood's own tendencies in portraying social conflict, closure, and resolution. A result, as in the melodramas of director Douglas Sirk such as *There's Always Tomorrow* (1956), *Written on the Wind* (1956), *All That Heaven Allows* (1955), and *Magnificent Obsession* (1954), was the critique both of romantic relations and standards of masculinity and of the artificiality of filmmaking conventions that portray them. *Rebel Without a Cause* took the provocation further by exploring the problems not of adults but of youth. A handful of earlier films had examined (for some, exploited) juvenile delinquency but these productions, such as *Youth Runs Wild* (Mark Robson, 1944) and *I Accuse My Parents* (Sam Newfield, 1945), had been low-budget efforts of smaller studios. *Rebel* was a major studio production that brought together social critique of teenage life with self-conscious attention to the role of popular cinema in portraying contemporary society.

Part of that self-consciousness, as described below, would emerge from James Dean's galvanizing use of method acting to break through conventions of Hollywood performance and to reveal what many perceived as the "authentic" pain and alienation felt by teenagers. In *Rebel* and other films made for and about teenagers, the realization that institutions like families to which instability and tensions were often displaced in the social problem film, and to which critical attention or responsibility for individual ills was shifted from society at-large, were nevertheless still defining social institutions. Compounding these tensions in the 1950s were the unprecedented challenges to popular film's preeminence as a cultural form through which social values could be contested and negotiated. Both society and cinema struggled at the time with the legacy of World War II on family life and, especially, the status of the young.

Jackie Byars claims that *Rebel Without a Cause* goes a step beyond melodramas like *The Man With the Golden Arm*: whereas the latter film "deals with rejection from and reintegration into the social and domestic order," the former "questions this order" itself.[15] The order achieves restoration only at the price of having its central conflicts and contradictions exposed. Even more, implicated in the questioning of social and domestic order is the *cinematic* order by which Hollywood had institutionalized itself as the nation's predominant storytelling and image-making apparatus. *Rebel Without a Cause* suggests not only contradictions and conflicts at the heart of the familial relations that constitute contemporary society but also the very narrative means by which society's cultural institutions organized and legitimized certain experiences.

Nicholas Ray

Raymond Nicholas Kienzle was born on August 7, 1911, in Galesville, Wisconsin, the youngest of four children and the only boy of a builder who died when the boy was fifteen. Growing up in the nearby city of La Crosse, Ray early expressed interest in literature and the theater, and he earned a college scholarship based on his proposal of a series of radio plays. He initially chose the University of Chicago, but attended only for a year before returning to the La Crosse campus of the University of Wisconsin. More familiarly, he also attended Taliesin, the artists' colony, where he studied architecture with Frank Lloyd Wright and served as a "master" in theater. Throughout these wanderings in formal education, Ray worked in theater, especially with traveling productions around the Midwest.

At twenty-one, Ray moved to New York and became associated with a number of left-leaning and even radical theater groups, including the Group Theater, the Theater of Action, and the Workers' Laboratory. Among those with whom he worked were some of the major figures in twentieth-century American drama: Elia Kazan, Lee Strasberg, Harold Clurman, Clifford Odets, John Houseman, and Joseph Losey. In the late

1930s, Ray would work for the Federal Theater Project under the sponsorship of the Works Progress Administration and traveled widely around the country, recording folk music and pursuing a love of folklore. He would continue his radio producing, becoming a notable figure in the rise of folk music around 1940. With the onset of the war and the establishment of the Voice of America, John Houseman appointed Ray to produce for radio about American folk music.

The postwar years saw Ray's initial encounters with Hollywood film, mostly thanks to former theater colleagues, alternating with returns to work on the New York stage. In 1945, he served as an assistant director for Kazan on *A Tree Grows in Brooklyn*, and in 1947, with Houseman as producer at RKO, Ray made his first feature, *Thieves Like Us*, which would be released two years later as *They Live By Night*. Ray directed eight films between 1947 and 1952, six for RKO and two for Humphrey Bogart's production company at Columbia. Of these, *Knock on Any Door* (1949) was especially well-received for its portrayal of juvenile delinquency. During these same years, the House Un-American Activities Committee (HUAC) investigated Hollywood and, especially, filmmakers like Kazan and Losey with roots in the political New York theater of the 1930s. Strangely for some, understandable to others, considering his wartime service to the Voice of America, Ray's name never appeared. By the early 1950s, Ray had established a reputation as an effective, workmanlike director that even earned him an invitation from studio owner Howard Hughes to become head of production; though Ray declined, he did contribute to a range of projects at various stages of production.

Ray's own films during this period ranged across conventional Hollywood genres but almost always revealed something of the director's individual vision and guiding concerns: the relations between individuals and cruel, unforgiving environments or authority—in particular, the status of adolescents as marginalized figures—the nature of masculinity, and violence as a defining attribute of social relations. A later critic, Dave Kehr, would offer a generally incisive observation about Ray's work when writing of *In a Lonely Place*, the 1951 portrait of obsessiveness and decay of the Hollywood dream factory: "the film's subject is the attractiveness of instability, and Ray's self-examination is both narcissistic and sharply critical, in fascinating combination."[16] To express and reinforce that thematic coherence, and corresponding to the emotional turbulence of characters and actions on the screen, his films also display a visual flair and recognizable style marked by restless camera movement and quick editing uncharacteristic for the wide-screen productions favored by the director.

Between 1954 and 1956, Ray directed six films that extended many of these concerns and demonstrated how they could be expressed through distinctive and often self-conscious revisioning of Hollywood genres and conventions. *Johnny Guitar* (1954) is a singular Western that features *female* antagonists vying for such generic objectives as property, law and order, and home and settlement, while *Bigger Than Life* (1956) showed the descent into megalomania of a small-town teacher and father who nevertheless fails in his grander schemes like sacrificing his son to escape his suburban life. It is worth emphasizing that these productions were each made with different Hollywood studios, both an indication of Ray's standing as an individual filmmaker and of the deteriorating control of the studio system over film production. It was also during this time that the championing of the director as cinematic poet and auteur by French critics, including later New Wave filmmakers like Truffaut and Godard, first appeared. In the United States, meanwhile, critics recognized the filmmaker's distinctive vision and, especially, his ability to elicit strong performance and the powerful use of wide-screen technologies to enhance the dramatic tensions of his narratives. Ray would direct another half-dozen films in as many years, still ranging broadly from the biting antiwar drama, *Bitter Victory* (1957) and the musical gangster romp of *Party Girl* (1958) to the biblical epic nearly played as Western in *King of Kings* (1961).

In 1962, Ray collapsed on the Spanish set of *55 Days at Peking*, alternately described as suffering a heartache or utter exhaustion. Whatever the precise cause of his collapse, the film, completed as it was by others, would be his last major Hollywood production. He looked forward, upon recovery, to continuing to develop and produce film projects, but, staying in Europe, found himself unable or perhaps not fully committed to filmmaking. The 1960s did witness a return to the passionate political activism that guided him in the 1930s and less able to follow through on productions. Ray claimed to be on the streets of Paris in May 1968, filming, and also shot some thirty thousand feet of film of the conspiracy trial of the Chicago Seven in 1969. A year later, rumors circulated that he would direct a reconstruction of the trial, titled "The Seditious Seven," but, like many other such rumors, they led to disappointment. Ray's renown among younger filmmakers continued to grow, however, and in the early 1970s he lectured widely at colleges and even taught filmmaking at Harpur College in Binghamton, New York. A film he made with those students, *The Gun Under My Pillow* (an allusion to Plato in *Rebel Without a Cause*), screened at Cannes in 1973. Working again in New York, Ray continued to try to develop new projects, appearing as himself in Wim Wender's *The American Friend* (1977), and then starting a new project, which became *Lightning Over Water* (1980), with Wenders. On June 16, 1979, having been withered by cancer, Ray died at age sixty-seven.

Ray's legacy turns most pointedly on his recurrent exploration of the relations between troubled or rebellious individuals and their unstable, even dangerous social or environmental settings. As a filmmaker, he underscored these narrative tensions by motivating vivid performances from his actors, themselves often cast against type, and often employed quick editing and close framings to contrast with the Technicolor and wide-screen formats popular during the 1950s. Ray practiced a self-conscious, often subversive awareness of working within Hollywood's relatively stable set of generic and institutional conventions, and production after production exhibits both dependence upon and departure from familiar filmmaking forms. Yet as critic Jonathan Rosenbaum has observed, "even within a vision as fundamentally bleak and futile as Ray's, a clear view of paradise is never entirely out of mind or definitively out of reach. This is the utopian promise of the '30s and the '60s that his work keeps alive."[17]

James Dean

James Dean was killed three days before the release of *Rebel Without a Cause* at age twenty-four. He had been born on February 8, 1931, in Marion, Indiana. Out of financial hardship, the family moved to Los Angeles five years later, but in 1939, Dean's mother died, and the boy returned to the Midwest—initially accompanying her body on a train ride back to Indiana. He was mostly raised on the farm of his aunt and uncle in Fairmount, Indiana, and, in high school, participated in basketball, debate, and drama. Graduating with honors, he left again for California, joined the father who had since remarried and was attempting to win back his son, and enrolled in the pre-law program at Santa Monica City College. Despite his father's resistance to the love of theater (as an unreliable career choice), Dean transferred to the University of Southern California, Los Angeles, to study the performing arts.

Dean appeared in one student production at UCLA, of *Macbeth*, and received mixed reviews. The performance was enough, though, to persuade one agent to represent him, and he thereafter left the university and pursued acting full-time. Dean then appeared in a number of bit parts in films and in television commercials, mostly as a fresh-faced All-American boy, and also began training in method acting from actor James Whitmore, who eventually persuaded the young man to attend the Actors Studio in New York. Borrowing money from his aunt and uncle in Indiana, Dean moved to New York in 1952. He began auditioning for roles in theater and television, studying acting, and reading widely, especially what was seen as the "culture of cool" of the day: Beat poets like Kerouac and Allen Ginsberg, and Gide, Sartre, and Camus. Dean also modeled himself as an actor after Montgomery Clift and Marlon Brando. He did receive a number of bit parts, though survived more on odd jobs like being a busboy and, according to some, a hustler.[18] Two Broadway roles, in *See the Jaguar* and, as a homosexual Arab youth in Gide's *The Immoralist*, impressed critics and led to a screen test for Elia Kazan's upcoming film version of *East of Eden.*

Dean earned the role and returned to Los Angeles in March, 1954, living on the Warner Bros. lot. His performance as the troubled son, Cal, in Steinbeck's tale of family jealousy powerfully conveyed the often tragic gap between restless youth and maturity. *East of Eden* premiered on March 9, 1955, and many reviewers singled out Dean, though, unkindly, for his derivative style. As Bosley Crowther put it bluntly in the *New York Times*, he "is a mass of histrionic gingerbread . . . all like Marlon Brando used to do. Never have we seen a performer so clearly follow another's style."[19] The shooting of Dean's second and third features would occur in short order in the spring and summer of 1955. *Rebel* was shot from late March through May of that year, and *Giant*, George Steven's epic production of Edna Ferber's novel of Texas life during the early twentieth-century transition from cattle to oil fortunes, would consume the rest of that summer. In fact, Dean had just wrapped his final scene of Stevens's film before leaving for a weekend road race on the drive that would take his life at the end of September. Both of the films would be released posthumously, *Rebel* in early October and *Giant* nearly a year later, in October 1956.

The outpouring of emotion following his death quickly transformed Dean's persona into popular cultural legend. Dean was nominated for a best supporting actor Academy Award for *Giant*, but beyond the quality of individual performances, his perceived embodiment of the rebellious, outsider roles he played was celebrated for its authenticity and power. Thousands attended his funeral in Indiana, tens of thousands of fan letters continued to arrive in Hollywood throughout the later 1950s, and fan clubs grew around the country and world. A documentary, *The James Dean Story* (codirected by Robert Altman), was released in 1957 and proclaimed its eponymous hero as "the First American Teenager." Writing in these expansive and celebratory terms about *Rebel*, Graham McCann claims that the film's theme is nothing less than

> the evolution of a new generation. The process is mythic (it takes place in a single day) and the young generation grows up at night (it is a night journey). The characters depict the biological, sexual and moral shifts of adolescence, the changes from child into adult. Jim Stark is the loner spirit of the adolescent retreat that reinterprets its

> isolation as a function of the world's defects. Everything around him seems "phoney."[20]

As enacted and personified by Dean, who employed method acting techniques unconventional for Hollywood to convey alienation and genuine feeling, the story of adolescent striving to strip away society's artifice could be viewed as having an "authentic" core. That relationship between story, actor, and historical moment retains its power as a statement about more timeless oppositions both between generations and between the genuineness of individuals clashing with the constraints imposed by society and its institutions.

Rebel: Production and Release

Warner Bros. had purchased the rights to Lindner's book in 1946. The case study documented the violent life of Harold, who had started a life of crime at the age of twelve. In it, Lindner defined the rebel as "a religious disobeyer of prevailing codes and standards . . . an agitator without a slogan . . . a revolutionary without a program."[21] When Ray wrote "The Blind Run," a seventeen-page original story idea, and submitted it to Warners in September 1954, they suggested the director adapt Lindner's case study.[22] Ray demurred, claiming the case of Harold was "too abnormal" and expressing his desire to make the project about "normal delinquents."[23] By the time shooting began on the film six months later, the director had eliminated everything but the title from Lindner's study, and declined even to use Lindner, who had volunteered to help with the movie, as a consultant.[24]

Ray later recounted that " 'The Blind Run' was an original idea for a film without a dramatic structure but with a point of view."[25] Initially composed of a series of vignettes, Ray proposed three possible lines of development for a plot involving three characters: Jim or Jimmy, Eve, and the Professor (who became Plato).[26] Ray wanted to work with Clifford Odets on the script but Warners assigned another of its top screenwriters, Leon Uris, to the project. With Uris and producer David Weisbart, Ray set out to do firsthand and on-site research in order to transform his story idea about juvenile delinquents into a screenplay.[27] They met and corresponded with judges, probation officers, criminologists, child analysts, and the California Youth Authority. The director also spoke to young offenders themselves: "What they felt, when asked about their families, was a bitter isolation and resentment. All told similar stories—divorced parents, parents who could not guide or understand, who were indifferent or simply 'criticized,' parents who needed a scapegoat in the family."[28]

The "normality" of delinquency, or at least of the social pressures within families to produce normal children and relations, consistently impressed Ray and shaped his thinking.

Uris produced a screenplay adaptation of the story idea, though it ended up being entirely unused. Ray then selected another Warners scriptwriter, Irving Shulman, who had impeccable credentials for the project: he had penned an early novel about "wayward youth," *The Amboy Dukes*, in 1946, which was adapted for the screen as *City Across the River* (Maxwell Shane, 1949).[29] Shulman produced a 164-page script that, almost immediately upon submission, he requested and received permission from Warners to reproduce as a novel, which appeared in 1956 as *Children of the Dark*.[30] It would also serve as the basis for Ray's and Weisbart's continued revision, as well as screenwriter Stewart Stern's further reworking (he saw the film as "a modern day *Peter Pan*: three kids inventing a world of their own"[31]). Stern's final effort, the shooting script, was dated March 26, 1955.

Despite such professional input about the problems of juvenile delinquency, the film suffered problems in production for its controversial central subject. As historian Jerold Simmons has shown, the Production Code Administration, and PCA chief Geoffrey Shurlock in particular, was preoccupied by films about delinquents, scandalous teen behavior seen as inappropriate or immoral, notably deviant sexuality, and also sought to regulate images of disrespect for authority.[32] Shortly before Warners submitted the *Rebel* script for PCA review in late March 1955, the *Saturday Evening Post* had inflamed public (and Hollywood institutional) fears about juvenile delinquency in a five-part series entitled "The Shame of America."[33] Following two routine script conferences between Warners and the PCA, the list of problems remaining numbered nineteen and addressed such issues as images of girls smoking outside the high school, the possible reading of homosexuality into Plato's relationship with Jim, and Judy's rebelliousness. In the dinner scene between Judy and her father, for example, where Judy is upset that her father will not kiss her, kisses him, and then he slaps her, Shurlock called for a more tasteful handling in which family strains and violence would not be so directly highlighted. Also of special concern was the possible illicit sexual relationship between Jim and Judy—particularly as suggested by the interlude at the mansion—and the scenes of violence such as the "chickie run" and the knife fight. Focusing on the latter scene, the "blade game" between Jim and Buzz at the planetarium, Shurlock insisted that there be no implication that high school kids really fought with knives. All of these addressed the causes of the juvenile delinquencies of such concern to the PCA.

With the script undergoing review, Ray was busy completing the casting of the film. The director had settled on James Dean for the lead role during a December 1954 trip to New York and the two agreed, reportedly with a handshake, on the arrangement despite there being only fifteen pages of solid screenplay at that time.[34] Auditions took place early in 1955 at UCLA and elsewhere in Los Angeles and yielded Corey Allen, Nick Adams, and Dennis Hopper for secondary roles as teens. Hopper was a leading candidate for the Plato role early on, as were Jeff Silver and Billy Gray (the latter known from his role in the 1951 *The Day the Earth Stood Still*), but a meeting featuring sparkling improvisational work with Dean led the director to select Broadway actor Sal Mineo for the part. For the last key role, of Judy, Warner Bros. preferred an established young actress and fixed on Debbie Reynolds, Carroll Baker, and Natalie Wood, who, at fifteen, was already a veteran of more than twenty Hollywood productions. Though experienced and interested, Wood had never before appeared as a mature adolescent and was anxious about taking the step from her image as a child star; ironically, Ray finally settled on Wood after the young actress was involved in an automobile accident (with Dennis Hopper) and informed her of his decision when she was still in the hospital. The choices of Jim Backus and Ann Doran as Jim's parents were also unorthodox, Backus especially being chosen to play against comedic type, but Ray prevailed in both cases.

Filming began on March 30, 1955, and was scheduled to continue for thirty-six days. Only four days later, however, an important decision was made: rather than the monochrome Cinemascope in which shooting began, the film would be made in Technicolor. The reasons vary by source, from Jack Warner claiming that Technicolor was appropriate for such an important project to Cinemascope asserting that their contract with Warners required Technicolor processing. Whatever the ultimate reason, the change was made and the remainder of the shoot went mostly smoothly and according to schedule. The script and story continued to be modified slightly based on the PCA's demands, as detailed earlier, with the knife fight, smoking scenes, and teenagers' intentions to kill each being softened to accord with prevailing standards. What had been Christmas in the original script also became Easter (to decrease the number of set changes). Other concerns also arose, such as Wood's lack of familiarity and seeming comfort with the improvisational technique preferred by Dean and encouraged by Ray, but the shoot concluded well, finishing eleven days behind schedule on May 26, 1955. A further, noteworthy upshot of the production was a recognition of the sensibility shared by Ray and Dean in addressing issues of alienation and individual marginalization; after their work together on *Rebel*, Ray developed at least two projects with Dean for Dean.

Rebel Without a Cause premiered on October 3, 1955. Reviewers most often fixated on the credibility of the narrative's presentation of delinquency and fallen youth. One *Variety* critic wrote that the plot was about "... what happens to three young people who are in great need of love and understanding."[35] Another *Variety* reviewer was preoccupied that the delinquents in the film come from a middle class neighborhood. "Does the contrast between their healthy-seeming exteriors and their restlessly cruel natures occasionally strain credulity? The debate could go on long into the night with newspaper clippings and police court statistics arrayed on one side and belief in goodness on the other."[36] In *Cue*, the reviewer inquired whether the word "delinquents" should be replaced with "mixed-up kids." He went on, "Some may share their elders' restlessness and uneasiness in the shaky times in which we live—and seek in sudden excitement and 'kicks' emotional release from pressures they cannot understand, or resist."[37] Many of the contemporary critical responses thus followed from the underlying logic of the social problem film that children transform into juvenile delinquents when they are not receiving guidance and attention from their families.

Other critics linked this sociological attention to issues of performance and visual style in the film. In the *New York Times*, Bosley Crowther fixated (again) on Dean's "imitating" Brando, though also at least suggested that such a choice might accord with the actions of teens being presented. "The tendency," he wrote, is "possibly typical of the be-havior of certain youths." More than typical, as we have remarked, Dean's emotionally tortured portrayal also challenged conventions of Hollywood performance for expressing emotion in ways with which many teenage viewers would identify. Interestingly, Crowther concluded his review with another pregnant but undeveloped observation, "There is, too, a pictorial slickness about the whole thing in color and CinemaScope that battles at times with the realism in the direction of Nicholas Ray."[38] That "battle," or, at least, frequent contrast, between wide-screen Technicolor melodrama and the depiction of contemporary social problems likewise offered a formidable and self-conscious critique of Hollywood's own mode of storytelling.

French director François Truffaut would comment at the time,

> In James Dean, today's youth discovers itself. Less for the reasons usually advanced: violence, sadism, hysteria, pessimism, cruelty and filth, than for others infinitely more simple and commonplace:

> modesty of feeling, continual fantasy life, moral purity without relation to everyday morality but all the more rigorous, eternal adolescent love of tests and trails, intoxication, pride and regret at feeling "outside" society, refusal and desire to become integrated and, finally, acceptance—or refusal—of the world as it is.[39]

To extend Truffaut's remarks, moreover, we might observe that it was through youth that the shifting postwar consumer society of the 1950s discovered itself. Dean's significance and legacy emerged in part because his persona was at the nexus of concerns about social relations and the status of new standards for normal and deviant behavior.

Contents

This volume brings together chapters—all original, save two—and an account of the film's origins by the director that reassess the film's layered meanings. They examine both the complicated historical moment in which *Rebel* was made and first appeared as well as its persistent resonance for filmmakers and audiences. They track how the film continues to speak to viewers about a complex range of contemporary experiences of adolescence, family, marginalization, rebellion, mass society, and the movies themselves. While employing multiple analytical approaches and ideological perspectives, these pieces also reveal the frequently personal responses evoked by the film among contemporary viewers and critics alike.

The volume opens with a rare piece of writing by the director of *Rebel*, Nicholas Ray, of his recollections of the preproduction of the film. Originally appearing in the British journal *Sight and Sound* in 1956, this account expands on the development of the script offered previously and details of filmmakers involved in the film's production. It also lends heft to those viewers who celebrate Ray's shaping of the production and who approach the film as an auteurist vision.

Murray Pomerance's chapter examines the construction and meaning of the "chickie run" sequence of the film. He does so, methodologically, through a virtuosic analysis of performance and, particularly, the reverberating portrayal of Jim Stark by James Dean. The result is an argument that grounds, in a close reading of the filmtext itself, the passionate if often unfocused reverence for Dean's stirring role.

In " 'You want a good crack in the mouth,' " Susan White assesses the place and meaning of behaviors interpretable as violent in *Rebel* and then offers a fascinating overview of how this range relates to images in Nick Ray's other films. Her work is at once a probing inquiry into the nature of violent individual and social actions of the postwar years *and* an appreciation for the constancy and power of the filmmaker's vision. The result demonstrates how one film may be used as the basis for considering basic questions about how images of interpersonal relations often turn on social constructions of violence.

Jon Lewis develops an original reading of masculinity by focusing on Jim's parents. "Growing Up Male in Jim's Mom's World" situates *Rebel*'s family drama in both cinematic and wider cultural histories, tracing the centrality of troubled mother-son relationships in "Cold War hate-mother films" from *While the City Sleeps* through *Psycho* to *The Manchurian Candidate*, and recognizing how unusual and meaningful Ray's film is for including a father in the relationship.

Drawn from his provocative study of point of view in cinematic storytelling, *Narration in Light*, the contribution by George Wilson reprinted here argues that *Rebel* is a "social problem" film. An insightful reading of the film as historical document, Wilson's piece also assesses how Hollywood reworked the depiction of social problems such that they would both be adapted to repetitive (for viewers, recognizable and dependable) popular narrative forms and yet remain a cause for controversy and scandal.

In "Jim Stark's 'Barbaric Yawp,' " Jon Mitchell explores the "Cold War crisis of masculinity" enacted in the film and, conspicuously, the characters of Jim, his father, and Plato. Employing cultural and gender studies to illuminate identity politics in the film, Mitchell probes links between social panics over juvenile delinquency and concerns over the meaning of masculinity in contemporary society. In the process, he critically considers the normative roles and behaviors associated with suburban family life in the 1950s and foregrounded by Dean's Jim Stark.

Attending to another major (and related) discourse of postwar cultural history, Mick Broderick considers how *Rebel*, and the "chickie run" sequence especially, can be read as allegories for the atomic age and nuclear arms race. While historically specific, this incisive reading of the film is also an exemplary instance of how film narrative and images can be linked to social and cultural contexts—both at the time of production and later.

The next chapter focuses upon the historical reception of *Rebel* in some Western European countries where the movie was the subject of both success and controversy. Indeed, Daniel Biltereyst claims that the very focus on censorship, controversy, and "troublesome images" in the film may have been productive in studying social response to the representation of core social and ethical issues. As background, Biltereyst's essay draws a wider picture of the influence of American movies such as *Rebel Without a Cause* on Western European youth culture in the 1950s.

Elena Loizidou turns to theorist Hannah Arendt's study of revolutions to assess how issues of alienation and estrangement from the encroaching consumer and teen culture of the 1950s can be understood in terms of citizenship and political participation. In the process, her elegant meditation scrutinizes the cultural and philosophical notion of rebellion itself as a mode of action and expression in the film and beyond.

Images of rebellion would become even more pronounced and graphic in later films about youth. Yet as James C. McKelly makes clear in his piece focusing on the 1989 film, *Heathers*, the debts owed to *Rebel* by makers of films about youth hostility and the social anxiety surrounding them are complex and unmistakable.

Timothy Shary's contribution assesses more broadly the extensive and continuing legacy of Dean's portrayal of teen rebellion and alienation in Hollywood films of the last five decades. In particular, he is interested in the characterization of the figure of the youthful rebel at the heart of many of these films and, he goes on, the understanding of youth widely propagated by these popular cultural productions.

The final chapter, by Claudia Springer, considers the cross-cultural reach of *Rebel* by considering how the iconic figure of James Dean's rebel and broader, Hollywood-inspired ideas about adolescence and rebellion circulate globally. Looking closely the 1973 Senegalese film, *Touki-Bouki*, and the 1995 French production, *La Haine*, she proposes that the "rebel film" is a far-reaching popular cultural form that both relies upon its early, notably American, formulation and is importantly adaptive to local contexts and conditions.

The reflexivity Springer identifies in later renderings of the rebel figure in productions set far away from 1950s Los Angeles can be seen to reiterate many of the same cinematic and social concerns at issue during the production and initial reception of the film. Her reading, like the other pieces gathered here, also affirms how diverse audiences—what scholars might call "multiple interpretive and viewing communities"—have continued to see *Rebel Without a Cause* as a touchstone for imagining anxieties over coming-of-age, traditional values of family and community, threats from abroad, and the provocations of mass or consumer society. Fifty years after it first appeared, the specific sources of individual and social insecurity have changed, some of the particular motivations for rebellion have shifted, and the role of cinema and its heroes in U.S. and other societies have been forever altered. What has persisted is *Rebel's* singular power both to represent rebellion in what could otherwise be seen as the everyday and to affirm the potential of cinema to be at once part of institutional culture and distinctly, authentically outside it. This volume celebrates that continuing legacy.

Notes

1. See Lindner.

2. See Roffman and Purdy.

3. Doherty (esp. 48–53).

4. Bird's epigraph is signed, " 'Born 1930: The Unlost Generation,' by Caroline Bird; *Harper's Bazaar*, Feb. 1951." See Mailer.

5. May (9).

6. May (20). To speak of "radical restructuring" is, perhaps, already to say too much. May goes on to claim that, "Even the most radical measures of the New Deal, created to alleviate hardship, failed to promote the possibility of a new family structure based on gender equality" (47).

7. Polan (76).

8. Elsaesser (15).

9. Wood (131, 135).

10. Biskind (199).

11. In this way, Ben Singer insightfully views melodrama as a "cluster concept," a term "whose meaning varies from case to case in relation to different configurations of a range of applicable features." He identifies five such constitutive features that are configured in different combinations in different works: pathos, emotionalism, moral polarization, nonclassical narrative structure, and sensationalism. Much attention to melodrama in film studies, he contends, has dwelled on the first two of these features. Singer (44).

12. Aristotle, quoted in Butcher (237).

13. Shattuc (152).

14. Mulvey (127).

15. Byars (129). The observation follows from a point made with some regularity by critics of the genre that melodramatic crises and conflicts occur within the social and domestic order. For example, Stephen Neale terms these crises and their resolutions "an in-house arrangement"; see Neale (22).

16. See Kehr.

17. See Rosenbaum.

18. See, for example, both Alexander and Spoto.

19. Crowther (March 10, 1955).

20. McCann (148).

21. Lindner (2).

22. Some have questioned Ray's "original story idea" credit, claiming that Ray adapted *The Blind Run*. See, for example, Eisenschitz (229–32).

23. Eisenschitz (231, 232).

24. The director even recounted later that he had met Lindner at a cocktail party, emphasized his decision not to base the film on the case study, and declined the psychoanalyst's persistent offers to offer guidance. "The idea of filming his study of the young delinquent who related fantasies of violence under hypnosis seemed almost to obsess him. He almost begged me to do it; he offered his services as a consultant." Ray (1956, 74; reprinted as chapter 1 in this volume).

25. Ray (1956, 72).

26. Eisenschitz (233).
27. Ray (1956, 72).
28. Ray (1956, 72).
29. Shulman's preoccupation would continue, as he later penned the novelization of *West Side Story* in 1961.
30. Shulman (1956).
31. Eisenschitz (238).
32. Simmons (56–63). See also McGee and Robertson (93).
33. Clendenen and Beaser (17–19, 77–78).
34. Eisenschitz (234–38).
35. Brog (October 21, 1955).
36. Land (October 26, 1955).
37. "What Makes Juveniles Delinquent?" (October 29, 1955).
38. Crowther (October 27, 1955).
39. Truffaut, quoted in McCann (141).

Works Cited

Alexander, Paul. *Boulevard of Broken Dreams: The Life, Times, and Legend of James Dean*. New York: Viking, 1994.

Biskind, Peter. *Seeing Is Believing: How Hollywood Taught Us to Stop Worrying and Love the Fifties*. New York: Pantheon, 1983.

Brog. Review of *Rebel Without a Cause*. *Variety* (October 21, 1955).

Butcher, S. H. *Aristotle's Theory of Poetry and Fine Art* (1895), fourth ed. London: 1927.

Byars, Jackie. *All That Hollywood Allows: Re-Reading Gender in 1950s Melodrama*. Chapel Hill: University of North Carolina Press, 1992.

Clendenen, Richard and Herbert W. Beaser. "The Shame of America." *The Saturday Evening Post* (January 8, 1955).

Crowther, Bosley. Review of *East of Eden*. *The New York Times* (March 10, 1955).

———. Review of *Rebel Without a Cause*." *The New York Times* (October 27, 1955).

Doherty, Thomas. *Teenagers and Teenpics: The Juvenilization of American Movies in the 1950s*, revised and expanded ed. Philadelphia: Temple University Press, 2002.

Eisenschitz, Bernard. *Nicholas Ray: An American Journey*, trans. Tom Milne. London and Boston: Faber and Faber, 1993.

Elsaesser, Thomas. "Nicholas Ray (Part I)." *Brighton Film Review* 19 (April 1970), 15.

Kehr, Dave. "In a Lonely Place," *Chicago Reader*. http://onfilm.chireader.com/MovieCaps/I/IN/04456_IN_A_LONELY_PLACE.html [accessed June 1, 2003].

Land. Review of *Rebel Without a Cause*. *Variety* (October 26, 1955).

Lindner, Robert. *Rebel Without a Cause: The Hypnoanalysis of a Criminal Psychopath*. New York: Grune & Stratton, 1944.

Mailer, Norman. "The White Negro: Superficial Reflections on the Hipster." *Dissent* (Summer 1957).

May, Elaine Tyler. *Homeward Bound: American Families in the Cold War Era*. New York: Basic Books, 1988.

McCann, Graham. *Rebel Males: Clift, Brando, and Dean*. New Brunswick: Rutgers University Press, 1991.

McGee, Mark Thomas and R. J. Robertson. *The J.D. Films: Juvenile Delinquency in the Movies*. Jefferson, NC: McFarland, 1982.

Mulvey, Laura. " 'It will be a magnificent obsession': The Melodrama's Role in the Development of Contemporary Film Theory." In Jacky Bratton, Jim Cook, and Christine Gledhill, eds., *Melodrama: Stage, Picture, Screen*. London: BFI, 1994.

Neale, Stephen. *Genre*. London: BFI, 1980.

Polan, Dana. *Power and Paranoia: History, Narrative, and the American Cinema, 1940–1950*. New York: Columbia University Press, 1986.

Ray, Nicholas. "Story into Script." *Sight and Sound* (Autumn 1956), reprinted as ch. 1 in this volume.

Rosenbaum, Jonathan. "Nicholas Ray," Senses of Cinema; http://www.sensesofcinema.com/contents/directors/02/raynick.html [accessed June 1, 2003].

Shattuc, Jane. "Having a Good Cry over *The Color Purple*." In Jacky Bratton, Jim Cook, and Christine Gledhill, eds., *Melodrama: Stage, Picture, Screen*. London: BFI, 1994.

Shulman, Irving. *The Amboy Dukes: A Novel of Wayward Youth in Brooklyn*. New York: Avon, 1946.

———. *Children of the Dark*. New York: Holt, Rinehart, and Winston, 1956.

Simmons, Jerold. "The Censoring of *Rebel Without a Cause*." *Journal of Popular Film and Television* 23.2 (Summer 1995).

Singer, Ben. *Melodrama and Modernity: Early Sensational Cinema and Its Contexts*. New York: Columbia University Press, 2001.

Roffman, Peter and Jim Purdy. *The Hollywood Social Problem Film: Madness, Despair, and Politics from the Depression to the Fifties*. Bloomington: Indiana University Press, 1981.

"What Makes Juveniles Delinquent?" [Review of *Rebel Without a Cause*]. *Cue* (October 29, 1955).

Wood, Michael. *America in the Movies*. New York: Basic Books, 1975.

Nicholas Ray (center) during the shooting of *Rebel Without a Cause*. *(Courtesy of Photofest)*

1

Nicholas Ray

Story into Script

1.

THE INNOCENT PUBLIC HAS LEARNED much about writers and pro ducers from the drawing room anthropologist, who arrives in Hollywood for a short visit and a series of brisk interviews and writes a book about the place with plenty of references to primitive society and the tribal unconscious. To say anything more is, perhaps, inviting confusion. Yet, though the parallels with initiation ceremonies in Polynesia may be exhausted, personal experience has still something to tell.

I have been lucky enough, in Hollywood, to work for two outstandingly good producers. "Producer" in this sense means not the executive in charge of everything that goes on at the studio, but a member of his staff delegated to supervise scripting, casting, budgeting, and the general approach to an individual film. Leo Rosten, whose book *Hollywood—The Movie Colony* contains the best straightforward analysis of producers I

The title of *Rebel Without a Cause* came from the book by the late Robert M. Lindner, a pioneer of hypnotic therapy. Warners had acquired the rights to this book (it concerns the fantasies of a young delinquent as revealed under hypnosis), and suggested it as a subject to Nicholas Ray. His main interest lay, however, in finding "something that would dramatize the situation of 'normal' delinquents," and he instead proposed a story of his own. This was "The Blind Run," a brief story outline setting out the situation and some key incidents later used in the film. Stewart Stern was finally assigned to the screenplay, after the search for a writer described here.

know, remarks that movies are what the executives "encourage or *allow* their battery of creative talents to make of them." True enough; but this privilege ideally belongs to the director, and his task is to take it over as soon as he can in the creation of a film.

A sympathetic and imaginative producer can be enormously helpful, not only in the creative ideas he brings to a picture, but in fighting the director's battles with the "desk set" for him. He needs, of course, courage as well as imagination and this is what makes him rare. The inept or insecure producer, unfortunately, is not so rare, and his existence formed the subject of a pamphlet by the Screen Directors' Guild a few years ago. Simply through what he cannot or will not do, he may cause much damage to a picture—by creating a climate of confusion and mistrust in which the director's relationship to his writers and technical crew, as well as to the front office, is affected.

At Warners I found another good producer. Rather to my surprise, the studio offered me a choice of any of their contract producers, and I decided on David Weisbart. He was the youngest; he had two teenage children, which made me think he would bring a personal interest to the subject; and he was also an excellent worker with the celluloid strip (a rare attribute among producers). Previously he had been a film editor and had cut *A Streetcar Named Desire* for Kazan, who told me he had liked working with him, thought he and I would get along, and that Dave would be a *contributing* producer. He was.

When Dave read the outline of "The Blind Run" and listened to me talk some more about it, his first reaction was as if he had swallowed a hot potato. (Later, of course, he knew he had.) This was not surprising. To begin with, he was faced with an original story—less a story at this stage than an idea—and not the comfortable basis of an existing novel or magazine story or Broadway play. Also, the subject itself was potentially explosive.

I think he remained in a state of shock for some time. But when the story was at last taking shape and we were nearly ready to start shooting, he became passionately involved in the film. Not the least valuable thing he did for me was to accept, with patience and understanding, the two false starts over finding a writer and allow the search for the right one to continue.

2.

Finding a writer is for many reasons more difficult than finding a producer. The producer, anyway, usually finds you. There is a traditional writer-director hostility in Hollywood, and it is a unique kind of hostility.

Basically, each resents his dependence on the other. The writer needs the director for his story to be realized; the director needs the writer to give him a story in a form he can realize.

From this situation springs a good deal of misunderstanding and bitterness. The writer claims that his creative contribution is underestimated—the director and stars nearly always receive more publicity and acclaim than he, and yet hasn't he created the characters and the story, written the dialogue, and evolved the structure?

If the writer's case were as simple as this, he would be the most ill-treated professional in the film industry. Unfortunately for him, it is not. First, there are perhaps a half-dozen first-rate writers in Hollywood. Most outstanding creative writers will prefer literature or the drama, to which their contribution creates no ambiguity. The famous novelists who come to Hollywood and write a script seldom arrive with an open mind about the new medium they are exploring, and seldom learn very much about it. Nearly all of them return with an ironic, rueful image of the monstrous director or producer. The writer, they claim, is not *understood.*

In the same way, a few writers who have attained fame and influence in Hollywood will turn to direction in order, they claim, to preserve the integrity of their scripts. This is an admirable theory but, on the whole, a deplorable practice. To bring it off requires the exceptional talent of a John Huston or a Preston Sturges at their best. There are many writer-directors whose films are unsatisfactory precisely because they overestimate the writer and underestimate the director. The writer-director is much too indulgent to the writer, reluctant to cut a word of that brilliant dialogue, a sentence of that verbose scene.

The most talented Hollywood writers are those who recognize the special nature of writing for the movies and acknowledge the creative claims of the director. ("One of the functions of the director," says Gilbert Seldes in *The Movies Come from America*, "is to save us from the writer enamoured of his own wit; another is to save us from the players enamoured of their own personality; and a third is to save us from the producers. . . .") This involves, sometimes, a difficult kind of abnegation for the writer, who is working in a medium in which the image and not the word has the final impact. "It was all in the script," a disillusioned writer will tell you. But it was never all in the script. If it were, why make the movie?

There is a revealing story told in this connection by the German director Fritz Lang. When he made his first Hollywood film, *Fury*, in 1935, he knew about thirty words of English. (This did not prevent him from working on the script.) The brilliant picture that emerged was considered too controversial and disturbing by a distinguished front-office executive. Irately he summoned Lang to his office and accused him of having changed the script. Lang replied that his lack of English made this impossible; comparing the script with the finished film, he showed that not a line of dialogue nor a situation had been changed. All the same, the executive complained, the film was entirely different from the script.

Starting from an original idea, the tendency of most writers is to make it "literary," to present situations primarily in terms of dialogue. The director has to fight against this and the result is often to make the writer accuse him of being illiterate. There may be a scene in which a writer is especially proud of his dialogue; it may be good dialogue, but what is really needed for the scene is not good dialogue but a visual conception. And the dialogue has to go. What replaces it may seem, to the writer, banal—and here another misunderstanding can arise. Someone remarked that a fundamental tenet of Stanislavsky's system is to help an actor say "What time is it?" and mean one of maybe twenty different things—"I want to leave" or "I want to stay," "I love you" or " I hate you," "I'm worried" or "I don't care," and so on. In this sense the most apparently banal line of dialogue can achieve dramatic meaning. Out of the inner moment, the state of being and the urgent need, comes the whole accent of what is said or done. Only the director is in a position to help the actor create this effect.

If writers were able to work more closely with directors from the beginning of a film's conception, the results and mutual understanding would improve. Most directors, when they start making films, are handed complete (though often impracticable) scripts a few days before shooting is due to start. Later, they still have to fight to work with a writer of their own choice. (Often the difficulty is that a studio likes to use one of its own contract writers, for obvious economic reasons.) This is a battle Hollywood directors have been fighting for twenty years, and it is not yet won.

The complaints are not all on one side. Studio executives work under the anxious pressure of having to account to their stockholders, and they can do this only by keeping up a regular supply of profitable product. An executive's first instinct is to oppose anything that will interrupt the supply or increase the budget. It is inconvenient and often wasteful to postpone a shooting date, to juggle with actors' commitments. Why can't the director get on with making the picture he has been signed to make?

Nobody sets out deliberately to make a bad picture, though a lot of people set out just to make a picture. The economics and the mechanization of the system demand it. The difficulty starts when a filmmaker's personal convictions interfere with the mechanisms of a business operated for profit. To object to the movies because they are "commercial" is idiotic; to accept that honesty and originality are necessarily "uncommercial" is impossible.

Yet good films somehow get made—and not, as some embittered humorists like us to believe, simply in spite of the front office. Producers, directors, and writers have many misunderstandings among themselves. For the front office this is merely an additional burden to bear. It has every reason never to take a risk. Yet it does, and surprisingly often. The decision that enabled a *Grapes of Wrath*, a *Citizen Kane*, or *A Place in the Sun* to be made uncompromisingly, the way their creators wanted, could not have been an easy one. And in one case at least it could not have been easy to appease the stockholders.

Production methods, then, are one factor. Another is human insecurity. In making films, creative people and businessmen and administrators have to work together. There is a hatchet of tradition to be buried. There is an intensely competitive atmosphere. Credit and fame are not only matters of personal pride but professional necessity. In the process of discarding ancient instinctive hostilities, some unexpected alliances may be formed. In the producer-director-writer triangle it is not necessarily the "artists" who form the base. To gain a point, the producer may decide to drive a wedge, and it is not difficult for him to do so; separately and secretly, writer and director may seek the producer's support in an unresolved issue.

An insecure producer tends, on principle, to keep writer and director apart—in some cases, even to the extent of refusing to allow the writer to visit the set, thereby making it virtually impossible for him to learn more about the medium.

An insecure writer always decides his first obligation is to the producer, rather than to the story or himself—except his economic self, that is, for a writer commonly assumes it is only the producer who gets him the job.

An insecure director has a wider field in which to operate. Basically he can be insecure because he doesn't know what he wants—from the writer or from the actors, from the technical crew or the cutter (and, in a few unfortunate cases, from any of them). As a result his potential victims are legion. The case has been finely put by Arthur Hopkins in his book, *Reference Point*. It is about the theatre, but the parallels are deadly and apt.

> He prays for delivery—
>
> From the director who inflicts his barbed jokes on defenseless people.
>
> From the director who suffers the tortures of the delivery room.
>
> From the hysterical director, a fugitive from the home for wayward girls.
>
> From the director who keeps actors waiting while he is prostrate with exhaustion.

> From the director who keeps actors sitting around while he tries to make up that rumpled bed—his mind.
>
> From the director who stages a big scene which he has planned for his own stellar appearance.

This makes it only too clear that we can be the most dangerous of all.

3.

"The Blind Run" was an original idea for a film, without dramatic structure but with a point of view. The problem in developing it was to create situations and dialogue that reflected this point of view. On occasion I have earned my living as a writer. For most of my films I have supplied ideas for situations or changed existing ones, and written some dialogue scenes. But I don't regard myself as a writer. (Ideally I would prefer not to write at all, being no doubt even more indulgent than a professional to the few lines I've written that have pleased me.)

Warners wanted me to use one of their contract writers, and suggested Leon Uris, whose *Battle Cry* had just made a successful film. This didn't prove he was the kind of writer I was looking for; but he was enthusiastic about the subject, seemed to share the point of view, and there was an intriguing episode in his personal history. Before becoming an established writer, he had been a distribution supervisor for a San Francisco newspaper. To the forty boys working under him, who came to him with their problems, he had acted as a father confessor.

Uris began by spending ten days as an apprentice social worker at Juvenile Hall, the detention center where all kinds of children and adolescents who have got into all kinds of trouble—from getting lost to setting fire to a house, or even murder—are held for examination and interview by social workers and psychiatrists before their cases come up in court.

We had first approached Juvenile Hall and the Juvenile Bureau of the city police department some time earlier, uncertain of the reception that might be forthcoming. Richard Brooks had told me that, through no fault of his own, he had failed to get any official cooperation on *Blackboard Jungle*. He had been advised to tell the authorities that he had no script, for fear that certain scenes would meet with objection or disapproval. This was bad advice, as the deception was discovered, the authorities were angry, and Brooks was refused even an interview and told by the police to expect no cooperation at all.

I could truthfully say, on my first visit there, that I had no script. But I knew what I wanted, and explained it frankly to Judge McKesson at Juvenile Hall, and to Dr. Coudley, chief psychiatrist there. They liked the approach and offered us everything we needed: talks with social workers and psychiatrists, admission to interviews with young delinquents and to courtrooms, going out on riot calls in a police car.

Out of all this had come confirmation of my original point of departure. In listening to these adolescents talk about their lives and their acts, two impressions always recurred. What they did had a terrifying, morose aimlessness, like the 16-year-old boy who ran his car into a group of young children "just for fun." What they felt, when asked about their families, was a bitter isolation and resentment. All told similar stories—divorced parents, parents who could not guide or understand, who were indifferent or simply "criticized," parents who needed a scapegoat in the family.

4.

Leon Uris approached his first treatment with diligence and research. As a way of feeling himself into the subject, he began by writing a short history of the imaginary small town in which the action was to be set: sketching the growth of one of those quiet "normal" communities now astonished by the number of juvenile delinquents in their midst.

The treatment itself, however, gave me the ungrateful task of explaining it was not what I wanted. One of the most difficult things for a writer is to try and follow somebody else's point of view, to create a story for an imagination not his own. On an adaptation, he can discover concrete instances of the director's attitude toward the material. On somebody else's original, he is working in the dark. It was like an eye test at the optician's—could he read the characters in my mind as he might a chart on the wall? We did not, it seemed, perceive the same characters on the chart. The search had to continue.

Of the writers available at the time, Irving Shulman seemed the likeliest. Apart from his work as a novelist and in films, he had been a high school teacher. He was also deeply interested in sports cars, which suggested a promising point of contact with Jimmy Dean.

By this time, I had seen *East of Eden*, had met Jimmy and knew he was the ideal actor for Jim Stark. It was still far from certain, although he was interested in the project, that he would play the part. One side of the difficulty was personal. Since beginning to know him a little, I had realized that, for a successful collaboration, he needed a special kind of climate. He needed reassurance, tolerance, and understanding. An important way of creating this climate was to involve him at every stage in the development of the picture. Accordingly, he met Shulman one afternoon at my home.

The result was disappointing. After a brief spurt, the talk of cars dwindled away to nothing. Suspiciously, rather menacingly, as happened when rapport was not forthcoming at a first encounter, Jimmy withdrew.

Shulman at once set about constructing a screenplay in some detail. Unlike Uris, he considered active research unnecessary and did not visit Juvenile Hall or talk to any of the people with whom I had made contact there. His talent for inventing or remembering incidents led us quickly forward, however, in some directions.

We started by discussing the school gang, and Shulman remembered a newspaper item about a "chickie run" at night on Pacific Palisades. A group of adolescents had assembled in stolen cars on the clifftop plateau. Drivers were to race each other toward the edge. The first to jump clear before the rim of the cliff, the drop to the sea, was a "chickie." On this night one of the boys failed to jump in time. The "chickie run" on the plateau replaced the original blind run through the tunnel.

We discussed Plato, the lonely boy trying to escape from his drab, indifferent family, and tried to find a more definite character for him. Although in Shulman's screenplay he became more overtly psychotic than in the final version, we arrived at a new background, a new basic situation, for him. His loneliness now came, like Jim's and Judy's, from a well-to-do home; hesitant, craving affection, filled with violent inner struggles, he lived in a large house with his neglectful, pleasure-seeking mother, and had contact with his father only from a check that arrived with a typewritten note pinned on it—*for support of son*. For some reason the front office at Warners had strong objections to this. I could only reply that for me it had an equally strong reality, as I have two sons in that situation, and it was an idea drawn only too directly from personal experience.

These were developments, but they did not reach the heart of the story. *Romeo and Juliet* has always struck me as the best play ever written about "juvenile delinquents." I wanted a *Romeo and Juliet* feeling about Jim and Judy—and their families. Out of this came a conviction about the shape of the story. "Try to follow classic form of tragedy," I noted one day, "Make sure the unities are comprehended." The main action should be compressed into one day, beginning for Jim Stark in trouble and confusion, but ending, for the first time, in something different. Another note was: "A boy wants to be a man, quick." The problem was to show, during this day, how he started to become one.

Weisbart and I also had an idea for a school scene. The students go to an astronomy class at the planetarium. Confronted with a giant replica of the sky, pinpointed planets and constellations glittering on it, they listen to a dry cosmic lecture. The voice drones on, of universality and space and the immense cycles of time, and concludes with a vision of the end of the world. Flashes of light explode across the sky. And while the other students mock or whisper, Plato suddenly shivers from an awareness of his own solitude.

Later, an idea for another scene at the planetarium occurred to me. At the climax of the story, when Plato believes that Jim, his only friend, has deserted him, I thought he should return to the deserted planetarium at night, seeking shelter under its great dome and artificial sky. It was the kind of unexpected dramatic reference I felt the story should contain; there was for me a suggestion of classical tragedy about it. Discussing the scene with Jim and with Leonard Rosenman—who, after seeing *East of Eden*, I had decided should be the composer for the film—I was encouraged that they agreed, and thought it would be one of the best scenes in the story. Shulman, however, tenaciously disagreed. He thought Plato should seek refuge in his own home.

This was a crucial point for me because it symbolized the more violent statement; the more sweepingly developed conflict that I was searching for and that Shulman seemed unable to accept. It was a gesture of anger and desperation that matched the kind of thing I had heard at Juvenile Hall.

The issue made me decide that our points of view were essentially different. In spite of the valuable things Shulman had brought to the screenplay, we were once again at a dead end.

5.

According to Robert Lindner, author of the original *Rebel Without a Cause*, we were at a dead end anyway. I met him at a cocktail party sponsored by the Hacker Foundation at the Beverly Hills Hotel. He was in Hollywood to give two lectures: "The Mutiny of Adolescence" and "Must We Conform?" There was, naturally, some tension to overcome at our first meeting. He knew I had rejected his book, though he soon made it clear he was not piqued by this—only genuinely bewildered.

His own book, he told me, contained the most searching basis possible for any film on delinquency. "You must do it this way. You must make a developmental film." In his lectures he was going to discuss the conflict between protest and conformity that faced young people today. The problem of the individual's desire to preserve himself in the face of overwhelming demands for social conformism was, he felt convinced, at the heart of the subject.

As this nervous, handsome man in his early forties (his remarkable career as a criminal psychologist was to be abruptly ended by death a year later) talked excitedly of protest and rebellion, I could not restrain the impression that he was grappling with a delayed rebellion of his own. The idea of filming his study of the young delinquent who related fantasies of violence under hypnosis seemed almost to obsess him. He almost begged me to do it; he offered his services as consultant.

I explained that one strong reason for my not wanting to film his book was that I had already made *Knock On Any Door*, about an adolescent who drifts into crime as the result of poverty and wretched upbringing, and I didn't want to repeat myself. His security, however, was unshakeable. So, in its way, was mine—though behind it lay some pressing doubts.

It was now toward the end of November. Nearly two months has passed and I was still without the script, or the writer, that I wanted. Not surprisingly, Warners was anxious to set a date for shooting to begin. As so often happens when preparations for a film do not run smoothly, the rumors had started that it would never be made. A technician at the studio, someone reported to me, had laid a bet of $250 to this effect. Dave Weisbart was having his front office troubles, and after we had started shooting, told me there had been talk of abandoning the project. On a higher level, Steve Trilling as executive producer was also having to justify his faith in an idea that, although money was being spent on it, was still no more than an idea.

I made another note: "Dave and I should be considering the new young writers as possibilities. Someone who will stay right there and work with us through the rest of the show. . . ."

2

Murray Pomerance

Stark Performance

Nicholas Ray is cinema as Bach is music.

—Jean Domarchi, "la loi du coeur"

The only child of ambitious, but also helpless, parents, Jim Stark (James Dean) is a kind of icon of modernism, having been forced to grow up in a perpetual state of motion as he is lifted out of one high school after another, transplanted from community to community, in order that his troublesome eruptions of temper and adolescent anguish do not tarnish his career options (or his father's).[1] Settled now in a middle-class district of Los Angeles, and being at heart a sociable young man of high ethical standing and pleasant personality whose goal is to fit in, Jim finds yet one more adolescent community he can join or hover outside, Dawson High.[2] The nocturnal (and, for Bosley Crowther, "shocking"[3]) "chickie run" we see early on in Nicholas Ray's *Rebel Without a Cause* is at once Jim's *rite de passage* and his social debut, then, a test but also a celebration of possibilities, determined in its form by the prevailing forces in the local gang and made urgent partly by Jim's fervent desire to be accepted by others once and for all as something other than a chicken and partly by the fact that Judy (Natalie Wood), a pretty girl who has caught his eye, will surely be there to watch.[4] In the run, Jim and Buzz Gunderson (Corey Allen) will race in souped-up, stolen jalopies toward the edge of the Millertown bluff. Whoever jumps from his vehicle first is the "chicken." Ultimately, this is a film in which only adults can be chickens. Buzz and Jim speed forward on Judy's ecstatic signal, their headlights cracking through the night, but as Buzz's sleeve is caught on his door handle so that he cannot get out and Jim self-ejects at the last possible moment, Buzz plunges over the cliff to his death on the rocks below. "Where's Buzz?" giggles Jim, picking himself up from the dirt and trying to get oriented. "Buzz's down there," one of the boys stammers. "Down there is Buzz."

I would like to examine the "chickie run" sequence as a kind of organic dramaturgical node in which all of the themes and plotlines of this remarkable film are knotted. While it is certainly possible to discuss *Rebel* as being a " 'sincere' social document" that fosters the social archetype of the "outsider" or "delinquent";[5] a treatment of eroticism, homophilia, and the fantasy family;[6] a sociology of deviance and the prevailing systems of social control;[7] a depiction of "mannered anomie,"[8] or a map of family dynamics;[9] not to mention the likely analyses of Ray's storytelling technique and the myriad possible interpretations of Dean's iconic characterization; nevertheless what intrigues me here are some aspects of the structural relationship between acting and performance—in social life and onscreen—and the ways in which the diegetic concerns of the characters, the extradiegetic concerns of the cast, and the metadiegetic concerns of the director are made especially tangible in a moment of profound action, drama, consequence, commencement, and termination. This is a film in which events of particularly pungent mortality are subjected to dramatization not, as is the case in historical epics or blockbuster action films, through the graphic spillage of volumes of blood by multitudes caught up in vast conflagrations but in a relatively intimate mise-en-scène that is especially notable for being up close and personal.

The quickness and vitality of what we see onscreen in *Rebel* is due to the filmmaker's particular concern to stage vivacity: his willingness (here as in his other films) to make a play of the elemental stuff of life, to "delineate the difference between *action* and *activity*."[10] As I hope to show, such an operation is very far from trivialization, and raises our attention to not only the vibrancy and vulnerability of the characters but also the alarming closeness to the surface of the actors who are portraying them. To my view, that Dean died accidentally only days before this film premiered adds not salaciousness but horrifying irony to the performance he gave in it.[11]

The "chickie run," what Jon Lewis calls "the most shocking set piece in *Rebel Without a Cause*,"[12] originally conceived for the Sepulveda Tunnel, was "virtually the only requirement" Nicholas Ray had for Stewart Stern when he hired him to write the picture.[13] Ray's "The Blind Run" in fact had been his "original idea" for a film, and while he was working it through with writer Irving Shulman (who followed Leon Uris on the project), Shulman

> remembered a newspaper item about a "chickie run" at night on Pacific Palisades. A group of adolescents had assembled in stolen cars on the clifftop plateau. Drivers were to race each other toward the edge. The first to jump clear before the rim of the cliff, the drop to the sea, was a "chickie." On this night one of the boys failed to jump in time. The "chickie run" on the plateau replaced the original blind run through the tunnel.[14]

Ray's talent for compacting a complex cluster of emotional motives in a brilliant, depictive scene is well demonstrated in this sequence; for him, *Rebel* was altogether about an oppressive, dynamic theme all of the elements of which could be drawn together in the "chickie run": "a boy wants to be a man, quick."[15]

As it proceeds to this confrontation on the Millertown bluff, the story is filled with moments that can be called tender or raw, situations and interactions built upon the direct and passionate revelation of elemental feeling, motive, logic, and politics. As a symbol, and also a case example, of such material we might consider an intriguing conversation between Jim and his father late in the afternoon of Jim's first day at Dawson High. Frank Stark (Jim Backus) is preparing to deliver a dinner tray to his wife (Ann Doran), dressed, as seems to be the custom for him in his home, not only in a frilly yellow apron straight from a Betty Crocker advertisement in the pages of *Good Housekeeping* but at the same time in his full business suit and tie. A paragon of 1950s gender identity (the businessman coexistent with the housewife who sheathes him), then, as Jim comes upon him—to ask for his advice about how to handle the chickie run challenge Buzz has presented, how to "be a man"—Frank has managed to spill the contents of the dinner on the floor and he is panicked about how, swiftly and invisibly, to clean it up. Jim has long been exasperated at his mother's demands and fastidiousness, and at his father's servility to her domineering ways. Now everything seems to swell to a

head. "Let her see it," he pleads. Ray stays on Frank's hesitation, and on Jim's pallid, desperate, glistening, querulous face. Then he cuts to an angle shot of the tray on the floor, with the dinner splattered around it. "Let her see it!" Jim repeats, as we stare at the atrocity. It is the perfect disestablishment of domestic hegemony, a violation of culinary art and etiquette, a deforming of civilization (in the precise Lévi-Straussian sense of shaped, prepared elements implicit in cuisine), while also being an apotheosis of expressivity, a pure concentration of authentic impetus, a gesture from the heart. The father, too, we suddenly know, is tired of this servitude (and of the paternal domination that ultimately engenders it, since there is guilt in his subservience to his wife). But now he must hide his resistance, mask it as does the wifely "good homemaker" he so resembles in so many homes just like this home all over the middle-class world.

Jim's behest to his father is significant too because it directs our attention to the crux of vision. "Let her *see* it." The mess of emotional truth has too long been tucked away from view. When she sees, she will fully acknowledge reality. Also, reality is not tidy but disorganized, expressive, uncontained: so this thing that will be the object of vision is what repressive social organization would call a "mess" but at the same time no threat to the eye. By being offered a glimpse of the "problem" ourselves we can see what Mrs. Stark will see if she is allowed to, and what Frank Stark will have to see her seeing, and in seeing the father stoop to clean it up, we catch sight of his own dark need to contain and masquerade the truth of his impotent brutality. Jim is living in a home where blindness is required, while he revels in seeing. Through the entire film—indeed, through Dean's brief career—there is no screen moment in which he doesn't see even more than the camera does, taking delight in what the world looks like when unadorned for presentation. His call to "Let her see it" and his posture in seeing thus signify for us an openness to the delights of viewing unmanipulated performance, suggesting that in order to be worth looking at, the world does not need to be manicured and made-up, costumed with garnishes, neatly carved and sauced. Dean was in general giving a radically new kind of performance, one based on open recollection, expression of feeling, and thought rather than upon mimicry of established templates of gestural form, posture, facial expression, vocalization, and attitude. This was no "Black Method," as Ray put it, "a phony naturalism born out of Strasberg and the limited imaginations and supplies of *audace* in the journeymen actors and actresses comprising the great majority of the profession,"[16] but a performance springing from an imagination "fresh as a new day."[17] But in *Rebel*, and in particular in this scene, Dean also models for the audience an appropriate viewer's attitude to exactly that kind of messy performance, a useful contribution since new habits of viewing were called for in order that "method" performance might make sense as stage style. The spillage, after all, is in itself a pure Deanism, something real, just as was a little blood on his cheek from a switchblade nick in one of the takes during his battle with Corey Allen at the planetarium—since the prop knives were left with tips. The spillage was real. Nothing real should be hidden, nothing real should be invoked as hidden; let them see it. "Goddamn it, Nick," he called to Ray when the director, seeing the blood, asked for a cut. "What the fuck are you doing? Can't you see this is a real moment? Don't you ever cut a scene while I'm having a real moment. That's what I'm here for."[18]

The pressure building in Jim, then, is to let everything of his sentiment and position be accessible to those with whom he interacts. In the opening sequence in the juvenile detention hall, we cut from a scene in which Judy is interrogated by a sanctimonious and solicitous youth worker (Edward Platt) to the sound of a nearby police siren and Jim, in the waiting room outside, slumped in his chair with his mouth wide open. At first glance we think Jim is playing out a game in which the siren is "coming from his mouth," that he is lip-synching to a siren outside in the street for the little audience of kids and parents in the waiting room and as a mockery of the rigid police procedure to which he must submit himself. But suddenly we realize the sound *is* coming from his mouth *as well as from outside*, that he is singing, or at least wailing, along, and that by becoming a siren he has become not only a functioning part of the police machine that has long stymied him but also a clown who undoes it all. Yet, too, as much as its contexting makes it apparent as a siren song, the wail coming out of his mouth is *no siren at all but precisely a wail*, so he is in pain and is expressing that pain directly. Let them see it. In the same sequence we learn quickly enough—since Nicholas Ray had studied architecture with Frank Lloyd Wright and knew how to sketch stresses in a few swift lines—the structural underpinnings of the overstressed Stark family: mother and father battling incessantly to shape and control the child-property in their respective images; father's mother with little regard for the wife as a social equal and the wife with no regard for her at all; the father buying the world off, a terrified appeaser, while the mother collapses in thoughtless surrender to any authority. "You're killing me!" cries Jim to them, again simply showing the direct and simple truth as openly as possible. The family is a world he must find a way to escape, and yet also an altar on which he must let his love be consumed. Before skipping off to meet Buzz at the cliffs, he grabs a kitchen knife from the dinner table and hacks off a mammoth piece of his mother's meat loaf to swallow as he goes through the door.

On his first day at school, it is plain that Jim wants nothing more than companionship. He bounces with eagerness when he sees that Judy lives next door. He tries to get with the spirit of the gang as they endure a tedious lecture in the planetarium in Griffith Park, mooing when the speaker mentions Taurus the Bull. Provoked into a switchblade fight outside, he tries to show Buzz and the others that he has skill, courage, and purpose but also that he does not want trouble, does not want to hurt anyone, and does not want to be antagonistic. His entry into the scuffle in the first place, and his eventual offer to meet Buzz "somewhere else," are motivated by his clear desire to get into the gang, all of this made explicit for us by Buzz's teasing comment, as he circles Jim with his knife outstretched, that Jim will indeed be inducted if he can cut one of Buzz's buttons and Jim then proceeding to go even further than the dare by flicking the knife right out of Buzz's hand.

I elaborate this description of the early scenes for the express purpose of showing that the chickie run is considerably more for Jim than a forced obligation. It is an event of central ethical importance, and therefore the crux of the film. The mise-en-scène of that moment is critical for us as a statement of the filmmaker's intent. And Jim's (read, Ray's) purpose here is not merely establishing his physical edge. As what Thomas Doherty called a "switchblade-brandishing menace,"[19] Jim has already demonstrated a competence that easily matches Buzz's, and so for Buzz and for the viewer, his masculinity must already be seen as unquestionable. The manhood he is having difficulty achieving, and in search for which he goes to his father for advice, has less to do with the capability to physically dominate other males—in this case, to outmatch Buzz—as with the spirit and savvy for socializing with them in terms that are not exclusively narcissistic and self-imposed. The chickie run is ultimately a kind of soirée to which he has been invited, attendance at which is a vital signal of membership. It is the perfect setting, "a dark and alienating milieu," for what Schatz labels "the efforts of a vaguely despondent male beset by postwar angst to 'find himself.' "[20] While by his flamboyance, his perceptivity, his forthrightness, and his self-choreography Jim is ostensibly, and unmistakably, one of those people initiated into what Johnny Depp has called "the mysteries of all things considered Outside,"[21] still it is a social life, a bond to other boys, that he needs and in the name of which he follows Buzz. Ray's chickie run sequence, then, is far more than a sociologically astute set piece, a dramatic tour de force, or a pretext for Jim's demonstration of his courage, skill, defiance, resilience, deviant attitude, derring-do, or willingness for self-sacrifice. It is a ticket to what he believes at the time to be a real possibility of real friendship with Gunderson, another "victim of failed bourgeois social institutions, particularly that of the family,"[22] and at the same time, of course, it opens the door to a friendship with Judy and to Plato's furtherance of friendship with him. What may eventuate from the evening's activity, if Jim can but formulate a plan for acting like a man, is the social life his parents have rigorously denied him in town after town as they keep him within their cloister of combative protection.

That the competition on the cliffs is framed entirely without hostility is worth considerable note, since the express sociability of the event gives direct indication that it is for what the boys would consider constructive purposes, rather than for what they would consider conflict, that the scene has been set. The initiation is rigorous, to be sure, but the intention is to produce a circumstance in which Jim will be added to the gang roster, the clearly implied solution to the chickie run riddle being that in the end both boys will escape from their cars but Jim will escape first and have to live with an epithet he detests. It is play, not killing, the boys have in mind. We see this demonstrated in the relative quiet of the behavior, the orderliness with which the boys follow Buzz's, then Judy's, commands to line up their vehicles, the civility with which Buzz asks Judy to give him dirt that he can rub into his hands and with which Jim mimics the request a few moments later, and Buzz's genteel—not sadistic—encouragement to Jim to rehearse opening the door and jumping. While it is a requirement of the opening of the mise-en-scène to our view that the escape maneuver be rehearsed in front of our eyes (during the race itself the necessary actions will be performed far too quickly for us to grasp, with the vital debility that we will fail to grasp the problem Buzz encounters when we see only the swift close shot of his caught wrist), still Jim can make the decision to have a rehearsal on his own, and can be cantankerous or malevolent when he does so; the civil gesture on Buzz's part is called for only by Ray's deeper intentions, which involve showing boys actually building a bond.

Nor is Dean's performance of the rehearsal ejection as it would be if Jim believed his opponent of the evening were trying to harm him. He would be secretive, diffident, unengaged, defensively private. Instead, he treats his body-in-action as yet one more natural reality that should be open to sight—"Let them see!"—by demonstrating the escape maneuver sincerely, simply, and with no reservation. While he will be racing against Buzz, because that is the regulation of the game in play, Buzz is not his enemy and both hostility and aggression are entirely out of place. While the sequence is filled with action and angle, then, it is lit and acted with a curious pacificity, an almost gracious self-possession and sociability. There is no boisterousness, only elegance and prowess. There is no frenzy, only concentration, discipline, and prayer.

In the middle of the sequence there is a curious little scene, some of the dialogue in which has provoked considerable scholarly comment as being especially revealing of the existential fundaments of 1950s urban adolescent life yet which as an integrated whole has passed virtually unseen by those who have admired this film. Its content, therefore, while apparently decorative, appears to further the story in no particular way. After Buzz has welcomed Jim and suggested and encouraged the escape rehearsal (a significant enough moment in itself, since Jim's survival of the competition turns out to depend on his having had benefit of practice), he makes a point of drawing him aside to the edge of the bluffs. As they walk together, reflectively, the camera dollies at a modest distance and the other young people drop away. Keeping his stride, and being cautious not to turn his head so that he must forwardly look Jim in the face, Buzz extends a hand and politely gives his name. Jim reciprocates. Now we cut to a crane shot peering down at the boys with their feet at the lip of the abyss, the surf far below crashing upon dark rocks. "This is the end," says Buzz. They pause in silence, in what Domarchi calls "an icy solitude much more irremediable than the infinite void of outer space."[23] And then, as we watch from up close, the lines by which the film has come to be known: "Why do you do . . . *this*?" says Jim, and Buzz answers him, "You gotta do *somethin,*' don't ya?" What is stunning in this scene is hardly the dialogue, however. Two qualities stand out distinctively. First, the speech is quiet, almost whispered; certainly intimate; *and not for anyone else's ears.* Second, Buzz has taken Jim off to a place reserved for only the two of them, not only in order to symbolically affirm to Jim that during the contest the line at the edge of the cliff is meaningful only for the two of them but also in order to create, at this critical locus, a space utterly different in kind from any other space inhabited by either boy in the film, a special limited territory. The crane shot is the director's way of affirming spatial discontinuity, the vocal technique is the actors'.

Surely here, alone with Jim and Buzz, we are backstage. There is a relaxation of stance, a characterological disrobing, in progress quite as though the "Buzz" and "Jim" we have seen until now are recognized by both boys as systematic performances now artfully put in abatement. The Buzz who introduces himself to Jim as "Buzz Gunderson" is by no means the cocky, self-promoting rooster who swerves his car around in the street before picking Judy up for school, or commands attention during the planetarium lecture, or struts on the balcony outside afterward prodding Jim's tire with his knife. Instead he is civil, even delicate in his manners; reflective, even philosophical in his demeanor; respectful, even affectionate in his regard for Jim as a professional equal. As the boys stand looking over the cliff, one comes very close to imagining Corey Allen and James Dean having a moment off-camera, as perhaps they may have done in shooting this scene. Gone, too, is the anxious Jim, the self-critical Jim, the Jim desperate to make his mark. For a moment we encounter a self-assured, tranquil, sweet boy who wants nothing more in life than to stand here with his friend in the darkness and breathe in the smell of the surf. As though to convey all this to us, we have the sound of the crashing water, the penetrating darkness, the stillness of the two bodies, the calm quiet of their voices, and the overwhelming quality of sadness that the moment must soon be transmuted to the business of putting on a performance again. Had they known one another for some time, perhaps the conversation could have continued; but they have said everything they have available to say. And it is for staging the characters Buzz and Jim that these two receive credit from their current or would-be friends, not for being the people they are (who must perforce go through life putting on characters).

In the limited analysis it receives from critics who pay no attention to the structure of this scene, Jim's question, "Why do you do . . . *this*?" is consistently taken to be a query about the purpose of chickie runs, masculinity contests, and power struggles for Buzz and his gang. There are three objections to making this the preferred reading. First, accepting Jim's question as an interrogation of gang practice distances Jim, the questioner, from the gang. It is the kind of interpretation, in short, Jim's father might make if instead of being Jim's father he were a kid dragged along to watch some Saturday night, or a critic watching this film. To read the question this way is to align Jim with his father, not with Buzz; and also to be as uncomprehending as Jim's father is about gang life. While the director is surely aware that most members of his audience are in fact bourgeois sentimentalists who may titter at Mr. Stark but who will thoroughly understand him nevertheless, still he is not adopting a bourgeois sentimental view of gangs himself and would never opt for the judgmental perspective at so critical a moment as this. Second, taking Jim as a boy who is unclear about why Buzz would initiate a chickie run takes the risk of assuming him ignorant of gang life in general. To this it can be answered, first, that he has many times before been called a chicken, and so he is fully aware of other boys' evaluative practices and able to discern that this game might be one of them; and next that nothing in his manner as he drives up to the bluff, gets out of his car, meets Plato and Judy, takes instruction from Buzz, and finally meets Buzz in private suggests that he is either unfamiliar with a scene like this or uncomfortable with it. It is not the chickie run itself that is bothering Jim, or that leads him to beg his father for advice. And I would argue it is not the chickie run itself that Jim is referring to when he asks, "Why do you do . . . *this*?"

My third objection may be the most revealing. It is that taking Jim's question as a reference to the chickie run as an exclusionary practice entirely neglects the dramatic context in which the question is posed. Jim and Buzz have lit cigarettes and are meditating at the edge of "the end." They are backstage. When the word "this" comes out of his mouth, Jim nods a little offscreen, referring by his gaze to the object of his utterance. But what is that object, if not the race? The "this" Jim refers to is the performance of macho dominance Buzz habitually gives in front of Judy and his gang, Buzz's public self, now lingering as a ghostly trace just behind them, and a reference to the theater of engagement in which all of the action of the film so far has been organized and which we have just departed for an aside the other kids cannot share. The "you" in the question—"Why do you do . . . *this?*—is the present Buzz, who has revealed himself to Jim privately backstage. When he replies, "You gotta do *somethin'*, don't ya?" Buzz is implicating Jim in the same kind of performance, his "you" being the present backstage Jim; and suggesting, further, that without performance of this kind, social life in the setting of the city and the school is unthinkable. Jim, however, does not implicate himself.

If Buzz's stance and attitude in the gang constitute a mask, they are surely accoutrements of a profession, no less than Mr. Stark's gray business suit or the juvenile detective's holstered gun that he makes a dramatic show of unfastening and slowly stowing in his desk drawer so that he can talk to Jim man-to-man. Jim Stark's ethical devotion is to an unperformed self, a liberated and also unconstructed capacity for committed response. Proscenium theater, the institutionalization of performance, is the mechanism of social repression as well as its symbol. It is constituted of a systematic and perduring commitment to denial through obscurity. Exactly as I take Jim to be questioning the relentless performance of strength and domination that Buzz gives, when it is plain Buzz is a civil boy with a graceful demeanor and a sensitive bearing, I take him to be asking as well why Buzz creates, and then retreats into, a backstage where he can make a show-behind-the-show of revealing an inner self he would never display to his other friends. It is the backstage that substantiates repression and performance, holding away from the audience's view what is real but contaminative, original but incoherent according to the terms of reference of the performance visible on the stage. If part of what is hidden behind performance is the feeling and need that motivate an actor to produce it—biography, political concern, economic conditions—part, too, is the application of technique by which the masquerade is effected. Involved here are professional knowledge of the body and the voice, adeptness at postures and posturing, precision of control of the musculature of the face, rhythm, disciplined self-consciousness, willingness to be regarded, and so on. Jim Backus affirmed that Dean

> Had studied ballet and modern dancing, and was no slouch at either. When he used to finish sparring a few rounds with [technical adviser] Mushy [Callahan], he would surprise onlookers by doing some beautifully executed leaps, glissades and *entrechats*. Under the great Marcel Marceau, he had studied pantomine. . . . [a]nd as a result, he had the greatest control over his body of any actor I have ever known.[24]

That Jim's actions at the edge of the cliff are notably less divorced from his actions in other circumstances than Buzz's are attests to his commitment to a style of performance in which very little is hidden, an "authentic" performance; Kazan might have called it natural, since according to him "Dean had no technique to speak of. He would either get

the scene right immediately, without any detailed direction—and that was ninety-five percent of the time—or he couldn't get it at all."[25] James Dean's *performance of* Jim Stark, indeed, is so masterful that for many critics Stark utterly disappears and Dean himself is attributed with the qualities one sees depicted on-screen. Because Jim Stark is so interested in "method" acting, in short, and because he seems so realistically portrayed by the actor James Dean, Dean himself is thought a "method" actor.[26] Susan Sontag so identifies him, along with Rod Steiger and Warren Beatty.[27] In truth, while he lingered around the Actors Studio, taking a few classes and affiancing himself to the idea of becoming Brando's friend even as he had become Kazan's protégé,[28] he did not stay long, sitting in the front row, "a surly mess," and once doing a self-written scene[29] for which Strasberg handed him a "scraping and slicing he couldn't sit still for"[30]; he walked, "furious with the criticism."[31] Moreover, he was a young man who affiliated most passionately not with any school or technique but with the "heightened moment."[32] In a biography of Dean no less eccentric than most, Donald Spoto quotes Nicholas Ray previous to the production of *Rebel* to the effect that Dean "could be absorbed, fascinated, attracted by things new or beautiful, but he would never surrender himself."[33] And Dean "swerved easily from morbidity to elation," Ray wrote in 1968, of a journey with him to see Jacques Tati's *Jour de Fête*:

> Unshaven, tousled, wrapped in a dyed black trench coat, glasses on the end of his nose, Jim's mood was dark as he entered the theatre. But after ten minutes he was laughing so wildly, the nearby audience complained. He ignored them, there was nothing else he could do, the spell of delight had got him. Before the film was over he had to leave, which he did in a series of leaps and hurdles through the aisle. Back on the street, he stopped at a pastry shop. Then down the sidewalk, éclair in hand, with the Grouchian walk and the inquiring, bulbous-eyed face, he turned into Tati's postman.[34]

Jim Stark's call for the spilt food to be left on the floor so that it can be seen is emblematic of what has often been labeled James Dean's honesty as a performer, his willingness to risk hiding nothing and let the eye of the viewer have complete access. "Don't act," he told Dennis Hopper, for example, "If you're smoking a cigarette, smoke it. Don't act like you're smoking it."[35] That viewer's eye will itself construct performance entirely differently than the actor does, of course, layering it in memory and thus entertaining it as mobile, a fragment subject to intertextuality and forgetting at once, as Lesley Stern points out;[36] but for the actor, in Dean's view, the performance is entirely existential and whole, the product without residue of a moment of live need.

In terms of both performance style in particular and the more general organization of social life that performance mirrors, what is typically hidden—what Dean wanted to reveal—is not only the filthy residue of the front, nor only the contradictory impulse that can belie the coherent presentation of self in which the performer is ostensibly engaged,[37] but also the capital and exploitation of capital involved in mounting the visible presentation. By capital I here refer to the whole gamut of resources an actor must use, from physique through cultural experience and education to carefully practiced techniques of movement, expression, and—as Dean learned from Kazan—emotional recall. What is backstage of the face, then, is work, and the theatrical repression in which Buzz Gunderson is involved, along with every other character in the film except, apparently, Jim Stark, is a system for camouflaging work and making the social construction of reality seem to be nothing more than what inevitably, automatically, directly, simply, naturally, and unselfconsciously occurs as an emanation of pure spirit. Often, writes one of Dean's biographers, "his preparations [for a scene] took a long time. He would go off alone and exercise, stretch out, shake his wrists, bounce up and down, kick the ground, and seem to pout. Or he'd disappear into his dressing room to meditate."[38] Jim Backus recalled that

> Before the take of any scene, he would go off by himself for five or ten minutes and think about what he had to do, to the exclusion of everything else. He returned when he felt he was enough in character to shoot the scene. . . . Jimmy would key himself up by vigorously jumping up and down, shadow boxing, or climbing up and down a fifty-foot ladder that ran to the top of the sound stage.[39]

For Stark, as for Dean, the spirit must be worked up and worked out; it is this working at expression simultaneous with expression that we see in him throughout the film.

What Jim Stark's mother would see, if his father would only cease his repressive cleanliness enough to let her, and more than the fact of the dinner spilled onto the floor, is the open display of labor required to satisfy the wants of the powerful, in this case, most evidently, Frank Stark's own failure to carry a tray properly but at the same time his own desperate (and too habitual) attempt. Since great care is taken by Ray to establish Jim's mother and grandmother as domineering women (women, indeed, who loathe one another), it is the familial power structure that is revealed in this particular mise-en-scène, and Frank's frantic race to clean up his mess is nothing other than a dutiful application toward repression of production in the name of absorption with tidy product. Normally, that is, dinner appears on her tray automatically and because the mother (passive-aggressively) wills that it should; it is a presentation on command. Surely part of what Jim Stark is fighting as he rails against his father's timidity and obsequiousness is the brutal exigency of the power behind such commands and the equally brutal expectation that anyone—his father, he himself—should be forced by fear or the force of authority to sacrifice arduously in order to meet that exigency. "Let her see it," then, means expressly, "Let her see the work she puts you to, the precise mechanism and choreography of it, and also the way you do that work, with a style of devotion, in order that it may appear that there is no work." The same can undoubtedly be said of the mother's role: exhausted from her domestic slavery, she cannot even feed herself, and Frank knows guiltily that even as she tries to dominate, nevertheless male prerogative has enslaved her. The action of secreting work, maintaining face, disguising the mechanism of performance, and in general cleaning up the mess of living life constitute together the pressures of ideology, which, for John Belton, "suppress signs of technique and technology." Addressing the technology of film (but, for me, intimating the technology of everyday life) he goes on, "The basic apparatus reflects the actions of bourgeois ideology in general, which seeks to mask its operations and to present as 'natural' that which is a product of ideology."[40] It may be argued that Mr. Stark's labor around the house in general—indeed, since he is mocking the stereotypical suburban housewife in his apron, we can adduce as well the labor of the domesticated woman—softens the jolt of the exigencies of reality by upholstering them culturally, and that his rush to clean up after himself in front of Jim's critical eyes upholsters a too-open revelation of that upholstering. On the origins of jolt-softening upholstery, actually in the nineteenth-century railroad carriage, one can usefully read Wolfgang Schivelbusch, who, beginning by quoting *The Lancet* on "a sufficient intervention of elastic materials [reducing] the movement, which in a springless railway wagon is inconceivably distressing, to a gentle swaying motion," concludes by noting that with the rise of the new industrial bourgeoisie such upholstery moves to the living room, "where there were no mechanical-industrial jolts or jerks to be counteracted. Thus the jolt to be softened was no longer physical but mental: the memory of the industrial origin of objects."[41] Repression is upholstery, ideologically hiding the industrial origin of social relations away from the awareness of those who engage in them.

Jim's father has no intention of allowing such a glimpse into his backstage as his son requires, anymore than Buzz Gunderson has intent to allow a glimpse into his. Jim's battle with his father and his battle with Buzz are one and the same battle, aimed at undoing the proscenium that keeps the backstage out of sight and opening all of production to the eye of the beholder: unwinnable. Similarly hopeless and unattainable, it would seem, is the bisexual family, a paradigm of which Ray arranges between Jim, Judy, and Plato in the deserted mansion as they hide from the vengeful gang and the cupidinous, insatiable police. Relations based on feeling and desire, on the full appreciation of the moment, rather than the fear of losing the future potentiality of power, in short, human feeling absent a plan of investment, design a social performance that must be kept from sight if sexuality is to lie properly buried in the name of the economic and military organization of kinship toward child-production, socialization, and marketable labor. To upholster and closet the homosexual implications of his gazes at Jim, Plato must seem to be infantilized as Jim and Judy's "kid"; and to upholster and closet Jim and Judy's need for one another, they must seem to be playing at the sorts of marriages their parents cannot sustain. This is the camouflage of the organic reality present to our eyes that is encapsulated in such critical appraisal as Thomas Doherty's: "Throughout, Stark and his alternative 'family' (surrogate wife Judy . . . and surrogate son Plato) lead an autonomous existence; the adult world is peripheral. Father Jim Backus has no idea what his son does outside the home, much less what his inner life is like."[42] Jim's father pauses to look at that dinner spilled on the floor, not because his gaffe has paralyzed him but because Jim's clarion call to freedom, "Let her see it!," has engaged his own imagination profoundly, just as it has engaged ours. He knows exactly what his son's inner life is like, having had one, too; but he has forsaken that life.

It is certainly easy enough to make an insensitive reading of this film as a documentary about, perhaps even a cause of, juvenile delinquency: Senator Kefauver did just this in June of 1955; as did the British viewing public, convinced by *Blackboard Jungle* and *Rebel* that "most United States children are maladjusted and often brutal delinquents"[43]; and *New York Times* reviewer Bosley Crowther, who found the picture "a violent, brutal and disturbing picture of modern teen-agers . . . young people neglected by their parents or given no understanding and moral support."[44] But such a view negates Ray's having configured the picture by presenting us with the secret tête-à-tête at the cliff, a moment that has no significance in the plot but which is of central significance in the overall vision, that has nothing of activity but a profound action. By showing the backstage as a possibility embraced by Buzz but relatively neglected by Jim, Ray brings not adolescence but performance to our attention and suggests two incompatible views as to its nature and importance. Buzz is an actor straight out of the nineteenth century. Jim's program, by contrast, if it liberates, also makes a real world impossible. "He wanted his self to be naked,"[45] Nick Ray wrote of either Dean or Stark, we will never really know which. But with a naked self, which everyone can see, with absolutely nothing hidden, the focused attention and selective disattention that make the escape of storytelling possible, the framing and bounding that make objects possible and therefore that define property and place, and the darkness against which it is possible for us to see light and be seduced or deluded, all dissolve in the entropy of experience. For his part, Jim Stark would never have drawn Buzz Gunderson aside to the edge of the cliff for a private cigarette—"Let her see it!" The wonder of *Rebel Without a Cause* is that Nicholas Ray drew the two of them off together.

Notes

1. "James Dean is a moving target (as Jim Stark and as an actor), dodging clichés like bullets. Part of the suspense of the film comes from watching Jimmy weave through the labyrinth of stereotypes that—as in some carnival game—are thrown in his path," writes David Dalton. Dalton and Cayen (96).

2. If, that is, he can find it. His first encounter with the local gang is a playful one in which they snidely misdirect him to the nonexistent intersection of "University and 10th."

3. Crowther (October 27, 1955, 28).

4. According to Hyams, Fay Nuell in fact stood in for Wood in the action shots. Rod Amateau doubled Dean (see Hyams [208]; while Jim Backus asserts by contrast that *Rebel* "is one of the films where doubles were never used. Backus (153).

5. Hatch (486); see, for more discussion, Doherty.

6. See Alexander.

7. See Kreidl (61–70). Venable Herndon calls it a "young-man-in-terrible-trouble project" (182).

8. Lewis (20).

9. "Obsessed with his own role as a father, Ray's films are parables about the endemic American conflict between fathers and sons which he believed hid at the root of all types of social unrest." Dalton and Cayen (87).

10. Ray (1993, 60).

11. Although other writers take quite a different view. Howard Lake, for instance, sees Dean's persona resting upon "recklessness, rebellion, and nonconformity," traits which were "contributory factors in his death" and that make the death "less shocking" (61–62). Tony Williams argues that the "chicken run" in *Rebel* "gained its share of morbid notoriety due to the death of its star, James Dean, in a road accident almost immediately following the film's release" (221; Williams has his dates wrong).

12. Lewis (25).

13. Rochlin (287).

14. Ray (1956, 73).

15. Ray (1956, 73). As A. Loudermilk notes, the "chickie run" sequence also dates the film, since "teens don't do scenes from *Rebel Without a Cause* anymore,

as drunk-driving hysteria has dampened thrills like drag racing and chicken-at-the-wheel" (14).

16. Ray (1993, 59).
17. Ray (1993, 106).
18. Hyams (208).
19. Doherty (51).
20. Schatz (369).
21. Depp (70).
22. McKelly (214; reprinted as chapter 10 in this volume).
23. Domarchi (36).
24. Backus (155).
25. Quoted in Hyams (132).
26. See, for example, Golds.
27. Sontag (285).
28. See Hyams (131–32) and Ray (1993, 59).
29. Hyams (66).
30. Dalton (92).
31. Hyams (67).
32. Hyams (169).
33. Spoto (225).
34. Ray (1993, 111).
35. Hoskyns (130).
36. See Stern.
37. On performance and the presentation of self, see Goffman.
38. Hyams (133).
39. Backus, (154).
40. Weis and Belton (63).
41. Schivelbusch (122–23).
42. Doherty (107).
43. See Ronan.
44. Crowther (October 27, 1955.
45. Ray (1993, 107).

Works Cited

Alexander, Paul. *Boulevard of Broken Dreams: The Life, Times, and Legend of James Dean*. New York: Viking, 1994.

Backus, Jim. *Rocks on the Roof.* New York: G. P. Putnam's Sons, 1958.

Crowther, Bosley. Review of *Rebel Without a Cause. The New York Times* (October 27, 1955).

Dalton, David. *James Dean: The Mutant King*. San Francisco: Straight Arrow Books, 1974.

Dalton, David, and Ron Cayen. James Dean: American Icon. New York: St. Martin's Press, 1984.

Depp, Johnny. "The Night I Met Allen Ginsberg." *Rolling Stone* 816–17 (July 8–22, 1999).

Doherty, Thomas. *Teenages and Teenpics: The Juvenilization of American Movies in the 1950s*. Boston: Unwin Hyman, 1988.

Domarchi, Jean. "La loi du coeur." *Cahiers du Cinéma* 59 (May, 1956).

Goffman, Erving. *The Presentation of Self in Everyday Life*. Garden City, NY: Doubleday Anchor, 1959.

Golds, Rosey. "Humiliation and Charisma: James Dean." www.sensesofcinema.com/contents/index.html#performance.

Hatch, Robert. "Theater and Films." *The Nation* 181 (December 3, 1955).

Herndon, Venable. *James Dean: A Short Life*. Garden City: Doubleday, 1974.

Hoskyns, Barney. *James Dean: Shooting Star*. London: Bloomsbury, 1989.

Hyams, Joe, with Jay Hyams. *James Dean: Little Boy Lost*. New York: Warner Books, .

Kreidl, John Francis. *Nicholas Ray*. Boston: Twayne, 1977.

Lake, Howard. "Jump On In, You're in Safe Hands." In Mikita Brottman, ed., *Car Crash Culture*. New York: Palgrave, 2001.

Lewis, Jon. *The Road to Romance and Ruin: Teen Films and Youth Culture*. New York: Routledge, 1992.

Loudermilk, A. "Clutching Pearls: Speculations on a Twentieth-Century Suicide." In Mikita Brottman, ed., *Car Crash Culture*. New York: Palgrave, 2001.

McKelly, James C. "Youth Cinema and the Culture of Rebellion: *Heathers* and the *Rebel* Archetype." In Murray Pomerance and John Sakeris, eds., *Pictures of a Generation on Hold: Selected Papers*. Toronto: Media Studies Working Group, 1996.

Ray, Nicholas. "Story into Script." *Sight and Sound* (Autumn 1956).

———. *I Was Interrupted: Nicholas Ray on Making Movies*, ed. Susan Ray. Berkeley: University of California Press. 1993.

Rochlin, Margy. "Stewart Stern: Out of the Soul." In Patrick McGilligan, ed., *Backstory 2: Interviews with Screenwriters of the 1940s and 1950s*. Berkeley: University of California Press, 1997.

Ronan, Thomas P. "British TV Shows Everyday U.S. Life." *New York Times* (April 9, 1956). Reprinted in Gene Brown, ed., *The New York Times Encyclopedia of Film 1952–1957*. New York: Times Books, 1984.

Schatz, Thomas. *Boom and Bust: American Cinema in the 1940s*. Berkeley: University of California Press, 1999.

Schivelbusch, Wolfgang. *The Railway Journey: The Industrialization of Time and Space in the 19th Century*. Berkeley: University of California Press, 1986.

Sontag, Susan. "Notes on 'Camp.'" *Against Interpretation and Other Essays*. New York: Delta, 1964.

Spoto, Donald. *Rebel: The Life and Legend of James Dean*. New York: Harper, 1997.

Stern, Lesley. "Putting on a Show, or the Ghostliness of Gesture." www.sensesofcinema.com/index.html#performance.

Weis, Elizabeth, and John Belton, eds. *Film Sound: Theory and Practice*. New York: Columbia University Press, 1985.

Williams, Tony. "Heart Like a Wheel." In Mikita Brottman, ed., *Car Crash Culture*. New York: Palgrave, 2001.

3

SUSAN WHITE

"You want a good crack in the mouth?"

Rebel Without a Cause, Violence, and the Cinema of Nicholas Ray

NICHOLAS RAY'S FILMS ARE DEEPLY concerned with the etiology and damaging effects of violence. These films depict a broad range of violent acts inflicted upon and by individuals caught in difficult or oppressive social situations. Often these are individuals, characters, who seem to be too tightly woven in the fabric of the societies being depicted, or who are, paradoxically, situated on the social margins. Both groups are shown in Ray's films to suffer from violence inflicted by social structures themselves. Violence may be, especially for male characters, a coping mechanism internalized only to go awry. What was meant to ward off a hostile environment becomes a means of inflicting on oneself or on one's near and dear the most intimate forms of aggression. This is a tragic story told again and again in Ray's films.

Although it is occasionally brutal and overt, much of the violence described by Ray's cinema is "symbolic," as Pierre Bourdieu describes the subtle violence that resides in social structures of domination.[1] Because of this emphasis on the social origins of violence, Ray has been considered (though not always in so many words) a "liberal" filmmaker—one who did not stray far from his 1930s roots in radical theater and folk music, and who barely escaped the fate of those blacklisted during the McCarthy period.[2] (One can easily imagine many of Ray's lonely heroes as figures in folk songs.) Ray's films explore many types of violence and present the perpetrators of violence with differing degrees of sympathy and condemnation. The social context of the films—even of the numerous period pieces Ray directed—resonates distinctly with the contradictory imperatives of the post-World War II period. Men in this period were encouraged to conform to male group behaviors perceived as helping us win the war, later adapting them to the new corporate context. But there was also a powerful unease about the potential violence of returning warriors, which created pressure for men to resist the male group's often violent bonding rituals by retreating into a domestic household presented as both comforting and stifling. Often the men in Ray's films spend a lot of time on the margins between these worlds. They are at once powerless to change the social structures that oppress them and uncomfortable with the considerable power they do have and sometimes abuse. Jim Stark, for example, is trapped in a tension-filled home, but is afraid of his own potential for violent lashing out. In *On Dangerous Ground* the protagonist, a police officer, is depicted as crushed in the small space of his apartment and locked in anger toward lawbreakers. But most dangerous of all is his own tendency to use his physical power and authority as a cop to destroy the very things he wishes to protect.

The middle-class home found in *Rebel Without a Cause* is a crucial icon in Ray's films. It symbolizes, on the one hand, utopian family and the stability sought by Ray's characters. As indicated above, it is also a symbol of failure for men who have succumbed to society's demand for stasis and predictability and a potential hotbed of abusive relationships. Ray's films, therefore, sometimes sketch an Edenic vision of alternatives to the middle-class home, such as the rebellious male-led group or the young couple on the run. *Rebel* examines the permutations of all of these images of stasis and movement, of family and escape from family.

The role of women in these films is also necessarily ambiguous. The ideal stable and understanding female partner is eagerly sought by most of Ray's male protagonists. But women also function as lures drawing men into the traps that lead to stasis and finally violent rebellion against that stasis. But Ray's cinema also presents the perspective of women confronted with men who are both desirable and problematic and homes that are attractive and threatening.

As has been amply discussed in the many works on film noir written in the past two decades, women in the post-WWII period were actively pulled from the workplace into homes and domestic roles that seem to offer them the only possibility for self-affirmation. But these homes also present (in films ranging from *The Reckless Moment* [1949] to *All That Heaven Allows* [1956]) a kind of understated Gothic menace:

> [I]n the postwar moment—in the moment of Kinsey and a new fictional awareness of sex and passion—there is also a reworking of the female Gothic genre in which the menace for the woman is not that of an exoticness intruding into ordinary life but, on the contrary, of a deadeningly dull emptiness coming from the man and threatening to crush the new sensual energy of the woman.[3]

In a Lonely Place, *Bigger Than Life*, even *The Savage Innocents* and *The Lusty Men*, all construct a domestic situation in which the woman is confronted with visions of domestic bliss, shaken by the prospect of violence and betrayal, and torn by the underlying fear of estrangement, boredom, and alienation from a male partner who is almost impossible to read and is certainly beyond her control. *Rebel Without a Cause* runs the gamut of the male sense of entrapment, his anguish at being forced to conform to a certain kind of domesticity, and the hope, on the part of both men and women, that loving and egalitarian relationships can be built in the aftermath of the explosions rocking the very identities of Ray's films' protagonists.

While striking out at restrictive social forces is almost always presented as to some extent justified, Ray places familial and domestic violence, especially male violence toward women and children, under relentless, quasi-ethnographic scrutiny.[4] Few films capture as compellingly as *Bigger Than Life* (1956) the terror of living with an unpredictable and abusive husband and father, while *In a Lonely Place* (1950) is a profound—and moving—study of the role of violence in constituting mainstream masculinity. Depicted with ambivalence, as well, are violence toward animals and nature (Plato's killing of the puppies in *Rebel* [1955], the taming of rodeo beasts in *The Lusty Men* [1952], the ecological concerns of *Wind Across the Everglades* [1958]); the almost ubiquitous motif of lynching and sacrifice;[5] male-male violence (particularly prominent in *Rebel* and *In a Lonely Place*); female-female violence (*Johnny Guitar* [1954]); police and governmental violence (*They Live by Night* [1948], *On Dangerous Ground* [1951]); professional and emotional rivalry leading to violence (*Bitter Victory* [1957]); criminal versus "legitimate" violence (*The True Story of Jesse James*

[1957]), and so forth.[6] In this essay I seek to clarify the role of violence in *Rebel Without a Cause* by placing it within the context of the broader discourses represented in Ray's films as a whole.

Ray's obvious condemnation of the social role played by violence is countered by his frequent romanticizing of characters who cannot resist the urge to take recourse to it. Perhaps most compelling are those characters in Ray's films who find that their adaptation to culture has produced in them an inner violence—and a shame-inducing tendency toward brutalizing those around them—against which they, often futilely, must struggle, as in *In a Lonely Place*, *On Dangerous Ground*, *Johnny Guitar*, *Bigger Than Life*, and *Rebel Without a Cause*.[7] As indicated above, Ray's exploration of violence also transcends the immediate social sphere and takes on historical or even cosmic dimensions. Humans are placed, for example, within the context of an overwhelmingly violent universe in *Rebel Without a Cause*, as is shown most starkly in the film's first planetarium scene, in which the teens sit frozen with terror as the cosmos explodes above them. "Man," in turn, inflicts violence upon nature—a violence shown to be as meaningless as the frivolous wiping out of entire species of birds, in *Wind Across the Everglades*, in order to decorate women's hats. A sometimes grudging admiration is paid in these films to those individuals who attempt, blindly and in error, to "tame" the natural world, as well as (less grudgingly, perhaps) to those who rebel against the apparent arbitrariness of human law. It is here that Ray remains true to the Western formula as it evolved in the 1950s to critique the white man's imperialist project, while mourning the demise of the individuals who pressed it forward.

Since the late 1950s, Nicholas Ray has been regarded as the consummate Hollywood auteur. Contributing to this myth of authorship are the difficulties Ray had achieving his personal vision, insofar as he was able to articulate such a vision or critics to discern one. As anyone familiar with Ray's career well knows, his creative control over the films he directed was constrained by production circumstances of all kinds. Ray has been described, notably by the critics of the *Cahiers du Cinéma*, as making a courageous stand against the tyranny of the moribund studio system and megalomaniacal independent producers of the 1950s and early 1960s. In the writings of historians like Eisenschitz and cinephiles like Truffaut and Godard, who famously proclaimed that "Nicholas Ray is cinema," we can detect a persistent perception of Nicholas Ray as the victim of both his own genius and the constant betrayals and humiliations he experienced in Hollywood. The production histories for a number of the later films read like transcribed nightmares, as Ray loses control of various aspects of his films and suffers personal crises, including episodes of binge drinking, while the studio system itself begins to unravel. Eisenschitz's biography of Ray enumerates countless frustrations that, in the context of the rise of auteurism and the love-hate relationship of French critics with the American film industry, took on a particularly dramatic coloring.

Such formulations feed into the Foucauldian view of the "author function" as upholding the bourgeois sensibilities of art in that they reify the view of the director as the "singular and great author of the text."[8] The beleaguered middle-class white male will tend to identify with the artist-as-individual, especially in a world that demands ever-increasing enslavement to the corporation, suburbia, and consumption. Nicholas Ray has come to represent this kind of outsider *par excellence* to the generation of filmmakers and critics who came of age in the 1950s and 1960s. Ray's clashes with studio executives, his battle with alcoholism, loss of control of "his" projects, the increasing pressure to take on international super-productions such as *55 Days at Peking*, and his decisive move away from traditional narrative films in the 1970s are among the factors that pushed New German filmmaker Wim Wenders to cast Ray as the iconic visionary artist at odds with the official art/cinema world in *The American Friend* (1977). In that film Ray plays a painter who must pretend to be dead in order to sell his canvasses. Wenders also exalts Ray to the status of fetish object in *Lightning Over Water* (1980), which documents Ray's slow death from cancer.

Recognition of the contributions of the writers and other personnel with whom Ray worked (including actors, decorators, and cinematographers) and who helped to shape his films to a much greater extent than is often acknowledged is an undramatic but important way of tempering the romantic auteurism to which studies of Ray's work are prone. *Rebel Without a Cause* is characterized by many of the problems associated with claiming "authorship" for an industrial group product like a film. Even if Ray had a good deal of creative control over the film, other influences, conscious and unconscious—perhaps even "stolen"—guided his hand. For example, screenwriter Sylvia Richards and her friend Esther McCoy claim that Ray took some of the most distinctive elements of *Rebel* from an original story the two wrote about juvenile delinquency, entitled "Main Street Heaventown," which Ray read and liked and even tried to sell to Universal for the two women.[9]

Still, although we would like to set the record straight and acknowledge all the sources of films, there remains some merit in using a director's (or producer's or writer's) name as a means of categorizing a body of works. In Ray's case, careful analysis reveals that his own tendency, even with studio assignments and without the influence of other writers, was to refocus the film's story at least in part upon issues of violence as a sociological and psychological phenomenon—something we might miss if we were not using Ray as an organizing principle in discussing this group of films. Nowhere is Ray's "refocus" upon the issue of violence more obvious than in his penultimate epic, *King of Kings* (1961), which gives an unusual slant to the tale of Jesus's life and death. In Ray's script the character of Barabbas is depicted (upon scant biblical evidence) as the leader of a large group of Jews rebelling against the Roman Empire. Barabbas is presented as Jesus's rival for the hearts and minds of his people: the man of war and rebellion is set in opposition to the man of peace.[10] Jesus's characterization as young rebel links the film to those by Ray, including *Rebel Without a Cause*, that treat the problems of maladjusted youth. (According to Andrew [181], *King of Kings*' "contemporary nickname" was *I Was a Teenage Jesus* and, significantly, *Rebel Without a Cause* begins on Easter.)

Ray's interest in the problems of the very young is evident from the beginning of his directorial career. The prologue of his first film, *They Live by Night* (1949), immediately makes it known that its youthful protagonists, Keechie and Bowie, live on the edge of a world to which "they were never properly introduced." This world has done them violence—the violence of poverty, of familial abuse, of intimate betrayal—and out of desperation they have responded in kind. So, too, in *Knock on Any Door* [1949], does attorney Andrew Morton (Humphrey Bogart) present the case of Nick (John Derek), the "pretty boy killer," as one in which the failures of social institutions to respond to human needs are tantamount to a kind of violence that brutalizes and renders brutal its victims. Thus, Ray came to the making of *Rebel Without a Cause* with a strongly developed sensibility about the social ills ascribed to and lamented by contemporary youth culture.

Nicholas Ray's *Rebel Without a Cause* is known to address the "social problem" of teen violence, as well as the psychological and physical violence that takes place in the middle-class home. Ray insisted that he wanted this film to document the lives of "normal" teenagers, by which he meant middle-class and (to some degree) mentally stable ones: "It was neither a psychopath nor the son of a poor family I was interested in now."[11] Thus, Jim Stark, the reluctant nomad and would-be pacifist, is the hero of the narrative, rather than Plato, whose psychological problems seem to be of a different order of magnitude than Jim's. (Plato might well be described as psychopathic, and in Ray's original story idea for the film Plato's character [Demo] is condemned to be executed for his crimes.) With *Rebel Without a Cause*, Ray shows that within the heart of the American family people can live strangely marginal lives, especially the young people who have the liminal or threshold status of teenagers (in transition from one stage of life to another)—or those whose desires do not conform to the norms of the period, including that of compulsory heterosexuality.

George Wilson has written, concerning Jim Stark's first violent outburst in *Rebel*, when he pounds his fists into the desk of the police youth counselor (Ray Fremick/Edward Platt), that this behavior seems to be an appropriate response to the claustrophobia experienced by the young people in this and other environments created by the film.[12] Ray's mise-en-scène and cinematography, particularly his use of the Cinemascope image in the film's early scenes, prime the viewer to expect and to sympathize with Jim's need to break free of the space closing in around him. Throughout the film we witness the teenagers' attempts to tear loose from their confining surroundings, only to find themselves staging tribal rituals of extreme violence in the wide-open spaces they seek (the outdoor plaza of the planetarium, the bluff where the chickie run takes place, the mansion that dwarfs the small family dwelling). Ray explores this tension between domesticity and the world at-large even more systematically in *Bigger Than Life*, which takes advantage of Ed Avery's drug-induced delusions of grandeur to depict his middle-class home, his marriage, his family, and his job as unbearably confining (the original story upon which the film was based was entitled "Ten Feet Tall," a title that points to both the man's grandiosity and his sense of not fitting into his environment). The travel posters on the wall of the Avery home, representing exotic destinations to which the Averys will probably never travel, introduce the image of the nomad familiar from Ray's other films—the lives of saddle broncs depicted in *The Lusty Men*, Dixon Steele's restless nocturnal peregrinations in *In a Lonely Place*—not to mention the obvious case of the gypsy lifestyle depicted in *Hot Blood* (1956) In Ray's films the car itself, that symbol of America's new nomadic lifestyle in the twentieth century, becomes a kind shorthand image for the rootlessness and potential violence of men. Thus it's not surprising that the most spectacular death scene in *Rebel* takes place as cars plunge over a cliff under the watchful gaze of the headlights of other cars, or that the first violence (the punctured tire) inflicted by the gang upon Jim is aimed at his car.

Rebel Without a Cause opens and closes on ritualistic actions performed by Jim Stark who, lying drunk on the ground in what becomes a fetal position, covers a mechanical monkey with a newspaper (or wrapping paper—for there is also ribbon and a bow). This is one of the images of the film that has become a textbook example of Ray's use of the long horizontal lines of the Cinemascope frame to express character psychology, in this case a sense of loss and devastation. James Dean's mobile face conveys anguish at the plight of his little monkey friend left to beat out his song under the open sky and, in a protective gesture repeated several times in the film, he attempts to cover him up.[13] The link between protection and danger is conveyed on the soundtrack by the wail of the police siren as it approaches Jim, a wail that forms a sound bridge with the next scene, set in the police station.

As Jim is brought into the station, the desk sergeant asks whether the boy is "mixed up in that beating on 12th Street." The arresting officer replies, "No, plain drunkenness." A number of important ideas are expressed in this simple exchange. To some extent *Rebel*'s plot represents a kind of initiation ritual or testing of Jim Stark's masculinity and worthiness to pass into adulthood. As Ray makes clear in such films as *On Dangerous Ground*, *In a Lonely Place*, and *Bigger Than Life*, the most dangerous aspect of the transition into adult masculinity revolves around the question of violence. Is Jim or is he not capable of brutality? The initial response to this question seems to be "no"—his is a case of plain drunkenness, a somewhat embarrassing inability to cope with life. But Jim is haunted by the fear of his own potential for violence. As he says after taking a punch at Ray in the police station: "Please lock me up! I'm going to hit somebody. I'm going to do something and I don't . . ." Dean frequently leaves sentences unfinished in this film—an effective technique for conveying the immensity of his character's feelings and his despair of being unable to communicate them.

Jim Stark seeks the confines of the lock-up in order to combat his fears of that enormous welling up of feeling transforming itself into violent action if he remains at-large. He will later seek out the shelter of the police station when he goes to tell Ray Fremick of the accident on the bluff during the chickie run. But the police station has no shelter to offer: Ray is not there, and on his way into the building he encounters some of the hooligans who have been seeking revenge on him for the loss of their leader, Buzz.[14] (This is neither the first nor the last time that Jim seeks refuge in the brick and mortar of the very social structures that oppress him.) Protectiveness is presented as the most noble of masculine qualities—and as the antidote for violence. Jim's protective desire to cover the monkey is repeated in his offer of his jacket to Plato in the police station. This offer is refused, but Plato's desire for Jim's love and protection are kindled by this initial interaction. Significantly, among the first words Jim speaks to his father (after "Happy Easter") is the sentence "You can't protect me." First and foremost among the failures of Jim's father in the film is this inability to protect, which is repeatedly conveyed as a lack of uprightness. Jim's sentences "Stand up" and "Dad, stand up for me" are spoken at moments of crisis later in the film, and the film ends on Plato, in death, assuming the prone position Jim had adopted in the first scene. As dawn breaks, Mr. Stark completes the ritual of bringing his son into adulthood by saying, "Stand up. I'll stand up with you. I'll try to be as strong as you want me to be." Jim is then able to stand tall with Judy by his side. In the scene at the police station Jim, who feels that he cannot achieve manhood without the example of his father, attempts to elevate the latter by enthroning him on the shoeshine chair, and then, later in the film, by pulling him up by the apron strings from his sordid cleaning task. But despite the optimistic tone of the final scene the film makes clear time and time again that a father cannot protect his son, and that one's efforts to protect are punctuated by betrayal and violence.

The deus ex machina quality of *Rebel*'s ending is made even more evident when it is placed in the context of Ray's other films depicting the struggles of men to mature within mentoring relationships. Male bonding and mentoring are explored in detail in a number of Ray's films, notably *Knock on Any Door*, *On Dangerous Ground*, *In a Lonely Place*, *The Lusty Men*, *Run for Cover*, *Bigger Than Life*, *Bitter Victory*, and *Wind Across the Everglades*. Most often such relationships end, as is partly the case in *Rebel Without a Cause*, with betrayal and death, but they are also presented as the only means for either the mentor or the one mentored to mature. Few filmmakers have portrayed paternal and filial love and disappointment as poignantly as does Ray. Many of his films explore the relatively uncharted territory of appropriate male parenting (the 1940s and 1950s being more fixated on bad and good mothering in general), taking note of the contradictions and aporia to which those relationships are prone.

In Jim's relationship with Plato in *Rebel*, as we have seen and as has been amply documented elsewhere, Jim tries to carry out the kind of protective "fathering" that he would have liked to receive from his own father, although he jokingly dramatizes his discomfort with Plato's declaration that he wishes Jim could really have been his father. It is also clear that in this film the protective relationship carries with it seemingly inevitable betrayals and bursts of violence, notably, in *Rebel*, when Jim is finally able to give Plato the jacket that has signified protection from the beginning of the film. But the red jacket, metaphorically linked to the jacket sleeve that catches on the door handle and causes Buzz's fiery death, is an ambiguous gift. It seems to pass along Jim's own rebelliousness to the younger teen, while it marks the substitution of Plato for Jim in death at the end of the film.[15] The violent heroes of *In a Lonely Place* and *On Dangerous Ground* also fail as mentors or saviors, although the latter film's cop protagonist (Jim Wilson/Robert Ryan) does come to question his own violent nature after the "sacrifice" of young Danny. In *On Dangerous Ground*, a project into which Ray had much personal input, the mentally defective young murderer Danny (Sumner Williams) plays a role similar to that played by Sal Mineo as Plato in *Rebel.* In both films, the rebellious male, who had been considered potentially violent and dangerous by those around him (Jim Stark and Jim Wilson), must become a role model or protector for a younger male who proves to be much more violent and unsalvageable than his mentor.[16] Similarly, in *Run for Cover*, Sheriff Matt Dow (Jimmy Cagney) takes moral responsibility for a young man (Davey Bishop/John Derek) who is finally unworthy of Dow's attempts to salvage him. One might say that the plot of *Rebel* is rewritten in *Run for Cover* with James Cagney in the role of both Jim and Mr. Stark, in that he is both the peer and the father figure for Davey. Davey also bears an obvious psychological and physical resemblance to Plato and to Nick Romano, the John Derek character in *Knock on Any Door.*

The plot of *Run for Cover* is rather convoluted, but in brief Matt Dow (Cagney) feels responsible for Davey's (Derek) life-threatening injuries at the beginning of the film because he had made the young man ride ahead of him during their return to town from—strange as it may seem—an inadvertent robbery of the mail train. In the style of true melodrama, Matt and Davey are the victims of a misunderstanding that conceals their innocence. The men on the train, having been robbed at the same bend in the railroad where the pair happens to be resting on their horses and taking potshots at a bird, assume that this is another robbery and, rather than waiting to be attacked, throw the money out to the two men. They then alert the townspeople, who form a posse—or lynch mob. Because Davey is riding ahead of Matt, he takes three bullets and breaks his leg while Matt escapes with a slight injury. Matt assigns himself a maternal, nurturing role as he nurses Davey back to health—until one significant moment when violence, at least, psychological violence—is shown to be an integral part of proper fathering. Matt and his soon-to-be love interest (Helga Swenson, played by Viveca Lindfors) have just learned from the doctor that Danny will never walk again because of the severity of his leg break. Matt refuses to accept this verdict. A crashing sound brings him and Helga back into the bedroom, where Davey has himself just made the discovery that he can no longer use his leg. Gathering his psychological force, Dow brutally sends the woman out of the room and commands Davey to walk, which he does. The overcoming of the self necessary to maturation is shown to be achievable only by means of paternal cruelty. This scene in *Run for Cover*, in which Matt Dow demands that Davey rise from the floor to prove his manhood, also reverses the configuration of that father-son confrontation in *Rebel* when Jim finds his father stooped on the staircase landing cleaning up broken dishes. Uprightness is in both instances connected to manliness, but in

Rebel it is the son who demands it of the father as a model for himself, whereas in *Run for Cover*, Dow demands it of his surrogate son as part of the architecture of hopes and wishes he has for the boy.

All of Dow's nurturance will prove to be for nought, not so much because of Dow's own hidden past redolent with violence, in the style of the Anthony Mann Western hero, but because of Davey's greed, self-pity, and ambition. The moral ambiguity of the film is underscored by Davey's final violent act (which reiterates the kind of interpretive error made by Johnny when he fires on Turkey in *Johnny Guitar* and the mistaken act of robbery at the beginning of *Run for Cover*). Davey pulls his weapon to fire—not on Dow but on Davey's own sleazy partner in crime, Morgan (Ernest Borgnine). Dow sees Davey draw and, believing himself to be in mortal danger, shoots to kill, thus committing the ultimate betrayal of his ersatz son. This killing will prove to be the salvation of Davey's reputation, however, as Dow describes him as a hero to the townspeople upon his return.

In a Lonely Place depicts Dixon Steele as abusive of women but (like Wilson in *On Dangerous Ground*) protective of certain men, especially his down-and-out actor friend (Charles Waterman, played by Robert Warwick) and his agent Mel Lippman (Art Smith). Predictably, this affection for his agent and other passive males in the film doesn't prevent Dix from occasionally roughing them up. Although male-female violence is most salient in *In a Lonely Place*, the film relies for its psychological density upon the breakdown of idealized male relationships—their deterioration into violence, narcissism, and mistrust. Of particular interest is Dix's relationship with Police Sergeant Brub Nicholai (Frank Lovejoy), whom Dix had commanded in an army unit during the war (WW II). Brub's admiration for Dix, a fine commander whose best qualities were revealed in the theater of war, is not diminished by his suspicion that the latter may in fact be the murderer of Mildred Atkinson (Martha Stewart).

In a Lonely Place is particularly poignant because so many of the relationships between characters, including the one of mutual respect and affection between Brub and Dix (like the love between Dix and Laurel [Gloria Grahame]) seem almost to succeed. Dix's paranoia, which is the immediate cause of his downfall (much as Othello's jealousy is of his), is a by-product of the contradictory social imperatives regarding masculinity and violence that he, like most of Ray's other male protagonists, has internalized. The absolute control, laconic style, and (it is implied) capacity to explode that made him a successful warrior in turn complicate his integration into the social nuances and interpersonal nastiness of the Hollywood scene. His response is to lash out at other men and at women, whom he views respectively (and perhaps accurately) as persecutors and betrayers. As in *Rebel Without a Cause* and *Bigger Than Life*, the home is the constricting space where misguided male mentoring and sexual violence are staged. Crucial to the meaning of this film is the scene in the dollhouselike Nicholai home where Dix theatricalizes his "crime" of killing Mildred Atkinson. Dix convincingly reenacts the crime, the strangulation of Mildred in a moving car, by having Brub act it out on his wife. Brub's overenthusiastic depiction of the crime—he has his wife pleading for mercy as he strangles her with a viselike grip—is cause for alarm. With his macho allure and a suave narrative style that echoes the compelling narrative structure that Ray creates in the film, Dix becomes a kind of Pied Piper of male violence toward women.

As mentor figure Dix represents the inverse of Frank Stark in *Rebel*, of whom son Jim states, "If only he had the guts to knock Mom cold once, then maybe she'd be happy and maybe she'd stop picking on him. Cause they [Frank's wife and his mother] make mush out of him." Young Jim's misogyny—his willingness to use violence as a solution to family problems—can pass unremarked upon (or may even be applauded) by spectators of the film who are unfamiliar with Ray's consistent indictment of male violence toward women in his other films.[17] In the context of the reality of male brutality towards women in *In a Lonely Place* and *Bigger Than Life* (to which I will return shortly), however, Jim's comment stands out as seriously in error. As Perkins notes, violence among Ray's heroes is "the index of weakness rather than of strength."[18]

In the case of *Johnny Guitar*, which ends spectacularly on a showdown between two women, gender roles are scrambled or perturbed regarding the image of the mentor as well as that of the gunfighter. While women generally play the role of peacemakers in the Western (when they are not the trigger for violent rivalry), Vienna (Joan Crawford), as the owner of a saloon and the employer of her former lover, behaves toward ex-gunfighter Johnny (Sterling Hayden) much as do the male mentors toward their young followers in Ray's other films. Her insistence on his giving up the gun reflects not so much the laudable pacifism of the mature male or enlightened female, however, as the kind of lack of resolve shown by Frank Stark in *Rebel*. Like Jim's father, Vienna would send her "boy" out into a violent world without protection, without a game plan for winning in the male jungle.

In *Johnny Guitar*, as in many of Howard Hawks's films, the love relationship between a man and a woman is characterized by the bonding more often found in male-male relationships. Like Jim Stark, Johnny is a veteran of strife who craves peace, and only become violent when driven past his limits. Johnny begins the film by acting as a mediator between hostile parties (balancing a fragile coffee cup in his hand as the objective correlative of the fragility of peace). But soon thereafter, he responds to young Turkey's (Ben Cooper) shooting demonstration by flexing his old gunfighter muscles and firing his gun with frightening rapidity and accuracy. When she witnesses this theatricalized reversion to violence, Vienna shows the kind of disappointment we see on the faces of male mentors like Matt Dow (*Run for Cover*) or Andrew Morton (*Knock on Any Door*) when their protégés have shown their true colors. Johnny should be *protecting* young Turkey, not firing on him, in Vienna's view. But Vienna herself will be humbled later in the film when she accidentally betrays Turkey to his murderers—and is in turn betrayed by him and almost lynched. In this way Vienna, whose difficult life as a woman has made her as hard as the rigid and paranoid males we encounter in some of Ray's other films, comes to understand and sympathize with the difficulty of Johnny's position—and with the difficult choices men must make regarding violence.[19] Vienna herself steps into the role of gunfighter at the end of the film and guns down her persecutor, Emma Small (Mercedes McCambridge), a woman's whose rage dwarfs that of the male characters in most of Ray's films.

Many of those who have regarded *Johnny Guitar* as a kind of *roman à clef* for the Hollywood witch hunts of the McCarthy era have seen in Emma the embodiment of the enraged anticommunist who enforces through violence what she regards as social norms. Robert Corber has termed the mostly unwritten social conventions of the 1950s the "Cold War consensus," an atmosphere of political conformity that favored the rise of the "organization man"[20] and condemned those who rejected the "postwar American dream of owning a home in the suburbs" as risks to the security of the nation. One of the most important threats to the "Cold War consensus" described by Corber is the alternative to the nuclear family offered by homosexuality. Ray's films, particularly *Rebel*, raise questions about this "heterosexual consensus" by depicting certain kinds of male relationships as desirable alternatives to the suburban lifestyle of the couple. Relationships between men in these films can work to reveal the fissures in heterosexuality. Thus Plato's homosexual longing for Jim is a threat to the formation of the Judy-Jim couple, but also seems to offer the possibility of an alternative and desirable kind of family structure for a brief period, when the three are alone together in the old mansion.

Male homosociality and homoeroticism as a means of resistance to the "Cold War consensus" are especially crucial to the meaning of those films by Ray that depict male mentoring relationships. Powerful and contradictory emotions define these relationships, and violence is an inevitable feature of men sorting out their feelings for one another in these films. Ray's most extensive examination of the role of violence in male mentoring may be found in *The Lusty Men*, one of the jewels of Ray's early film career. With economy and restraint, the first few scenes sketch the end of a rodeo career and the laying to rest of Jeff McCloud's (Robert Mitchum) dreams of glory. After his career-ending fall from a bull, Jeff is shown walking across the empty rodeo ring. Bits of paper and other debris (anticipating the crumpled wrapping paper that figures at the beginning of *Rebel*) blow aimlessly around him as he leaves through the stock exit—having been reduced to the status of one of the rodeo animals, or simply making another "stock exit" as seen so many times in films when defeated men ride off into the distance. In a scene that seems to condense into a few frames all the longing for home expressed by the characters in Ray's other films, Jeff crawls underneath the old house where he had lived when he was a child, and takes out of a hidey-hole some of the talismans of his youth: a tobacco can with two nickels in it, a rodeo program, a broken toy gun.

It is the female protagonist in *The Lusty Men* who *seems* most concerned with establishing a stable home, but in point of fact broken saddle bum Jeff McCloud is just as interested as she is in domestic happiness. All would be well except that Louise Merritt (Susan Hayward) is married to—and in love with—Wes Merritt (Arthur Kennedy), who promised her a home but falls in love with the tinsel charms of the rodeo circuit. Jeff is the rare Ray hero who has learned his lesson about the wandering life. But Jeff's desire for home doesn't find a direct expression. Instead he falls in love with the female half of the young couple who come to look at the old homestead, now owned by crusty Jeremiah Watrus (Burt Mustin). Arthur Kennedy plays Wes Merritt, a young man who, like Davey in *Run for Cover*, does not want a regular job, especially one as a cowhand. He seems, rather, to be an adherent of Nick Romano's (*Knock on Any Door*) motto, "Live fast, die young, and have a good-looking corpse," as he decides to apprentice himself to the famous Jeff McCloud to learn the dangerous sport of bronco busting.

The use of space in *The Lusty Men* is particularly revealing in its alternation between enduring but barren and run-down houses, the cars and trailers of the rodeo circuit, and the open arenas where the men demonstrate their prowess. Jeff is an interloper even in his old family home: Jeremiah confronts him with a shotgun under the house and treats Jeff to some cynical comments about marriage, home, and Jeff himself. Jeff is also linked to a past that is forever gone, but the young couple who come to visit the house represent the kind of future widely advertised as desirable in the 1950s. They are aspiring homeowners and parents, planning to have their own farm, thus working, in a small way, as entrepreneurs. Louise dominates the confined domestic space of their rented frame house, which is located on the ranch where Wes works and where he finds a job for Jeff, despite the suspicions of the ranch foreman, who disapproves of rodeo types. The rental space is an interesting category in Ray's films. It is itself a kind of liminal or in-between space, where courtships occur and plans for the future are formed, as in, most strikingly, the bungalow apartments in *In a Lonely Place*. This rental home is Louise's pride, for it represents the investment in a future that will include the kind of home about which she has always dreamed. But no sooner has Jeff appeared on the scene than Wes (played with Arthur Kennedy's expertly shallow charm and boyish enthusiasm) quits his job and takes a portion of their savings to enter a rodeo contest, which ultimately leads to leaving their home and going on the road.

Naturally, Louise considers Jeff, who takes half of Wes's rodeo winnings as his agent's fee, her enemy, for he represents the nomadic and violence-filled life of the rodeo circuit follower. But Jeff reenters the world of the rodeo only reluctantly—and, one senses, mostly because it is a way of being close to Louise. Although Jeff comments a number of times during the film that he enjoys the comforts of domesticity (particularly in one scene where Wes does not appear for dinner and Jeff waxes eloquent about pot roast), to be a homebody is dangerously feminizing for men of the 1950s. Jeff has proven his masculinity and can afford to say that he wants to stay home, but the image of the aproned, henpecked man we see in *Rebel Without a Cause*—or in the case of *The Lusty Men*, the man who does dishes—haunts the edges of this narrative, as well. The desire for home and stability are "appropriate" to Louise's gender, but Wes, who begins his rodeo career by having the purchase of the old McCloud place as his goal, finally feels that to save his money for a home diminishes his masculinity and freedom, which are inexorably linked to his remaining a nomad. Again, this desire for permanent wandering is expressed through the kind of dwelling Wes chooses. He purchases a house trailer from Grace (Lorna Thayer), the widow of Buster Burgess (Walter Coy), a man who was killed by the most violent of rodeo creatures, the Brahma bull. And soon after this purchase of the home-on-wheels, Wes himself begins bull riding, in this way bringing into Louise's life a daily spectacle of terror and violence as she fears for her man's life each time he enters the arena.

Like Jim Stark, Jeff McCloud is lured by male derision back into the kind of behavior he despises. When Wes accuses him, during a drunken party, of "dragging your foot in my stirrup," Jeff rises to the bait and enters a bull-riding contest the next day. This moment of machismo will cost him his life. Geoff Andrew's description of the rodeo performances in the film could apply just as well to the kinds of activities engaged in by the young men in *Rebel Without a Cause*: "Shown over and over again, the achievements of the competitors are exposed as almost absurd: futile, foolhardy rituals performed for no purpose other than to demonstrate the contestant's virile prowess to a crowd hungry for thrills."[21] Still, as is often the case in Ray's films, violent death is a sacrificial ritual that will permit the remaining characters to find a more peaceful way of life. Upon Jeff's death in a shadowy rodeo office, Wes abruptly quits the rodeo to return to the McCloud ranch. As he and Louise leave, they are joined by the father-daughter pair, Booker (Arthur Hunnicutt) and Rusty (Carol Nugent), shelterless eccentrics of the type dear to Ray, and to whom the young couple will now provide a home. The film ends where it began, as characters leave behind the rodeo arena and the rodeo itself. Although this departure is marked as a positive beginning, Jeff's self-sacrifice in the interest of Louise's happiness imbues with particularly Rayian melancholy the familiar Western topos of the death of a too-rugged masculinity. And as with the deaths or departures of Shane, Wyatt Earp (*My Darling Clementine*), Tom Doniphon (*The Man Who Shot Liberty Valance*), or Ethan Edwards (*The Searchers*), there is every evidence that the man who had finally learned to value domesticity is the one forever banned from its comfort. The violent sports defining masculinity continue to draw the unwary: as the foursome leaves the arena, the young men are lining up for the next contest.

The violence that dogs the lives of marginal groups—screenwriters, bull riders, and so on—is used in Ray's later films to recharacterize the middle-class home and relations between family members. The desire for and suspicions about domestic stability in *The Lusty Men*, *In a Lonely Place*, and elsewhere illuminate similar themes and patterns in *Rebel Without a Cause*. As in the earlier films, the Stark family is represented as nomadic, moving from place to place to escape the consequences of Jim's violent acting out. The nomad's dream of finding a stable home common to most of Ray's early films is shattered in *Rebel* and *Bigger Than Life*, which reveal that nomadism is not the *cause* but the *result* of the inability to mediate the contradictions presented by family relationships and gender roles. But the dream dies hard. Despite his attempts to flee his family's tension-filled home and his discomfort in its cramped space, Jim Stark, like Plato and Judy (or Jeff and Louise), longs for home, and his longing propels the narrative.

Rebel's best-remembered illustration of the longing for home is the tour of the abandoned mansion, where the three characters role-play about family, children, and social class. But there are moments, as well, in both Jim's and Judy's homes where their desire to *feel* at home is expressed through dense icons and powerful language. The kitchen, where

Jim is always alone in the film, is a place where the teenager seems to reach out for the literal and spiritual nourishment that his parents have trouble providing him. (When Mrs. Stark packs a sack lunch for Jim, he grimaces at the contents and the lunch becomes a bone of contention between mother- and daughter-in-law.). But the cold, smooth surface of the milk bottle, as well as its symbolic contents, provides a kind of comfort to Jim that he can no longer ask of his parents. On the way out of the house later that night, Jim pauses as his parents bicker off-screen to cut, in an oddly balletlike pose, a piece (I assume) of the applesauce cake made by Grandma for his lunch. Jim's relationship with his grandmother (played by Virginia Brissac) seems to be rife with bitterness and disdain, and it is only at the knife's edge and as he runs out of the house that he is able to partake of what she has to offer him. (In a parallel gesture, when he leaves the house again later that night Jim kicks a hole in a portrait of Grandma.) Judy, on the other hand, can't take part in the family meal, not even the fish soufflé proudly announced by her mother but made by the servant, Bertha, because her need for her father's affection is even greater than her need for food, and this affection has been denied her since she entered puberty. "This isn't my home," she cries, as she runs out the door to take part in the chickie run. The inability of the inadequate home to contain its inhabitants contributes directly to the genesis of violence.

The male apprenticeship relationships we have described in *In a Lonely Place*, *The Lusty Men*, *Rebel Without a Cause*, and elsewhere, are worked out with very different stakes and consequences in three of Ray's later films, *Bigger Than Life*, *Bitter Victory*, and *Wind Across the Everglades*. In all cases, these relationships are marked with extreme forms of violence. The dream home sought in *The Lusty Men* and hinted at in *Rebel Without a Cause* has been achieved in *Bigger Than Life*, though it is a struggle to keep up with the economic demands it makes of the middle-class family. Husband and father Ed Avery (James Mason) works two jobs (school teacher and taxi dispatcher) to make ends meet. One might say that Ed is making every effort to conform to the Cold War consensus, in which commodity culture—consumption at the expense of production—threatens to "feminize" the American male.[22] Early versions of the script hint that part of the problem for this family is Lou Avery's (Barbara Rush) extravagant spending and fascination with consumer goods, although this caricature of the consumerist housewife almost disappears from the final version of the script, in which it is Ed whose megalomania leads to careless spending. The suburban house itself is presented as a kind of ailing and needy body—broken water heater, aging refrigerator—that anticipates the failure of Ed's own body when he is diagnosed with a potentially fatal disease of the vascular system. The cortisone treatment (experimental in the 1950s) required to keep Ed alive also slowly renders him psychotic. Ed's psychosis, brought on by a deliberately self-administered overdose of cortisone, takes the form of delusions of grandeur: he grows too "large" for the middle-class home and family that limit him and his intellect to a second-rate existence.

As Ed's psychosis advances, *Bigger Than Life* encapsulates with uncanny accuracy the atmosphere of a household in the grips of an abuser. Eye-line matches and other cinematographic techniques help to establish a language of complicitous looking between mother and son (Richie Avery/ Christopher Olsen). The alliance against an abuser (in that case a female abuser) that Jim Stark sought but failed to achieve with his father is forged successfully between Lou and Richie, who alternately try to humor or flee from Ed's verbal and physical assaults. As his mental illness progresses, Ed becomes more and more obsessed with "educating" Richie. This process of education is less a reasonable program of pedagogy than the kind of "foolhardy ritual" described by Andrew as characterizing *The Lusty Men*'s rodeo stunts. Hours of football practice, both inside and outside the house, and exhausting mathematics sessions comprise Richie's indoctrination into appropriate masculinity. Props and other elements of mise-en-scène resonate with symbolic meaning in this drama of a family in extremis. Football is associated with the vainglory of Ed's youth; in fact, Ed's old winning football is displayed on the mantle at the beginning of the film in a sadly deflated state. When he leaves for the hospital, Ed gives the ball to Richie as the legacy of a father who may not return. But he does return, and when he does Ed is no longer willing to accept the deflation that age and limited economic resources have brought about. He pumps up the football and begins to torment his son with his own deflected ambitions, finally rejecting the boy as having been ruined by an overindulgent mother.

Milk is an important prop in both *Bigger Than Life* and *Rebel*. In the former film it comes to represent Richie's dependence on his mother when Lou sneaks a glass of milk into the room where Richie is working, far after the usual dinner hour, on a difficult math problem. Sharp-eyed Ed spots the subterfuge when Lou later pours milk from the pitcher on the dinner table and he sees that one glassful is missing. This incident leads Ed to declare angrily that he no longer considers himself married to Lou. (One is reminded of the absurd paternal thought patterns of Inuk/Anthony Quinn in *The Savage Innocents*, when he becomes upset because his son is born without teeth. Ironically, as George Wilson pointed out to me in conversation years ago, the liquid that Ed must drink for his X-rays is a good graphic match for the milk he so despises Richie for consuming.) The next day the family attends church. This is a scene filled with understated irony, for what should be a refuge—filmed in straightforward, high-key lighting—is no refuge, but simply a grown-up version of the school Ed reproaches earlier in the film as productive of mental midgets. Nevertheless, under the influence of the sermon, which he labels "feeble-minded" but which obviously marks him, Ed recasts his thinking in a religious mold, revisiting Abraham's sacrifice of Isaac as a means of expressing his own disappointment in his son.

This final escalation in violence takes place, appropriately, on the staircase, in a mother-father-son scene that reconfigures the staircase scene in *Rebel Without a Cause*. (What would happen if father *were* strong and authoritative?) When Lou pleads with Ed, pointing out that God had commanded Abraham to spare Isaac, Ed reaches the chilling climax of his megalomania: "God was wrong." Another kind of deus ex machina, in the form of Walter Matthau as the friendly gym teacher, saves the day, but this film's conclusion remains among Ray's most pessimistic. Geoff Andrew succinctly sums up the conflicts of the film:

> Because Ed feels himself alienated from the kind of life he has to lead, he resorts—like so many Ray protagonists—to aggressive rebellion. At the same time, however, he is unlike Bowie, Nick Romano, Dixon Steele and others in that he has a family, friends and material comfort; since he rejects what other Ray protagonists dream of, he is more complex than they, and the film is all the more subversive, since it fails to find consolation from despair in an ordinary, middle-class lifestyle.[23]

The furnishings and props of that middle-class lifestyle (furniture, television, food, mirrors) are revealed to be either too fragile for the rough demands of the family (ergo the breakage during Richie and Ed's indoor football romps), or to be mindless, noisy distractions (the television, also prominently present in *Rebel*'s living room), or even to be productive of terror (the glass of milk is in its way as uncanny as the one found in Hitchcock's *Suspicion*). Ed's despair, which is tempered but not gone at the end of the film, is always closely linked to violent retribution against those who anchor him to the home. The very fact that wife and child can give (or take away) meaning from a man's life—sometimes a cause for rejoicing in Ray's films—is during his protagonists' worst moments the target for a destructive identity crisis. That Ray's films are ultimately male centered is indicated by the fact that women's home- and identity-related crises are seldom the central concern of the narrative, although Ray's frequent use of the tropes of melodrama does introduce these issues. And, as we have seen and shall see again, Ray's films often blur gender boundaries by casting doubt on the moral or psychological tenability of masculinity and femininity as traditionally defined.

Another of Ray's films featuring the middle-class family home and what may well be the only "normal" family in Ray's oeuvre is *Flying Leathernecks* (1951). In making this film, a patriotic vehicle for John Wayne and for one of Ray's favorite actors, Robert Ryan, the director was fulfilling a contractual commitment to RKO. One can detect in every scene the limitations imposed by producer Howard Hughes's reverence for the American military, especially its flying forces. But the film is intriguing in its effort to put a lid on the kinds of conflicts that in other Ray films are "tearing [everyone] apart." In endorsing state-sanctioned violence and the male military hierarchy that ensures its proper enactment, Ray is forced to obviate criticisms of masculine authority and violence in evidence elsewhere in his films. What we have in *Flying Leathernecks* is that impossible creature desperately sought in Ray's other films, the man who has somehow sorted out his relationship to authority, violence, the law, sexuality, and family. But the strain lines in the creation of such a character, though subtle, can be detected. Major Dan Kirby's (John Wayne) struggles in the film are potentially those of every other Ray protagonist: he is a visionary (as much as is Ed Avery in *Bigger Than Life*) and an idealist (like Jim Stark) whose ambition is to persuade the military authorities to adopt his system for protecting ground troops with close air defense. Kirby is the ultimate protective Rayian male: he wants to institute a kind of strategic air defense that will keep the troops he loves (with "tough love," of course) from being slaughtered. The brass is recalcitrant, but Kirby takes an attitude of tolerant understanding toward the unwieldy military—it's a system he endorses—but only at the price of some rather amazing logical contortions throughout the film.

These contortions are of interest in themselves. In order to construct Kirby's character Ray resorts to a melodramatic framework he often uses, but seldom exactly in this way. Kirby is the "misunderstood" hero whose virtue, like that of Lillian Gish in *Way Down East*, is only made fully apparent by a series of revelatory plot twists. The traditional melodramatic "spectator within the film" is represented by Griff (Robert Ryan), who poses questions regarding proper male behavior that one would expect to hear from Jim Stark. In *Flying Leathernecks*, though, it's not being "chicken" but what Griff sees as its excessive opposite that is perceived by the rebellious younger man as problematic, even scandalous. Griff views Major Kirby as overly willing to sacrifice the lives of the young soldiers under their joint command, and literally does not see the otherwise loudly broadcast emotional toll this command and these sacrifices take on Kirby. Kirby manages the contradictions inherent in authority through a kind of dissociative process. By day he is the tough commander, willing to place his men in harm's way at moments when Griff would have chosen otherwise. Numerous scenes demonstrate this conflict: for example, when Griff attempts to pull one man from the day's flight operations because he has been vomiting, Kirby abruptly nixes this decision—"We're all sick"—implying that the man is sniveling and that Griff is too soft. But when that very flyer dies during the day's combat, Kirby is shown by night grieving in his tent, writing a letter to inform the boy's parents of his death, confiding his lack of confidence in his own decisions to the outfit's doctor, and so forth, while Griff is off getting drunk on sake.

The fact that Griff does not observe Kirby's anguish has several functions. First, the melodramatic plot demands that Kirby's virtue only be revealed to his detractors at the end of the story. Then, of course, Kirby's maturation into proper manhood must have the traditional delays, or peripeteia. But at another level this concealment is itself part of the lesson Kirby conveys to Griff on masculine hierarchal etiquette. An officer does not allow his subordinates to witness his indecision and his emotional conflicts. While Griff serves to some extent as cocommander, he is outranked by Kirby and this ranking takes precedence over their bond as officers in Kirby's treatment of Griff. To some extent the film is structured around Griff, who must learn both proper leadership after having once been passed over for promotion to major/commander of the Marine outfit, and the proper way of interpreting Dan Kirby's behavior. First and foremost, Griff must be taught the lessons of manhood. And the most important of those lessons is his appreciation of Kirby.

We are given even more clues about the "proper" way to interpret the "father-son" relationship Kirby adopts with his men, and to some extent with Griff, when we are given to observe Kirby's interactions with his own young son, who seems already to have adopted the proper attitude toward his father. When Kirby is eventually relieved of his command and sent back stateside, his wife (Joan/Janis Carter) and son (Tommy/Gordon Gebert) welcome him home. These domestic scenes, like Kirby's personality, seem peculiarly sanitized when examined with the hindsight provided by of our knowledge of Ray's later films. Still, Kirby's homecoming uncannily repeats some of the themes and even some of the dialogue found in *Rebel Without a Cause* and *Bigger Than Life*.

The main difference between *Flying Leathernecks* and the later films' depiction of domesticity seems to be the role of the military within the context of the family. Because military values and hierarchies are accepted almost unquestioningly by the Kirbys, it provides a structure that makes feasible the roles family members must play in order to conform to the “normal” American nuclear family of the 1950s. After Dan enjoys a tender reunion with his wife, the couple moves into their son’s bedroom. This bedroom is almost interchangeable with that of Richie in *Bigger Than Life*, and in color and furnishings also resembles that of Jim Stark (the “generic” boy’s bedroom of the fifties, dominated by browns and oranges, by sports equipment and school banners). (Art director Albert S. D’Agostino, who worked on this film, did three other films with Ray, though not *BTL* or *RWC*.) Whereas in the later films we sense the irony of such attempts to normalize a child by normalizing his surroundings, here we find that everyone conforms perfectly to the conventional setting and is able to express familial warmth and find his or her place in the family thanks to the military metaphors that pepper their conversation. The use of academy ratio rather than Cinemascope, deployed to often “estranging” effect in *Bigger Than Life* and *Rebel Without a Cause*, may also contribute to the greater sense of intimacy we find in this bedroom. Entering Tommy’s room and bending down over the bed (as Kirby had bent over the beds of his wounded soldiers), the parents awaken their son.

Tommy: Hello, Major.

Dan: A little formal, aren’t you? But then it has been a long time.

Joan: Tommy, give your father a kiss.

Dan: Aw, he’s too old to go around kissing men, aren’t ya, boot?

[Tommy wrestles Dan down to the bed.]

Tommy: Do you surrender?

Dan: Unconditionally.

Joan: Look what he brought you.

[Dan gives Tommy an ornate Japanese sword.]

Tommy: Gee, thanks. How’d ya get it? Buy it off some of the mud marines?

Dan (indignant): I took it off a Jap officer whom I defeated in single combat hand to hand.

[Joan flashes the bedside lamp in what is clearly a bedtime ritual.]

Tommy (protesting): Ah, Mom!

Joan: Lights out.

Tommy: How about some cocoa, huh? I'm hungry.

Joan: No—and no raids in the middle of the night. The kitchen's out of bounds for you.

Dan: Well, I could use some cocoa—and then you can bring him a cup.

Tommy (to Joan): Your order's countermanded!

Joan: Not even a four-star general outranks me in this house . . . but I'll bring you a cup.

Because Joan is able to take the role of a military commander, Dan may take that of the merciful "mother," a role he only allowed himself to play secretly back at Guadalcanal. His upcoming promotion to colonel, and Joan's toughness, insure that Dad is not feminized by his tenderness. (When Dan announces the promotion, his son proudly asks if he will be a "chicken colonel"—an interesting contrast with the symbolic use of the chicken in *Rebel*). When Joan leaves the room, Dan goes back for a good hug from his son—the kind of emotional expression that can only occur in *Rebel Without a Cause* after violent deaths have taken place (as indeed they have in this film, but in another country). The problematic regarding Judy and sexuality in *Rebel* (when is one too old to kiss father?) lightly evokes a homosexual rather than heterosexual threat in *Flying Leathernecks*: Tommy's too old to "go around kissing men." We might find something of a parallel to Judy's father's relationship to his son, Beau (about the same age as Kirby's son, Tommy), in the psychological dynamics of the father-son relationship. Beau's dad can cuddle him, but Beau is holding a noisy toy machine gun while his father does so—much as Dan Kirby can only cherish his men or express affection to his son within the context of the violence of war looming in the background (and, in this scene, a Japanese sword in the foreground). As is so often the case, war is an alibi for expressions of emotional warmth between men. (The war metaphor is extended to Judy's behavior, as well: when Mom tries to comfort Dad by saying that it's the "age" that is making her behave so, Beau blurts out "the atomic age" and fires his machine gun.[24])

The home scene in *Flying Leathernecks* ends with a discussion that is also typical of conversations between men and women in Ray's films. Dan announces that he has a "station job"—he will literally be stationary rather going into battle—and Joan is thrilled. She is even happy about where they will be: "Goleta? That beautiful, hot, dirty little town! We'll probably have to live on the wrong side of the tracks. Darling, I'll never complain about Goleta again." Dan replies, "You're not the complaining type." Like Keechie in *They Live by Night* or Louise in *The Lusty Men* (or even, pace Perkins, Mel in *In a Lonely Place*), and in distinct contrast to Mrs. Stark, Joan is willing to live anywhere as long as she can stay in one spot with her man.

In this body of films, male apprenticeship or mentoring relationships of the type just discussed in *Flying Leathernecks* are, as we have seen, most often forged within a violence context, whether it be war, teenage gangs, the rodeo, the swamp—or the family. I mentioned earlier in this chapter various categories of violence that may be found in Ray's films, among them "legitimate" and "illegitimate" violence. To a certain extent, the question of what constitutes legitimate violence is the most basic of all questions about violence in Ray's films. When, if ever, should a man (or a woman) use violence? What if, as Jim Stark says, it's a matter of *honor*? While Jim's father could not answer this question, Howard Hughes could. Thus, one feels, with *Flying Leathernecks* (and this is true of many films depicting World War II as the "good" war) that Ray is "suspending disbelief" and making the film as if war could be considered a legitimate form of violence—and a form of violence without toxic consequences for the men fighting it. In *Flying Leathernecks* Ray depicts a kind of *directed* violence that does not spill out of its legitimate context to poison men's relationships with other human beings, as opposed to say, the "socially legitimate" though excessive violence of police officer Jim Wilson in *On Dangerous Ground*, which is constantly threatening to spill out in contexts other than that of law enforcement—and to make law enforcement itself a kind of thuggery. It is only through the process of a *hunt*[25] that Wilson's twisted idealism is purged, as he comes to understand the humanity of his prey.

The eviscerated war story and tale of one man's raising to manhood of another that is *Flying Leathernecks* is revisited with much more personal input from Ray in *Bitter Victory* (1958). While the war film is generally structured as a kind of hunt, the pursuit of prey has a particular significance in Ray's films. Hunts, ending as often as not in some form of individual or mob violence, are at the heart of most of Ray's films. *Bitter Victory*, which takes place in Northern Africa (Libya), is no exception. It depicts the rivalry-unto-death between two soldiers, Captain James Leith (Richard Burton) and Major David Brand (Curt Jurgens) who, like Kirby and Griff in *Leathernecks*, are very close in rank. Early in the film the brass has difficulty deciding which of the two men should command a top-secret desert operation. Brand, a desk jockey and political player, is finally chosen, but some ambiguity remains as to who is really in command of the outfit. The least one might say is that the hierarchy that places Major

Brand over Captain Leith is not as clear-cut as is the command hierarchy in *Leathernecks*. It becomes obvious, as *Bitter Victory* progresses, that the "better" man and the more "natural" commander—Leith—was given the subordinate position. In addition to the military matters at hand, the men happen both to be in love with the same woman (Jane Brand/Ruth Roman). Jane, we learn, married Brand only after having been abandoned by Leith. The film makes much of Brand's cowardice—he is truly "chicken" in Jim Stark's sense of the word, as he first demonstrates when he is unable to kill a man in hand-to-hand combat (unlike Kirby, although his story of killing the Jap officer seems invented for the occasion), and then, paradoxically, by responding too readily to a dare silently presented by his doubting men. (The dare, perhaps the most childish of male rituals, figures prominently in many of Ray's films.) To prove that he is not afraid, Brand rashly drinks water that may be poisonous.

In all his dealings with Leith, to whom he feels inferior, Brand is conniving and underhanded. He finally succeeds in killing Leith, not through explosive violence, but passively: Brand fails to warn Leith that a lethal scorpion has crawled into his pants leg. Thus, *Bitter Victory* has a kind of "double hunt" structure: the men are on the hunt for the Germans' secret papers and then are hunted by the Germans. And Brand "hunts" Leith, who, because of his own nihilistic and even masochistic worldview, allows himself to be hunted and destroyed. Neither Brand's cowardly form of violence nor Leith's "noble" but finally meaningless response to that violence is endorsed by the film, although Burton's striking profile makes a very "good-looking corpse."

An even more ambiguous representation of two men who alternately take the roles of hunter and hunted can be found in *Wind Across the Everglades* (1958), a film written by Ray and Kazan collaborator Budd Schulberg. Burl Ives tears up the Florida Everglades as Cottonmouth, a poacher and backwoods king of a troop of misfits, which includes characters played by such oddly assorted actors as Peter Falk and Emmett Kelly. Christopher Plummer plays the role of Walt Murdoch, a schoolteacher who has just arrived to take over his nature studies teaching post in Miami, Florida. After witnessing a massive bird slaughter from the train, Walt takes on the role of "protector" of these helpless creatures. When one woman's garish feather display brushes against his face at the train station, Murdoch plucks the feathers out of her hat. Although this action makes him an "outlaw"—he is jailed for the offense—and gets him fired from his teaching position, it gains Murdoch a job as the game warden for the Audubon Society, whose members are impressed by his defense of birds. Soon Murdoch is headed out into the swamp, where almost immediately he comes up against Cottonmouth, the leader of the poachers—a bunch of swamp rowdies who live with the kind of ostentatious fecklessness found among Peter Pan's Lost Boys.

Wind Across the Everglades is an imperfectly achieved film, but it manages to convey a sense of visceral horror at the spectacle of the birds' slaughter while delivering an homage to endangered humans, as well. As the voice-over at the beginning of the film notes, "Nearly everyone conformed to the fashion and few connected its gaudy demands with the plight of the vanishing birds." Thus, although one might condemn the violence of the lower-class scofflaws who butcher the birds, leaving fledglings chirping and limping pitifully around broken nests, it is clear that the real social problem being indicted is the ignorance of the general public regarding the underlying violence of its own whims and fashions. But Walt's job is to protect the birds at the source, and so he must come into conflict with the men who inhabit that source. Cottonmouth is a powerful and attractive character, whose moral flaw lies in his not seeing the difference between natural and human violence. His philosophy of life is "Eat or be et," and by living according to this credo he believes that he remains in balance with nature. His nickname, "Cottonmouth," links him to the natural world, as does the white feather incongruously worn in his hatband.

Toward the beginning of the film, just before we see him and his men carry out a brutal killing spree upon the birds, Cottonmouth delivers his own eulogy: he will die with swamp cabbage seed in his belly and become a part of the natural world. Walt attempts to bring to Cottonmouth the awareness that human violence is not the same kind of violence as that of the animal predator, who need not wonder about the morality of preying on the weak. It is perhaps this new awareness that will kill Cottonmouth. In a give and take of predator and prey, Walt pursues Cottonmouth and is in turn pursued by him. In just such deadly games of pursuit, as well, the teenagers from *Rebel Without a Cause* use animals, living and depicted, as symbols for their own tribal affiliations and positions in (so to speak) the pecking order. Thus Jim is either a bull, like Taurus the bull in the planetarium sequence—or else he is "Moo," the cow, an insult coined by the boys who hear him bellow. Cottonmouth's totemic animal is, of course, the snake, and he keeps a real one in his pocket. While *Wind Across the Everglades* points to the error of wearing the feathers of dead birds with no consciousness of their origin in suffering, it presents the more conscious totemism of Cottonmouth—who loves the natural world even as he misunderstands his relationship to it—as less morally reprehensible. In some rather astonishing scenes later in the film, filled with the kinds of hazing rituals and man-to-man confrontations to be found in *Rebel*, Cottonmouth becomes, in effect, Walt's mentor in drinking, singing, and swamp dwelling. Their catchword is "protest," a "protest agin' the whole overgrown web we call civilization." It is with regret that Walt destroys this world of male derring-do, ritualized fights, and good, clean swamp living—for the lawlessness and violence of the outlaws is only truly destructive insofar as they are tied to the larger capitalist world of human greed and vanity. Like most of the other "natural" men in Ray's cinema, Cottonmouth must die and take his way of life with him.[26]

One senses that Ray would have preferred to depict the triumph of *Wind Across the Everglades'* ragged outlaws. In a limited way *The Savage Innocents* (1959) offers hope that some will continue to resist the forms of real and symbolic violence exercised by dominant culture. *The Savage Innocents* systematically examines the relationship between violence, law, and culture. It pits the symbolic violence of the white man's law, which comes from books and has the terrible power of outliving the humans that made it, against the laws of the Inuit people, whose civilization and legal system are adapted to the realities of their environment. As an "anthropological" look at Inuit life, *The Savage Innocents* runs the risk of parody (although it is clearly meant to be a respectful and moving depiction of the Inuit people). Anthony Quinn, who plays Inuk, the Inuit protagonist of the film, was used as the all-purpose "ethnic" character in Hollywood films of the period, and in his way Inuk is as baroque a character as *Everglades'* Cottonmouth. But *The Savage Innocents*, despite its title, does not depict the Inuit people as immune from that which Ray condemns in white civilization. Crucially, the Inuit are shown to share the human affliction of violence that is disconnected from nature and thus culpable. And just what is culpable violence is shown to derive from a complex cultural relativity. At one point in the film, for example, Inuk decides to kill another Inuit man for possession of the woman he desires. Somewhat mysteriously he changes his mind at the last moment and decides to keep as his wife the woman he had considered less desirable (Asiak/Yoko Tani). Inuk makes a moral decision, perhaps based on tribal law, that to kill with sexual desire as a motive is wrong. ("A man is not a seal.") Later in the film Inuk does kill, motivated by a clash of cultural norms. He offers his wife's sexual favors and other prized possessions to a visiting missionary and is, he feels, rudely refused. When he reacts by bashing the missionary's head against a wall, Inuk is surprised by the fragility of the man's skull, for the action (which we have seen Inuk perform before without such dire consequences) kills the man and makes Inuk a murderer according to white law—though not according to Inuit law. He is from this point a hunted man. Peter O'Toole plays a trooper who must bring Inuk to "justice" (a character similar to that of Christopher Plummer in *WAE*). It is O'Toole's character who tries to explain to

Inuk the astonishing fact that the white man's law will live on even if the individuals involved may die.

Because of this attempt to make its laws and cultural norms universal absolutes, the civilization that O'Toole represents seems to Inuk—and, perhaps, to the viewer of the film—an almost incomprehensible perversion in a world of contingency. The law, in imposing itself as an absolute, corrupts the human spirit and imposes its system of symbolic violence, in Bourdieu's sense, on those who come under its sway. The trooper, whose life Inuk has saved during the course of the narrative, does practice a kind of street justice, finally allowing Inuk to remain free. But despite Inuk's temporary reprieve, the future of the Inuit is writ large in the film. We see it in the pathetic reality of the trading post where Inuk and his wife had gone earlier in the film to trade fox pelts for a rifle (the sheer volume of pelts needed for human ornamentation marks white culture as perverse in its relation to goods and wildlife, as is also the case in *WAE*). At the trading post, Asiak gives away Inuk's rifle in disgust. But rifles, intransigent laws, and commodity culture will continue to invade the North. The relationship to the world that Ray depicts as that of the Inuit is doomed, and no real alternative to their cultural demise is offered.

As much as he espoused the cause of the protester, of the rebel who finally does have some cause for his violent rebellion against a stultifying or inherently violent social system, Ray remains a man of his generation. Although, as we have seen, they also stand in opposition to the social consensus of the period, which positioned men as cogs in larger organizations and isolated middle-class families in suburban homes, and which accepted as inevitable the replacement of diverse civilizations with global commodity culture, Ray's films are bound by the Hollywood system, the mores of the 1950s American middle class, and a sentimental yearning to refurbish the nuclear family and the white man himself.[27] Ray's films thus span the horns of a dilemma. In *Wind Across the Everglades*, Billy, the Seminole member of Cottonmouth's band, declares exultantly that Walt taught him that not all white men are the same: some understand the beauty of birds. But even as the gross violence of the social misfit is shown to wreak havoc on the most vulnerable, as in Plato's shooting of puppies, a greater and more subtle violence persists when these misfits are gone. For those who can see the beauty of birds, the lone man who learns to turn violence to protection and who tries to form alternative, more just, and more liberating family structures is reabsorbed into the mass of those who can only conform to the murderous indifference of fashion.

What had been, in American culture, a kind of escape into more or less permissible homoeroticism, into "going native" (*Huckleberry Finn*, *Last of the Mohicans*), into the wilderness as outlet for "acceptable" violence, has reached the end of the line. Ray seeks, in his depiction of the ambivalences of relationships between men under conditions of hardship, to heighten and thereby resolve the conflicts inherent in the homosocial both within and at the edges of cultures. Like *Wind Across the Everglades*, *Bitter Victory*, and so on, Ray's 1954 television adaptation of Evelyn Waugh's 1933 short story "The High Green Wall" for the *G.E. Theater* series deals with issues of wilderness, boundaries, male-male relationships, and the written word. Joseph Cotten (in his first television appearance) plays Henty, who is "fed up with the jungle of the civilized world" and decides to "explore the real jungle." But the jungle proves too much for him and he collapses as he reaches the clearing where McMaster (Thomas Gomez) has built a compound inhabited by himself and the local Indians. After four days of unconsciousness, Henty awakens to find that McMaster has plans for him. McMaster, born of an American father and an Indian mother, is passionately fond of Dickens but refused to let his father teach him to read.[28] This peculiar combination of traits leads to McMaster's dependency upon the literate speakers of English who stumble into his compound. During the course of the play, Henty is compelled to read Dickens's complete works to McMaster in a sort of endless cycle, beginning and ending with *A Tale of Two Cities*. Eisenschitz notes that Ray "enhanced the counterpoint between the plot development and the Dickens quotations (not featured at all in Waugh's story),"[29] noting that Waugh did not even mention *A Tale of Two Cities*, which is emphasized in Ray's version of the story. Franz Planer's cinematography emphasizes the sense of entrapment that Henty finds behind his "high green wall." As Eisenschitz comments, "Here the protagonists are already driven and rent by two forces, the rejection of civilization and the trap set by nature"[30]—but it is of course the written word, the letter, that comprises the real trap in this tale—as is so much the case in *The Savage Innocents*, in which the written law's cruelty and perversion invade the wilderness. As he slowly discovers, first by finding the grave of the "visitor from Venezuela" who had been McMaster's previous reader, Henty will no doubt spend the rest of his days reading Dickens to his smiling and good-humored captor.

Civilization in "The High Green Wall" is far from rejected—or, rather, it has been unsuccessfully rejected. In true Borgesian style, "white" culture has been boiled down to the works of one author, which serve as a kind of obdurate and persistent skeleton of civilization in the midst of the jungle. It is no wonder that Ray chose to place emphasis upon the "two cities" in Dickens's title: for this is the story of McMaster's city away from the city. McMaster (whose amusing name may recall Nabokov's humorous use of the name "McFate" in *Lolita*) is obviously caught (even more than is Cottonmouth) in a liminal state between races and cultures whose respective hegemonic positions are curiously tied together. As an "Indian" he is master of the jungle; as a white man he is master of the Indians around him. In a sense, "The High Green Wall" achieves a kind of negative utopia with respect to Ray's works: a homoerotic bond based on a foundational relationship to the wilderness and to a distant, authoritarian masculine Word comes to substitute for that other negative utopia found in *Rebel Without a Cause* and *Bigger Than Life* (in which the male protagonist is unhappily bonded to a woman and is himself obligated to represent the Word and the Law).

In 1974, after spending two years teaching and working on an ultimately unfinished film with his students at Harpur College, Ray shot a porn film entitled "The Janitor," as Episode 12 of *Wet Dreams*. This was an omnibus film produced by Max Fischer in Amsterdam and featuring the work of artists and filmmakers including Ray and Dusan Makavejev. It is tempting to see "The Janitor" as a true auteur film. As Eisenschitz puts it:

> It is a personal film from the word go. Not only does Ray, with rare complacency about his image, award himself both leading roles—complete with eyepatch, missing tooth, and socks tumbling down about his ankles—but he mentions his psychoanalyst Dr. Vanderhyde by name, he refers to his divorce, and he is playing the role of teacher-guru that he had filled for the past two years.[31]

The story of the film involves Ray as a doubled character, a janitor and a fiery preacher, whom the former regards with resentment and suspicion. After resisting the advances of his young daughter, who wishes to perform fellatio upon him, the preacher delivers a sermon in which he condemns the commandments brought down from the mountain by Moses. The preacher then succumbs to the desires of his racially mixed flock, several members of which ask and receive permission to carry out fellatio on him, only to be shot at and destroyed in effigy by the janitor, who fires at the film screen with a shotgun.

As a document of the seventies, "The Janitor" is only moderately shocking, despite Fischer's testimony that Ray had an erection during the whole of the filming. Read in conjunction with Ray's other films, it is perhaps his most explicit condemnation of Judeo-Christian law and of the violence of the word as delivered by the preacher. The doubling relationship between the two characters played by Ray reiterates the self-imposed violence also in evidence in the suicide scene in *We Can't Go Home Again* and critiques the position of director/mentor held by Ray during the making of the latter film. More importantly, *Wet Dreams* echoes the causal connection made in *Bigger Than Life* between religious authority and family violence, in this case incest. There is no nudity in this porn film, only Mosaic law and a divided self. The Word, for Ray, is the ultimate obscenity—and the most significant incitement to self-inflicted and social violence.

And so we return to the Easter setting of *Rebel Without a Cause*, to the role of male authority in its household, to the sexual tensions in the suburban homes the film depicts, to the death of the beloved rival, the other self. Jim leaves the "wilderness" of Griffith Park, having purged his own murderous rage and the violence of his thirst for approval in the eyes of men. Having surrendered himself to the tender mercies of the law and his father, Jim takes his place beside Judy, wearing his father's jacket. The family enters an unmarked police car, which moves off into the dawn as Plato's only mourner watches them with tears in her eyes.

Notes

1. In *Masculine Domination*, Pierre Bourdieu defines symbolic violence as "a gentle violence, imperceptible and invisible even to its victims, exerted for the most part through the purely symbolic channels of communication and cognition . . . recognition or even feeling" (1–2). While the violence wrought by and to characters in Ray's films overwhelms symbolic channels, it is through those channels that *potential* violence, more terrible in some ways than achieved violence, institutes its reign. Bourdieu also states that "[t]he effect of symbolic domination (whether ethnic, gender, cultural or linguistic, etc.) is exerted not in the pure logic of knowing consciousnesses but through the schemes of perception, appreciation and action that are constitutive of habitus and which, below the level of the decisions of consciousness and the controls of the will, set up a cognitive relationship that is profoundly obscure to itself" (37). Certainly it is this sense that the violence of domination is carried out as an expression of that habitus, visible in mise-en-scène, despite the will of these characters and yet not beyond the range of their responsibility, that gives Ray's films their peculiar pathos. As he clutches the steering wheel of his car in an excess of rage, Dixon Steele's character is a study in such obscurity.

2. For details on Ray's life and the making of his films, see Bernard Eisenschitz. Eisenschitz discusses in detail (119–26) Ray's somewhat mysterious escape from the kind of political persecution suffered by those who were blacklisted (including fellow La Crosse, Wisconsin native, Joseph Losey). Like Ray himself, Eisenschitz attributes Ray's relative immunity to the Hollywood witch hunts to Howard Hughes's patronage. Hughes's protection of Ray is especially odd considering the latter's refusal to direct *I Married a Communist*, a film that Hughes had used more than once before as a litmus test for the political tendencies of RKO directors.

3. See Polan (21).

4. On the ethnographic quality of Ray's films, including their tendency to describe particular social rituals, see Polan (29–30).

5. See Andrew (19–20).

6. Jean Wagner briefly but effectively summarizes the role of violence in Ray's films (30–34).

7. As V. F. Perkins eloquently comments, many of Ray's characters are "tortured male romantics looking for redemption from their own ferocities and driven by the contradiction between what they knowingly desire and what they, in fact, pursue or provoke" (224).

8. Gerstner (4).

9. See Eisenschitz (232–33).

10. Bernard Eisenschitz notes that "Ray approached the film with a seriousness and a fervor difficult to imagine in view of the completed artifact. According to Renée Lichtig, the original editor: 'He oversaw everything, sets, costumes. . . . At home he had two walls covered with books on the life of Jesus, in every language. I never saw such documentation in my whole life' " (365). On the Jesus-Barabbas "twinning," see Andrew (182).

11. See Eisenschitz (231).

12. See Wilson, chapter 5 in this volume. My discussion of *Rebel* is heavily indebted to Wilson's extraordinary essay.

13. The monkey motif is reiterated several times at key points in the film.

14. The title of my chapter comes from this section of *Rebel Without a Cause*. As Jim arrives at the police station, several of the other teenagers are leaving. One of the teens, Moose, tussles with an older man who asks him if he "wants a good crack in the mouth." Another middle-aged man intervenes, "Ah, take it easy, Ed. Can't you see the boy's on edge?" Ed replies, somewhat surprisingly, "He shouldn't talk to me that way. After all, I am his father." What may look like random aggression toward their elders on the part of the teens turns out to be intrafamilial violence. This is one of the many times in the film that characters are enjoined to "take it easy" or to "relax"—a kind of coded antidote to impending violence. V. F. Perkins comments that "Repeatedly, Ray's hero gives, receives and gives himself one simple piece of advice which also sets a goal beyond price or power: 'Take it easy' " (225).

15. Perkins notes the many acts of betrayal in Ray's films, singling out in *Rebel* Jim's "well-intentioned deception" of Plato when he disarms him (230).

16. The opening scenes of *On Dangerous Ground* spell out Wilson's problems with violence. His two partners are first shown in their homes as they get ready to go on duty. In both cases, and in contrast to Wilson, who is eating his dinner alone, the violent potential of the cops is mediated by their women, who hand them their guns as part of the leaving-for-work ritual. Wilson's contact with women is as violent as it is with men: in a paired set of scenes early in the film, Wilson's interrogations of suspects and informers take on overtones of sexual aggression. Myrna (Cleo Moore) shows Wilson the bruises inflicted by her boyfriend and invites him to do the same in order to elicit her information: "You'll squeeze it out of me with those big strong arms, won't you?" "That's right, sister."

When he catches up with the boyfriend, Bernie (Richard Irving), the latter also begs to be hit, inspiring Wilson's anguished outcry: "Why do you make me do it?" The relationship with Mary (Ida Lupino) echoes in visual terms (including one scene of physical restraint reminiscent of the scene with Myrna) the violent potential of these earlier encounters, but presents the opportunity for Wilson to adapt to a space controlled by a woman—in this case, importantly, a blind woman. By the end of the film Jim is straightening up the overturned furniture in Mary's home, having come to understand the need not only to protect the weak, even the culpable weak, but to maintain domestic order as well. This putting-into-order of the household stands in contrast to the disruptive behavior of Jim Stark in *Rebel* and Ed Avery in *Bigger Than Life*.

17. In "Documenting Domestic Violence in American Films," Phyllis Frus observes that although to some extent *In a Lonely Place* reinforces the myth that women "find violent men attractive," it also expresses a "proto-feminist theme: that it is impossible for a woman to redeem a violent man by her love, because it is unlikely that such a man can change even when he has found the 'right' person—the one he's been looking for, in Dixon's case, 'all his life' " (232). For an excellent in-depth analysis of the film, see Polan.

18. Perkins (226).

19. Perkins argues convincingly that the vehemence with which Vienna defends her hard-won position in this troubled (fictional) community is one of the self-reflexive elements of the film, insofar as Crawford, already in her late forties when this film was made, was publicly perceived as having to defend her star status. Thus her role as Vienna "exploits the resonances of [Crawford's] screen persona" (1996, 224).

20. Corber (2).

21. Andrew (79).

22. Corber (34–35).

23. Andrew (135).

24. Within the formulaic confines of the Jesus story, *King of Kings* explores some of the taboos that are evoked but skirted in *Rebel*. For example, Salomé's interactions with her stepfather sketch an uncensored and unrepressed version of those between Judy and her father in *Rebel*. Much has been written about the way in which Judy's juvenile sexuality obviously tantalizes her father, who feels compelled to reject her "advances" with brutality: *King of Kings* seems to illustrate the especially lurid fantasies that may be lurking at the edge of Judy's father's consciousness as he draws back from her too-red lips. The scenes leading up to the beheading of John the Baptist play in *King of Kings* as particularly neurotic family scenes. Salomé (played by seventeen-year-old Brigid Bazlen, who bears more than a passing resemblance to the seventeen-year-old Natalie Wood in *Rebel*) gives free reign to her sexual expression (in a dance choreographed by Betty Utey, Ray's wife at the time) in order to win John's head. Her desire for John's head is presented as a nexus of perversions—she wants to look at it, she says—but most of all as a means of defending her mother from further defamation by John—thus keeping the gesture within the territory of the family romance.

25. Andrew (14).

26. Walt plays, to some extent, a structural role similar to that of Farrell (Robert Taylor), the mob lawyer in *Party Girl* who acts as the vantage point from which to watch the gangsters' mayhem. Farrell, like Johnny Logan as Johnny Guitar, has surmounted the violence of his background, but other moral conflicts remain. He acts as a locus from which to observe the violence of other men.

27. The 1999 film *American Beauty* is another work where we witness a particular kind of virile protest to the feminization of men in suburban culture. What makes that film less interesting to me than *Bigger Than Life* is that *American Beauty* seems to endorse the male protest against suburbia at the expense of the rest of the family. The audience, it seems, is meant to applaud the male protagonist's sexual fixation on the young teenaged neighbor and his newly formed habit of smoking pot (as compared to cortisone addiction) as a sign of his rejection of the phony and emasculating values of suburban culture. Another 1999 film that specifically condemns as emasculating the grip of consumer culture is *Fight Club*. The protagonist (it seems) regains his masculinity by throwing away his Ikea catalogue and embracing extreme violence. Whether that film stands as an indictment or a celebration of male violence is not clear, but it certainly bears comparison to Ray's representation of masculinity and violence as social conundrums.

28. As Eisenschitz notes, the extent of Ray's involvement with the script for this teleplay is not entirely clear, but this detail (McMaster refusing to be taught to read by his father) is not in the script and is thus, presumably, one of Ray's additions (222). Eisenschitz also comments in some detail on the plot and stylistic similarities between this teleplay and, for example, *Wind Across the Everglades*.

29. Eisenschitz (227).

30. Eisenschitz (227).

31. Eisenschitz (451).

Works Cited

Andrew, Geoff. *The Films of Nicholas Ray*. London: Charles Lett and Co., 1991.

Bourdieu, Pierre. *Masculine Domination*, trans. Richard Nice. Stanford: Stanford University Press, 2000.

Corber, Robert. *Homosexuality in Cold War America: Resistance and the Crisis of Masculinity* Durham and London: Duke University Press, 1997.

Eisenschitz, Bernard. *Nicholas Ray: An American Journey*, trans. Tom Milne. London: Faber and Faber, 1993.

Frus, Phyllis. "Documenting Domestic Violence in American Films." In J. David Slocum, ed., *Violence in American Cinema*, 226–44. New York and London: Routledge/AFI Film Readers Series, 2001.

Gerstner, David A. and Janet Staiger, ed., *Authorship and Film*. London: Routledge/AFI Film Readers Series, 2003.

Perkins, V. F. "*In a Lonely Place*." In Ian Cameron, ed., *The Movie Book of Film Noir*, 222–31. Dumfriesshire, Scotland: Cameron Books, 1992.

———. "Johnny Guitar." In Ian Cameron and Douglas Pye, eds., *The Book of Westerns*, 221–28. New York: Continuum, 1996.

Polan, Dana. *In a Lonely Place*. London: BFI, 1994.
Wagner, Jean. *Nicholas Ray*. Paris: Rivages/Cinema, 1987.
Wilson, George M. "Nicholas Ray's *Rebel Without a Cause*." In *Narration in Light*, 166–90. Baltimore and London: The Johns Hopkins University Press, 1986.

(Courtesy of Photofest)

4

Jon Lewis

Growing Up Male in Jim's Mom's World

Fritz Lang's 1956 film noir *While the City Sleeps* tells the story of a serial killer who, as something of a theatrical exit line, writes in lipstick on a mirror in his victim's home a simple phrase: "Ask Mother." The killer's name is Robert Manners and B-movie actor John Drew Barrymore plays him with exaggerated effeminacy. Robert we figure early on is a "momma's boy." The brutal mix of violence and sex that fuels his crimes stem from his frustrations at being mom's own "Mr. Manners," a man like too many men in the fifties all too dependent upon his mother.

Robert Manners is an important fifties type if only because he offers a first step on the road to Norman Bates (Anthony Perkins in Alfred Hitchcock's far better known film *Psycho*, 1960); indeed they share a similar sociopathology. In order to execute his victims, Norman becomes "mother"; as Norman, Norman wouldn't hurt a fly, but as mom . . . well, "she" is capable of anything. The film invites us to look not only at what Norman has done as mom but what mom has done to Norman as well, what she has made of her little boy.

By the time we meet him in the film, Norman is like Robert Manners, an emasculated momma's boy. His gestures are feminine; he learned them from mom. Just watch the way he eats, the way he minces as he walks. And look at what he does for a living. He's a boy in a man's body doing a girl's job: dutifully changing the linens in a motel that is a sort of shrine to his mother's perfidy (it is after all the business mom ran with her lover, the man mom chose over him). The daily grind at the hotel is dutifully supervised and scrutinized by mother's stuffed corpse, an oddly talkative, nagging ever-presence that nonetheless reassures Norman, a man singularly incapable of acting without her "help."

We get the distinct sense that, like Robert Manners, Norman hates what he has become, what mom has made of him. When the detective Milton Arbogast (Martin Balsam) shows up looking for Marian Crane (Janet Leigh), he makes fun of Norman's feminine gestures and bullies him. Later, Norman (as mom) will kill Arbogast to prove, he thinks, that he's no momma's boy. But he does so dressed in women's clothes so the argument seems altogether lost. Norman's dress-up routine is a projection of his hatred of mom; as mom he is capable of killing just as, alas, mom has already, metaphorically speaking, killed him. But the dress-up routine is also an act of profound self-loathing. Norman hates himself because he knows Arbogast was right—he is a mincing little momma's boy.

Robert in *While the City Sleeps* wants us to ask mother because maybe she knows why he has done what he has done. But finding mom to answer the question is beside the point. The message he writes on the mirror is offered less as a request than as an explanation. For Robert, once the deed is done, all that is left to do is affix the blame. He is asking us, his audience, to "blame mother." Because he already does.

Of the handful of Cold War era hate-mother films, *The Manchurian Candidate* (John Frankenheimer, 1962) is the most complex and interesting. Eleanor Shaw Iselin (Angela Lansbury) has plans for her son (Raymond, played by Laurence Harvey); lots of mothers do. And while there are plenty of people to hate and be scared of in the film, the plans Eleanor has for Raymond (an assassination that might prompt a political retrenchment) makes her the scariest player of all. She plans less to live through her son than to use him to get what she wants for herself.

The plot in the film becomes clear—as clear as it ever becomes—when Eleanor holds Raymond's face tenderly in her hands and gives him a kiss. The only other screen kiss freighted so in film history is Michael's buss with Fredo when he knows for sure his brother has sold him out to his rival, Hyman Roth. The kiss in *The Manchurian Candidate* sends Raymond finally on his way to kill for mom. And he can't help himself, because of her.

Depending on how you read the film and its bloody climax, Raymond may be spared the heartache Robert and Norman bear—the heartache of the post-pubescent momma's boy. At least he doesn't live very long knowing what mom has made of him. As the cultural historian Greil Marcus writes of the film's ending: "As Raymond goes off to his assignation with his mother, we know that he is carrying images of what he has done in his head as surely as we are carrying them in ours—and thus he is no longer merely a weapon, a mechanism, or a prig. We see him as an individual who might possibly have a life to live—so when he commits the crime, when he kills his mother, in that instant the movie stops. You stop: as you realize what has happened, the horror of every death is doubled. His father-in-law, his wife, his stepfather, his mother, then himself—he has to kill them all."[1]

The inappropriately erotic kiss, mother to son, is of course "wrong." But its erotic content stems less from incestuous desire—that's the easy reading, but there's more to this than initially meets the eye—than from the excitement Eleanor feels at the unfolding, finally, of her political and professional ambition. Eleanor may be stuck behind the scenes. She is a woman and that's her place. But there is a pleasure in being the kingmaker. Eleanor is like Lady Macbeth, willing, even anxious to use a man she loves to get what she wants. (When Macbeth falters in a killing that must be done to gain him the throne, Lady Macbeth forces his hand; she calls him a momma's boy to get him to act, to kill for what *she* wants. "Art thou afeard To be the same in thine own act and valor As thou are in desire? And live a coward in thine own esteem, Letting 'I dare not' wait upon 'I would,' like the poor cat in the adage." [The adage in question is that of the cat who wants to eat a fish but is afraid of getting its feet wet.] Macbeth responds; he wants to be king, kind of, but most of all he wants his wife to lay off. "Prithee peace," he says, "I dare do all that become a man." To which Lady Macbeth replies: "When you durst do it [when you kill those between you and the throne] then you [are] a man.")[2] When Eleanor holds Raymond's face close to hers, she sees him as merely a means toward an end, an end she has foreseen and engineered. Raymond is the quintessential momma's boy, brainwashed to selflessly do what mom thinks is best for the both of them.

You Want To Kill Your Own Father, Part One

Conspicuously absent in these Cold War era films about boys and their mothers is dad. He is either irrelevant (*While the City Sleeps*), dead (*Psycho*), or mom's puppet (the stepdad, an ideologue but at bottom a dolt, played by James Gregory, in *The Manchurian Candidate*).

The vaunted crisis of masculinity observed by cultural historians of the 1950s is rooted in a growing distrust of women in post-war America. You want to know why fathers fail so miserably? Check the mirror: "Ask mother."

A pivotal scene in *Rebel Without a Cause* finds Jim (James Dean) and his father Frank (Jim Backus) tussling at the bottom of the stairs. In hysterics Jim's mom (Ann Doran)—she gets no name in the film or in the script, she is just Jim's mom—screams: "Do you want to kill your own father?" To her this is perhaps a rhetorical question (as it would be for Freud, I suppose—though their answers would be different). To be fair, Jim doesn't want to kill his father, really. He just wants to knock some sense into him. He's already tried talking.

To the film's lasting credit, this oedipal confrontation does not immediately solve anything. Indeed it sends Jim off to see firsthand how hard it is to be a father. When he fails even more miserably than his dad, he too will get to blame mom.

Near the end of the film, Jim, Judy (Natalie Wood) and Plato (Sal Mineo) head up to an abandoned mansion to hide out from the late gangleader Buzz's thugs. They play-act as suburban parents with Jim as the dad, Judy as his wife, and Plato as their son. All three kids are reeling from some family nightmare. Jim has just "tried to kill" his dad; Judy has been slapped by her dad after she's kissed him on the cheek, and Plato is devastated (yet again) after discovering a child support check from his absentee father. Together they run an "adult" scene (like in acting class). Plato plays a realtor showing suburban newlyweds (Jim and Judy) the mansion. When the conversation gets to the subject of children, Jim and Judy quickly agree that they don't want any. (As the father, Dean goes so far as to imitate Mr. Magoo, the blissfully blind cartoon character voiced by the actor who plays his father in the film). The teenagers feel much the same way about kids as they assume their parents do: "so noisy," et cetera.

Plato's relationship with Jim is complicated; it is impossible to miss the homoerotic tension (more on that later), but more superficially what's at stake is a kind of surrogacy with Jim standing in for Plato's absentee father. But while Jim has warmly accepted his role as Plato's protector, Plato's friend, and perhaps even Plato's object of erotic fascination, the retreat to the mansion finally affords Jim with an opportunity to spend some quality time with Judy. And he is, after all, a healthy teenage boy. And she is, after all, Natalie Wood.

The play-acting gives way—or perhaps it just continues in earnest in separate sites—as Jim and Judy tuck Plato in on the ground floor and then head upstairs. "You want to explore?" Jim asks Judy before they ascend the stairs. "Uh-huh," she replies quickly in the affirmative. It is 1955 so after some pillow talk ("you've got soft lips," etc.) the camera takes us back to Plato and what else goes on upstairs is left to our imagination. By the time Jim and Judy return from their liaison upstairs, intruders have awakened

Plato; we see him fighting them in the emptied out pool. Soon enough the cops arrive to sort things out. (Ultimately some sort of institutional authority is necessary. It always is in the teen film.)[3]

Plato's death, dressed in Jim's coat, delivers the director Nicholas Ray's liberal Hollywood message that even in good neighborhoods basically good kids go very wrong when left too much on their own. To blame for these wayward kids are neglectful, self-centered parents. And to blame for this larger family culture of neglect is mom.

When Plato exits the mansion and is gunned down by trigger-happy cops, Frank briefly mistakes Plato for Jim. At this moment Frank realizes that he should have helped Jim sort out his problems with Buzz and the gang. Frank is willing in this instant to take the blame for his son's death. But he is spared such a reckoning because it is Plato who is dying.

Frank's relief is palpable and he fully embraces a second chance to be a man, to be Jim's dad. Plato in Jim's coat carries a second message, one that complicates things as we look for gender roles and rules. The coat is at first a security blanket (Plato play-acting as Jim's son, being tucked in by Jim and Judy), but then a symbol of Plato's hero worship of Jim. Plato has a photo of Alan Ladd in his locker. It is the classic movie star glossy—something a young girl might pin in her locker. The hero worship Plato holds for the star of *Shane* (George Stevens, 1953) finds a more proximate target in Jim (and by extension James Dean). As Plato's affection veers into the (conventionally speaking) inappropriate, he is killed, sparing himself the embarrassment at the inevitable discovery of the reasons behind his affection.

Jim and Judy's play-acting as newlyweds out house-hunting evolves steadily from the moment Plato identifies himself as their child. He is a handful, they should know that; years of neglect have left him insecure and vulnerable. "Why'd you run out on me?" Plato asks Jim when things go wrong at the mansion, and then adds, cynically "you're not my father." Later Jim will recall that Plato "tried to make us his family," but Jim and Judy are not ready for parenthood. Their only models are their own parents, disasters one and all.

Plato is not a momma's boy, exactly. His mother is nearly as neglectful as his father. She at least lives where he lives some of the time, but she has not found the time or interest to make Plato "her" boy. Plato's female guardian is his nanny, a heavy-set African American woman referred to in the script as his "nurse" (Marietta Canty). She is cut from the classic Hollywood mammy mold; big, benevolent, and dedicated. When Plato gets in trouble in the beginning of the film, it is the nurse who arrives at the police station to sort things out. She tells Ray (Edward Platt), the earnest cop, that she's "been like a mother to the boy." Plato's father's absence is a matter of divorce and abandonment, but in many other such boys' lives, like Jim's, dad sort of lives at home but is otherwise committed at work. The absence of a male role model at home has contributed to Plato's effeminacy and his (hinted at) homosexuality, a fate (the film implies) awaiting all too many suburban momma's boys in the 1950s.

Plato's death resolves Jim's family conflict. In the film's denouement, the family ideal—the ideal family—is restored. Jim puts his arm around Judy, an adult gesture that speaks to their interrupted sojourn "upstairs," and affirms that being a teen outsider is not romantic at all. Teen audiences in 1955 failed to follow the conservative message of *Rebel Without a Cause*—its paean to conformity. What they saw in James Dean's face and gestures was the torment, the discomfort so many of them felt inside. And that profound recognition and identification transcended the film's pat melodramatic plot. But if we stop here and look closely at the plot we see that what Jim Stark wants and what he gets at the end of the film is nothing short of a restoration of the fifties' suburban ideal. He wants his father to act like a man and he seems to know what that means long before his dad does. And he wants his mother once and for all to shut up.

Relieved that someone else's son is dead, Frank decompresses as Jim introduces Judy, his "friend." It is a strangely anticlimactic moment, and yet it is the only scene in which Jim's father takes control. (Even the staging and blocking signals a change, as Frank no longer shrinks behind the two women in his life, his wife and mother.) Frank's innate kindness—previously in evidence as a sign of his weakness—comes in handy as he asserts himself as the family patriarch. In doing so, Frank makes the return to more traditional family roles seem not only logical but also easy. When Jim's mom tries to interject, Frank tells her firmly to "get back." The last shot of the film is of the cop cars leaving the scene, but the film's payoff is Frank's assertion of patriarchal control. And even mom seems happy that he's finally come to his senses.

You Want To Kill Your Own Father, Part Two

Let's return to the scene in which Jim and his dad struggle at the foot of the stairs. When mom shouts "You want to kill your own father?" she appears to be hysterical. Nicholas Ray foregrounds such a loss of control with oddball camera angles (looking up the stairs upside down, camera tilts off the 180 degree line) and with the seeming desperation in Dean's performance.

"You better give me something right now," Jim says to his father. But Frank is a middle manager and as such he is not used to making decisions. At work, the boss makes decisions. At home, mom calls the shots because in the domestic space she is the boss. Jim rejects such a family dynamic—a man has to be in control someplace, doesn't he—which explains why Jim asks Frank (and not mom) for an answer.

Earlier in the film, when Jim asks Frank what it takes to be a man, it is clear that Frank has no idea. When Jim debates going to the chickie run, Frank suggests making a list (of the pros and cons—again the sort of stuff middle managers deliver to their bosses so they can make decisions). Jim ends up at the chickie run *because* Frank fails to tell him not to go. (This is not so secretly what Jim wants in this earlier scene; he wants dad to take control and tell him what to do. When dad fails to assert his authority, Jim decides to take his chances on the cliff because, as Buzz affirms, in the absence of patriarchal authority, a man's got to do "something.")

After Buzz is killed, Frank tries to diminish the importance of Jim's complicity by copping the familiar parental position: "In ten years you'll never remember that anything happened." But Frank's waffling is no match for mom's heightened hysteria and her decision—she's the boss, after all—that the family must move *again*.

When mom says "we're moving," Frank doesn't argue the point, he just wonders when that decision was made. (Sometimes middle managers have to play catch-up. Bosses don't need to explain themselves and they don't need to keep underlings informed.) But while Frank will no doubt go along with whatever mom says, Jim makes it clear that he has had it with running away; he knows enough about being a man (from the movies, perhaps) to want to stand his ground and fight. Jim begs his dad: "Stand up for me." But even though we've passed the one-hour mark, it is still too early in the film for that.

Pointedly, Jim isn't asking Frank to stand up for him against Buzz's friends. He is asking Frank to stand up for Jim against mom. But Frank is too weary to comply. The pressures of middle-class life have seen to that. The surrender of control over the home has its benefits for men like Frank. It is one less thing to worry about. But that surrender costs boys like Jim dearly—that's the message here—and Frank's retaking of the home (from mom) at the end is where the melodrama inexorably leads. Jim is the same character at the start as he is at the finish. He is a confused, troubled teenager desperately crying out for help. Frank is a sad excuse for a man at the start, badgered mercilessly in the police station by his wife and mother. But in the end he takes charge, having narrowly escaped the most unthinkable of consequences for his indecision and cowardice, the death of a child.

"How can a guy grow up in a circus like that?" Jim asks Ray as they both watch the women boss Frank around at the station in the film's opening scene. "Beats me," Ray replies. The remark establishes a bond between the two men (Ray and Jim) that temporarily stands in for the bond that must finally exist between Frank and Jim. When Plato is brought in to the police station he states simply: "No one can help me." He is right. His dad is never coming home. Jim's frustration is more temporary. "I just want to hit someone . . . I don't know what to do anymore, except maybe die. . . . If I only had one day when I didn't have to be all confused. . . . " His dad must someday come around and we wait out the full length of the film for that to happen.

In the meantime—in the world in which teenagers are being, in Jim's words, "torn apart," mom rules. And hysteria is just one of her many tools. Earlier in the film she uses a headache to reduce dad to the woman's role in the house. Jim stumbles upon dad wearing an apron carrying and then dropping a food tray. Jim begs Frank to stand up to his wife, but he won't; he can't (yet).

The scene at the bottom of the stairs shows mom at her very worst. We see her descend the stairs in a point-of-view shot (Jim's); she is upside down (because he is)—a visual marker of a world turned on its head, no doubt. As the camera rotates (and Jim rights himself) Jim's mom expresses concern (but for whom?): "I was going to take a sleeping pill but I couldn't until you got home." In a skewed three-shot (one of many off-angle shots in the scene), Jim tries to tell his parents what his night was really like. But when he tries to tell them about the accident, mom takes it the only way she is wired to take it. "That's a fine thing," she says, "do you enjoy doing these things to me?" When she tries to talk him out of going to the cops ("Why should you be the only one?"), Jim questions her motives. Mom turns to Frank and plays her trump card: "Remember how I almost died giving birth to him!"

What Jim does not understand when he begs his father to tell him what it takes to be a man is that his father is in the process of discovering the answer. The film is about Frank's journey, not Jim's. Like a lot of men of his generation, Frank thought that marriage would make him a man. As the cultural historian Barbara Ehrenreich contends in *The Hearts of Men: American Dreams and the Flight from Commitment*, reluctance to commit (to marriage, to a suburban middle-class home) was seen in the post-war years as a sign of weakness. Bachelors, at least aging bachelors, were regarded as weak-willed or worse, momma's boys. In the pop psychology of mid-fifties America, the irresponsible male ("afraid" of commitment, of marriage, of settling down in the suburbs) courted talk among his fellow adults about possible homosexuality.[4]

To make this point, Ehrenreich offers a deft reading of the popular melodramatic novel *Marjorie Morningstar*, written by Herman Wouk (of *Caine Mutiny* fame) published in 1955 (thus reaching the American popular audience the same year as *Rebel Without a Cause*).[5] In the novel Marjorie ardently pursues Noel Airman, a handsome, glamorous, irreverent, and ultimately vain young ladies' man. He is, as Ehrenreich affirms, everything Marjorie thinks she wants in a man and everything her mother, who's seen his kind before, wants her daughter to avoid. For the better part of five hundred pages, Marjorie doggedly pursues Noel. But though Noel seems occasionally on the brink of relenting, he clings to his bachelorhood. Through these first five hundred pages Noel resists Marjorie's persistent effort to settle (him) down, referring to, even bragging at one point of the "narrowness" of his "escapes."

In the novel's denouement, Marjorie tracks Noel to Paris where he at last gives in. "I'm ready to quit Marjorie. That should be good news to you. All I want is to be a dull bourgeois. I've finally and irrevocably realized that nothing a man can do can make him stay twenty-two forever. But more important than that, and this is what's so decisive; I've decided that twenty-two gets to be a disgustingly boring age after a while. Staying up all hours, sleeping around, being oh so crazy, oh so gay, is a damned, damned BORE." Ironically, at the very moment Noel seems to have come around, Marjorie loses interest in him. At the heart of romance and melodrama is a woman torn between the romantic, glamorous man she probably can't have and the true-hearted but bland guy back home who will take her just as she is. The choice is difficult for the heroine, so long as the men stay put. They need to be essentially the same from start to end. But in *Marjorie Morningstar*, Noel breaks from type. He becomes the bland guy back home—or at least he professes a desire to become him: "I want to get some dull reliable job in some dull reliable advertising agency, and I want to drudge like a Boy Scout, nine to five, five days a week."[6]

What Noel has spent most of the novel avoiding is, according to Ehrenreich, "the responsibilities of breadwinning," in and of itself a potentially emasculating experience (just look at Frank Stark; there's no question he earns money enough to take care of his family, but at what cost?). But by the time he comes around to Marjorie's way of thinking, his many years lived outside the firm gender identification provided by marriage has left him vulnerable to his worst instincts (at least according to the mores of the day and according to the woman who once adored him, Marjorie Morningstar).

Prepared to become a bourgeois, suburban, middle-manager husband, Noel invites Marjorie to dinner. He is at the time living with a heavy-set, lantern-jawed German woman. She works. He cooks and cleans. Marjorie is duly mortified by the domestic "situation," put off by how much Noel seems to know about the cut of Marjorie's suit, his ease around the kitchen. As Ehrenreich pithily concludes, "Marjorie can forgive him for his domineering Aryan roommate, but not for the chicken in burgundy sauce."[7] Marjorie returns home and marries the first decent guy she meets. She settles down in New Rochelle (a upscale suburb of New York City) and gets the life she more or less wanted in the first place. Noel is stuck with the big German woman, having surrendered his masculinity for a life of supposed freedom and leisure.

What *Marjorie Morningstar* shows us is the problem faced by so many Frank Starks in 1955. At a moment when masculinity seemed so tied to marriage, was there any way to break with the breadwinner role and still hold on to one's manhood? (Frank poses the converse: was there any way to hold onto your masculinity in a suburban marriage?) According to Ehrenreich, it was this very frustration that gave shape to Hugh Hefner's *Playboy* philosophy, a mid-fifties promise made to men who dared not to be Frank Stark or Noel Airman.

Hefner's vision of perpetual bachelorhood may well have been swathed in an apparent love for women (at least an appreciation of how they looked and what they did in bed). But the fear of becoming Frank Stark that made the Playboy image so popular with a generation of American men was rooted in a distrust of women like Jim's mom, like Marjorie Morningstar, women who made it their business to domesticate their men. Consider the following remarks written by *True Magazine* editor Burt Zollo in *Playboy* in June 1953: "Take a good look at the sorry, regimented husbands trudging down every woman-dominated street in this woman-dominated land. Check what they're doing when you're out on the town with a different dish every night." And should these regimented husbands, these Frank Starks tell you how happy they are, what a blessed circumstance marriage is for them, they're lying. "Do you expect them to admit," Zollo bristles, "they made the biggest mistake of their lives."[8]

Hate Mom

In a screed on American hypocrisy titled *Generation of Vipers*, first published in 1942 (during the war) and in its twentieth reprinting by 1955, the popular writer Philip Wylie took aim at mom. "She is a middle-aged puffin with an eye like a hawk that has just seen a rabbit twitch far below," Wylie writes in a chapter titled "Common Women." "She is about twenty pounds overweight . . . [and] in a thousand of her there is not enough sex appeal to budge a hermit at ten paces off a rock ledge. She none the less spends several hundred dollars a year on permanents and transformations, pomades, cleansers, rouges, lipsticks and the like—and fools nobody except herself. If a man kisses her with any earnestness, it is time for mom to feel for her pocketbook. . . ."[9]

For Wylie, the suburban married formula is simple. It all comes down to dollars and cents: "it is her man who worries about where to acquire the money while she worries only about where to spend it." Mom's control over the household is absolute. She is "the American pope," the comptroller of the American "gynecocracy."[10] A 1958 study of household finances backs Wylie up: mom made 60 percent of all family purchases; and she handled the purse strings in 71 percent of America's households.[11] For Wylie, moms were slothful, "clattering ciphers" forming together an "idle class, a spending class, a candy craving class."[12]

For the 1955 edition of *Generation of Vipers*, Wylie ruminated upon his reputation as "woman's nemesis" and the whole "momism" business that took shape after the publication of *Generation of Vipers*. Claiming that he loves women more than most men—Hefner makes the same claim; ditto Larry Flynt—Wylie insisted that his gripe was just with suburbanized moms. Suburbia was the real target, as it is in *Rebel Without a Cause*. The suburban social contract (reduced by Wylie to a matter of spineless male wage earners and grasping, cloying, sexless moms running and ruining everyone's lives) degraded American society. In his 1955 commentary, with thirteen years to rethink his screed, Wylie holds fast. Suburban moms are "hen-harpies," "ridiculous, vain, vicious, a little mad." In a land that no longer has any use for "mature men," moms maintain control by a sort of "psychic umbilicus," by which they exert control over millions of men stuck in a sort of "diseased serfdom."[13]

Teen Anomie

Rebel Without a Cause poses the following question: why is Jim—a handsome, upper-middle-class teenager—so sad? James Dean's expert use of "the method," his ever-so self-conscious style of acting the part of the tormented teenager quickly became a hallmark of the American teenpic (see, for example, Keanu Reeves in *River's Edge* [Tim Hunter, 1986], or Christian Slater in *Pump Up the Volume* [Allan Moyle, 1990]). It also became a model for the way lots of real kids carry themselves in the real world.

We see throughout the film Dean journeying inward (part and parcel of the method) to solve the crises of "momism" and suburban ennui. Dean's tough-teen introspection is akin to the style of the strong, silent hero in the American Western (also very popular in the 1950s). Hamstrung by a turn to the domestic all around them, the Western gunslinger and the fifties' male teenager use a journey inward—a silent brooding—

as a means of escaping the "gynecocracy," the feminized world that so threatens to emasculate them.

That lots of kids emulated Dean's stylized performance of anomie suggests at the very least the recognition of a shared condition. Dean made moping stylish; he made anguish cool, even macho. But he also staged for kids already in the throes of anomie a stylized form of refusal, a means by which a certain way of carrying oneself signaled a rejection of an adult society presided over by mom and populated by fathers cowed by her.

In the introduction to their influential anthology on contemporary alienation, *Man Alone*, Eric and Mary Josephson offered, by way of definition, a list of symptoms, a checklist of sorts: loss of self, anxiety states, anomie, despair, depersonalization, rootlessness, apathy, atomization, powerlessness, meaninglessness, isolation, pessimism, loss of beliefs or values, disequilibrium, strangeness, and dissociation.[14] Lots of kids in the fifties would have recognized themselves in this list of symptoms. Dean's performance gave these symptoms a public face. The gestures (head tilted to the side as if trying to understand, head down to avoid eye contact) provided a physical performance of a psychological condition, the exterior manifestation of an inner torment.

As to what might drive a teenager to feel this way, the sociologist Robert K. Merton pointed to "a breakdown in the cultural structure . . . an acute disjuncture between the cultural norms and goals [of a society] and the capacities of members [of a given social group, in this case teenagers] to act in accord with them."[15] In his landmark work *The Lonely Crowd*, sociologist David Riesman makes much the same argument. For Riesman, anomie was not at root a psychological problem (as had been assumed), but instead a cultural problem.[16]

The adolescent psychologist Erik Erikson, whose work in the 1950s remains the foundation for contemporary work on adolescence, insisted upon a psychosocial, developmental model that focused on "life-stages." "It is the young," Erikson writes in his essay "Youth, Fidelity and Diversity," "who by their responses and actions, tell the old whether life represented by the old and as presented to the young has meaning."[17] The sociologist Kenneth Keniston echoed Erikson's contention that if alienation is a psychological problem, it has at its roots a profound social cause. "Alienation," Keniston writes in *The Uncommitted: Alienated Youth in American Society*, "is a response of individuals especially sensitized to reject American culture by their early development, a development which in part reflects their families' efforts to solve dilemmas built into American life."[18]

The notion that stylized teen behavior is an inarticulate but nonetheless dramatic expression of dissatisfaction, refusal, or rebellion is at the heart of Dick Hebdige's take on youth culture in his punk-era classic of cultural study *Subculture: The Meaning of Style*. Erikson and Keniston laid the groundwork for such an argument when they wrote about teen anomie in the first few years of the 1960s. Keniston again: "A complex and heterogeneous culture like our own of course offers many different paths to acculturation; but insofar as ours is a culture, these paths share common, socially learned assumptions about what is important, meaningful and right. When this learning is incomplete, as with alienated subjects, we can speak of a failure of acculturation. On the most conscious level this failure involves the explicit rejection of the most fundamental tenets of the 'American way of life.' "[19] In Dean's performance of teen anomie, we find a dramatic refusal to conform, a refusal to accept the basic principals of an adult society represented by the likes of Frank and Jim's mom.

Psychoanalyzing Jim

Rebel Without a Cause was released into a pop culture primed for the delinquent teenager. In 1954, Fredric Wertham published *Seduction of the Innocent* and it became the most talked about book of the year. Wertham, a respected psychoanalyst, put forth the argument that there is a causal relationship between comic book consumption and juvenile delinquency, an argument built upon his many professional encounters with real juvenile offenders. *Seduction of the Innocent* helped build the public image of the American teenager as a delinquent, an image furthered by the much-publicized Congressional hearings on juvenile delinquency (also in 1954).

The youth offender was given human form by Hollywood with the 1954 release of *The Wild One* (Laslo Benedek), starring Marlon Brando, who played Johnny, a young motorcycle gang leader.[20] *The Wild One* was based on a 1947 incident involving a motorcycle gang's takeover of Hollister, a small town in California. The film posed a cautionary fable; noting in a disclaimer at the head of the film: "It's up to you to prevent this from happening elsewhere." *The Wild One* proved to be at once sensational and documentary, a combination that would come to characterize teen films for over a generation to come.

Despite its embrace by the young, rock and roll subculture of the mid-fifties, *The Wild One* is a politically conservative film. It is structured like a Hollywood Western. The bad uncivilized gang rides into a town populated by weak, civilized, basically good adults. The townspeople don't want trouble and they are willing to make a deal rather than fight the young self-proclaimed outlaws. The town's policeman is weak and he attempts to befriend the gang. It backfires. They see only his fear and he becomes like the rest of the town's terrified adults, a patsy. When the local café owner sees the gang ride into town, he gleefully remarks to a coworker, "Better put some beer on ice." But he soon learns the cost of doing business with outlaws when the gang trashes his establishment.

It takes a sheriff from out of town to tame the wild youth in the film. (Institutional authority is necessary—remember.) The sheriff arrests Johnny and interrogates him. "I don't get your act and I don't think you do either," the sheriff says, but then shifts gears: "I don't know if there's good in you, but I'm willing to take a chance." So long as Johnny understands the rules, understands the rationale for conventional male authority, he is free to go.

As a teenager in fact or at heart, it is impossible to watch *The Wild One* and not side with and perhaps even identify with Johnny/Brando. Though the narrative attends the rescue and restoration of adult society now somewhat wiser for having endured the gang's siege, Brando's charisma as a star makes *The Wild One* paradoxical to the point of incoherence. Because of Brando, *The Wild One* was widely viewed as a celebration of the very outlaw behavior it purportedly condemned.

Rebel Without a Cause follows the formula set by *The Wild One*; it follows a similar theme (regarding the young male hero's quest for meaning in a corrupt and corrupted adult world) with a handful of clever variations. First and foremost among these variations involves setting. *The Wild One* is set in a rural backwater, a place where working-class folks live in Hollywood movies. The Starks live in a clean, upper-middle-class suburb, a place fifties' filmgoers were asked to recognize as their own. Johnny in *The Wild One* is a damaged young man on the run from his parents, from the law, from the responsibilities of adulthood. His outfit (leather jacket, gang colors) marks him as an outsider. Jim is the boy next-door, dressed neatly, basically courteous and (dare we use the word) "nice." That both Johnny and Jim feel just about the same way about the future was meant to appear alarming.

Both boys struggle with father issues. Johnny's dad beat him. Jim kind of wishes his dad would do something, anything, to set him straight. Both young men are charismatic, but uncomfortable asserting their masculinity. When Jim first meets Judy, she rebuffs him. "You live here?" he asks. "Who lives?" she replies. Sure, this expresses her alienation, but it also puts him off. There's not much he can say to keep the conversation going. It is only after Jim prevails at the chickie run that Jim and Judy get together. And by that point—because these are the rules she has set—she belongs to him.

Johnny is surrounded by willing and able biker chicks and their promise of nearly anonymous, consequenceless sex. But he is nonetheless alone and lonely. When a waitress (played by Mary Murphy) sees in Johnny a potential ticket out of her lonely little town, she tries to break down his defenses. "I want to touch you," she says, "but I don't know how." From the start Johnny is confused by all that a liaison with the waitress might involve. Sensing his reluctance, she again says what's on her mind: "It's crazy . . . you're afraid of me and I'm not afraid of you." At first Johnny replies to such a notion with violence. But when the waitress seems to lose interest (in what begins to look a little like a rape), he backs off. In the game lovers play—a game we see time and again in movies where love goes kiss/slap/kiss—Johnny is too screwed up to keep up. He drives the waitress back to town because he can't figure out what else to do with her. His smoldering machismo is in the end just a pose.

Judy is a far less confident young woman than the waitress and thus a better match for the tortured teenaged male hero. In a private moment, Judy sees her image in the mirror and frowns. She is in public the prize for which the alpha males (Buzz and Jim) fight, but she is also a teenage girl caught between a self-image as daddy's little girl (an image daddy rejects outright) and as a young woman (God forbid, just like her mother). When she says, "Who lives," she really means it—she is, at sixteen or so, just biding her time, waiting to live. At the chickie run Judy gets caught up in the excitement, lets down her guard, and finally expresses the sexual longing that's been weighing on her all film. The look on her face as she drops the flag to start the contest (the headlights lighting her face for an instant), the way the wind rushes by, the way her skirt swirls up is all teenage sexual anticipation, sexual excitement. It is the one moment in the film where Judy seems to feel alive. This is a far cry from the young woman we find in the police station at the start of the film. Out past curfew, her first line in the film is delivered to the cops: "He [dad] must hate me . . . he called me a dirty tramp." Ray is at first sensitive to the situation: "Do you think your father meant it?" he asks, implying that her dad probably didn't. But soon Ray is making the same sorts of insinuations. "You weren't looking for something [walking the streets] were you?" he asks.

In the sentimental denouement of *The Wild One*, Johnny returns to the café and settles matters with the waitress. He sits across from her and smolders but says nothing for an inordinate amount of time. (It's another method exercise, really.) And then, finally, we get the payoff; a smile. There is no promise of a future together; he is about to hit the road and she is doomed to a boring but safe life in her little town. At the end of *Rebel Without a Cause*, Jim and Judy make every effort to look toward the future by establishing a more conventional relationship, albeit one that seems to take shape in reverse. First they pretend at marriage (and all that that may involve) and then get around to the introductions to the folks.

Jim is handsome, charismatic, smart, and sensitive . . . he's James Dean. But even he (with all the advantages of good looks and upper-middle-class money), is troubled, tortured. In the course of the 110-minute film, and the twenty-fours hours the film depicts, Jim gets arrested for public intoxication and being out after curfew, has a knife fight, gets suckered into a chickie run with the leader of the tough gang at school that leads to his rival's accidental death, trespasses and hides out at an abandoned mansion where he probably has sex with a girl he's just met, and then gets shot at and gets to bear witness to his friend's death in his arms. What, to bastardize a speech made in jest in the parodic teen film *Repo Man* (Alex Cox, 1984), has "brought him to this sorry fate?"[21]

In an essay written in 1961, adolescent psychologist Bruno Bettelheim offers insight into the fictional character Jim Stark and the generation of teenagers posed in his image. "A youth expected to create a new but not yet delineated society finds himself a rebel without a cause," Bettelheim writes, alluding to the film. The generational "struggle," Bettelheim posits, is essential for adolescent development. And there are proscribed roles: "age provides the direction . . . youth the leadership."[22]

For Bettelheim, the absence of "something to push against" is at the heart of Jim's problem. When Johnny in *The Wild One* is asked what he is rebelling against he replies, "what have you got?" It is the key exchange in the film because audiences inevitably find Johnny's reply hip or cool. But in terms of the film's narrative, the dialogue denotes Johnny's reluctance to take a stand. Jim is anxious to take a stand, but he can't make up his mind. Should he or shouldn't he respond to the taunts of "chicken"? Should he or shouldn't he go to the cops when things go wrong at the chickie run? Jim finds an adult society (borrowing Bettelheim's terms) "more than ready to give way." Denied some established order to push against, Jim hits the streets in search of a meaningful act. And he finds meaning in a series of events that involve personal risk and in two cases climax with the death of kids quite like him.

Bettelheim pondered the contemporary absence of rites of passage into adulthood. Absent a walkabout or some other ritual signal of the end of adolescence, Jim wants desperately to find some definition for the nowheresville of his teenage years, this transitional stage between childhood and adulthood that is all too much about biding one's time. The film ends not with Jim finding or establishing a rite of passage, but with a reprieve in which Jim gets to be a teenager a little longer while his parents finally learn to get along and take better care of him. Adolescence becomes in the end of the film a time for parents to grow up.

Jim's Mom

All tolled, Jim's mom is in five scenes (early on in the police station, at home at breakfast before Jim's fateful first day at school, the confrontation at the bottom of the stairs, when Buzz's cronies show up looking for Jim, and the last scene outside the mansion when Plato is shot and killed) and has appreciable dialogue in just three of them. Yet she is the film's most memorable adult character—a caricature of suburban matriarchy, the very sort of creature Philip Wylie so reviled in *Generation of Vipers*.

What's made mom so awful is obvious enough in the opening scene. First off, she knows Frank for the simp he has become. After however many years together, she resents having to be married to him. Trying to joke with the humorless Ray in the opening scene, Frank reminisces about getting a little drunk in "his day." "When was that [his day]?" mom asks. Frank makes excuses for Jim's behavior; mom wants Jim to answer for himself. "Can't you answer the man?" she implores Jim, and then he goes silent, "What's the matter with you anyway?" Perhaps she sees a little of Frank in Jim and it makes her uneasy. (That the men in her life act this way is all her fault, or so the film makes clear, but that's beside the point.) When Jim breaks down and cries out: "They're tearing me apart," mom admonishes him: "That's a fine way to behave." She's right; Jim's behavior is unmanly (and she's seen that sort of behavior before now hasn't she).

Frank's mom, dressed in a mink stole and flower corsage (just like Jim's mom, a detail of some significance to the status conscious suburban audience of 1955 and an eerie generational commentary) puts in her two cents: (looking at Jim's mom) "We know who he takes after." On that sorry note, Ray takes Jim into his office and leaves the family to sort things out on their own. If Frank is weak, and of course at this point in the film he is, we can see why: it all goes back to mom. Jim's mom recognizes Frank's mom as a rival, but she never seems to realize (until the end, perhaps) that if she's not careful she will become to Jim what Frank's mom is still to Frank.

Mom's instinct in the police station is to make things right. When Jim exits Ray's office she says simply "It's all right Jim," even though she knows it isn't all right at all. Frank's mom is the most assertive of the three adults and she acts as if she is used to getting her way. "Mr. Officer," she says to Ray, "this was all very unfortunate. But he made a mistake and he's sorry." We then cut on image to Dad, Ray, Jim, and Jim's mom (glaring back at Frank's mom) as the speech continues: "So we're not going to have any more trouble. He was always such a lovely boy." Frank, the middle manager, fumbles about trying to befriend Ray, but even his offer of some good cigars gets him nowhere. When Jim's mom lays into Frank, Frank begs her: "Can't it wait until we're at home?" What Frank wants most is to save face.

The subsequent domestic scene après breakfast repeats the family dynamics staged in the police station. Jim's mom and Frank's mom vie for

Jim's approval and Frank can do little to compete with the two women. Meantime, Jim is distracted by a third woman, Judy, who he spies outside looking for her younger brother. Though mom has made him breakfast, Jim can't eat. He says he's nervous about the first day of school, but it is the sight of Judy that gets the better of him.

The scene at the bottom of the stairs sets in motion mom's ultimately willing surrender of authority. By the time the young thugs come looking for her son, we see her in this moment of crisis instinctively following Frank's lead, dashing about the house looking for Jim, knowing all too well he's not there and why.

The film ends with a series of still frames: Jim and Judy, Plato's nurse, Frank and Jim's mom. Jim and Judy appear smug; why after all has it taken Plato's death to get their parents to pay attention. Plato's nurse looks off into the distance; she has lost what may as well have been her own child, but she looks a little like she knew it would all end this way anyway. Frank and Jim's mom both start to say something but then stop and decide not to say anything. They instead smile at each other for the first time in the film. Everything is going to be all right, so long as everyone understands who's really the boss.

Notes

1. Marcus (54).
2. Shakespeare (67).
3. This is an argument I make at far greater length, and with regard to most if not all teen films, in Lewis. (1992).
4. Ehrenreich (16–25).
5. Ehrenreich (27–28).
6. Wouk (530).
7. Ehrenreich (28).
8. Zollo (37).
9. Wylie (189).
10. Wylie (189).
11. Moskin (77).
12. Wylie (49).
13. Wylie's 1955 commentary can be found on-line at: http://www.library.csi.cuny.edu/dept/history/lavender/momism.html.
14. Josephson and Josephson (12–13).
15. Cited in Josephson and Josephson (13–14).
16. Riesman (257).
17. Erikson (24).
18. Keniston (391).
19. Keniston (197).
20. *The Wild One* was released on December 30, 1953, but it was seen by most audiences in its first run in January and February 1954.

21. Otto, the punk hero of *Repo Man*, gets caught in the crossfire of a convenience store robbery. His old nemesis Duke is mortally wounded and offers as his last words a ridiculous commentary on "the life of crime that has led to this sorry fate." Otto admonishes Duke: "You're a white suburban punk, just like me." He's right, but so is Duke with his last words: "Ya, but it still hurts."

22. Bettelheim (89–90).

Works Cited

Bettelheim, Bruno. "The Problem of Generations." In Erik Erikson, ed., *The Challenge of Youth*. Garden City, NY: Doubleday, 1961.

Ehrenreich, Barbara. *The Hearts of Men: American Dreams and the Flight from Commitment*. Garden City, NY: Anchor, 1983.

Erikson, Erik. "Youth, Fidelity and Diversity." In Erik Erikson, ed., *The Challenge of Youth*. Garden City, NY: Doubleday, 1961.

Hebdige, Dick. *Subculture: The Meaning of Style*. London: Methuen, 1979.

Josephson, Eric, and Mary Josephson. "Introduction." In Eric Josephson and Mary Josephson, eds., *Man Alone: Alienation in Modern Society*. New York: Dell, 1962.

Keniston, Kenneth. *The Uncommitted: Alienated Youth in American Society*. New York: Harcourt, Brace and World, 1965.

Lewis, Jon. *The Road to Romance and Ruin: Teen Films and Youth Culture*. New York: Routledge, 1992.

Marcus, Greil. *The Manchurian Candidate*. London: BFI, 2002.

Moskin, J. Robert. "The American Male: Why Do Women Dominate Him?" *Look* (February 4, 1958).

Riesman, David. *The Lonely Crowd*. New Haven: Yale University Press, 1950.

Shakespeare, William. *The Tragedy of Macbeth*, Act 1, Scene VII. New York: Lancer, 1968.

Wouk, Herman. *Marjorie Morningstar*. Garden City, NY: Doubleday, 1955.

Wylie, Philip. *Generation of Vipers*. New York: Rinehart and Co., 1942.

Zollo, Burt. "Open Season on Bachelors." *Playboy* (June 1953).

Frank Stark (Jim Backus) and Ray Fremick (Edward Platt) look on Mrs. Stark's (Ann Doran's) embrace of Jim (James Dean) in the opening sequence at the police station. *(Courtesy of Photofest)*

5

George M. Wilson

Nicholas Ray's *Rebel Without a Cause*

Even more than *You Only Live Once*, *Rebel Without a Cause* has the characteristic format of an American social problem film from the classical period.[1] Its narrative surface specifies a familiar social problem, identifies a set of factors out of which the problem is supposed to arise, and suggests a means by which the problem might be solved or ameliorated. Moreover, I shall argue that *Rebel* is like Lang's film in its ultimate rejection of the social message it seems to proclaim so overtly. Nevertheless, the way in which this rejection is registered is quite different in the two films. *You Only Live Once* is rhetorically unreliable and leaves the competing possibilities of closure it invokes utterly suspended. From the film's perspective, they are all equally suspect. *Rebel*, however, belongs with *The Searchers* as a film that *does* establish a favored, explanatory coherence, although that coherence is presented opaquely. And yet, the respective strategies of opacity are distinct.

The question of Ethan's obsession in *The Searchers* is answered by a global pattern whose elements become intelligibly complete only when the crucial action at the conclusion has occurred. At that point, an answer to the key narrative question (albeit a surprising one) is supplied. In *Rebel*, the ending is a final working out of processes whose character and whose bearing on the narrative questions can be understood only after the viewer has learned, through the film, to reframe those original questions in a fundamental way. The social problem of ostensible concern is one that would require the delineation of responsive social action. But *Rebel* depicts a world in which no such response would be possible or relevant. The film affirms that to conceive the dramatized situation in terms of social problems that have social solutions is to hide from ourselves a much deeper truth about the sources and nature of social bonds, a truth that shows the problematic situation to be essentially inevitable. Therefore, the very *issues* that *Rebel genuinely* attempts to explicate are themselves raised opaquely. The viewer must come to give up his or her ideas about what a dramatic and thematic resolution should be in such a case, locating, instead, the perspective that *Rebel* will accept on this.

The difference between *Rebel* and *The Searchers* poses puzzles about some key point-of-view distinctions. For it is unclear that we should not say that Ray's film is, after all, rhetorically unreliable *with respect to* its social problem framework even if it is reliably coherent *with respect to* the questions that are opaquely posed. Either some modification of the relevant categories seems required or rhetorical unreliability and opaque closure may not be mutually exclusive.

I do not intend, however, to pursue the needed refinements. The difficulties can be met in several satisfactory ways, none of which would alter significantly my overall account. More importantly, the open-endedness of the larger taxonomic enterprise that these remarks have been meant to illustrate would still remain, and I prefer that the emphasis should be on the extensive work that is left to be done. Because *You Only Live Once* served as the initial motivation for the kind of theory of cinematic point of view I have developed, it seems fitting that a film of the same genre should remind us that the progress we have made is provisional and incomplete.

The social problem in *Rebel Without a Cause* is, of course, juvenile delinquency or, more specifically, the incidence of troubled teenagers among middle-class American families in the fifties. The teenagers in this 1955 film are presented as rebelling against their parents and their way of life, but, as the title suggests, not out of any identifiable cause or counterideology and not out of any generalized dissatisfaction that they can state. The film thus invokes the perception, widespread at the time, that the issue of teenage rebelliousness had an especially enigmatic character. Here were young men and women, popular wisdom declared, who had been provided with "everything" and still were prone to alienation, rejection of authority, and outbursts of violence. Because, by hypothesis, there was nothing that these adolescents could possibly want, their actions could not be motivated by any intelligible desire. Although these notions are called up in the film, the story, at the same time, hastens to dissipate any possible sense of paradox. The problem-defining format purports to lay bare the real sources of teenage disaffection. Moreover, it accomplishes this aim in a way that is designed not to be too provocative in relation to entrenched social values and beliefs. It is overtly postulated that the difficulties that are on display are produced by the individual domestic failures of the parents. The parents have only to act with more sensitivity, insight, and moral decisiveness in order for the tensions with their children to be eased.

The causes of the problem are therefore made out to be extremely well-defined and localized, and, like the film's initial statement of the problem, its genetic analysis conforms broadly to conceptions common in the period. What might appear, on the face of things, to be a somewhat serious reaction to the ongoing social order is revealed to be nothing more than remediable psychological maladjustments within the family. The remedy is to be found in what amounts to a renewed commitment to traditional American family structures and ideals. In this regard, *Rebel Without a Cause* seems to operate as a fundamentally reassuring contemporary morality play. The characters, parents and children, act out the semiofficial version of "the youth issue" and, in the course of the plot, come to discover an ideologically acceptable resolution of the conflict. Considered in this light, the following rather standard assessment of the film appears just: "With hindsight, the problem of juvenile delinquency seems naïvely treated, the relationship between parents and children schematically drawn, and the preoccupation with psychological fixation superficial."[2] However, such an assessment ignores so much that is most striking and idiosyncratic in the action, dialogue, and, above all, the narration of *Rebel*, that judgment is best deferred. I shall argue that the patent foregrounding of ideological elements in the film constitutes a misleading temptation to the viewer: a temptation simply to accept those elements without looking for a wider filmic framework within which they are subsumed and qualified. Indeed, of all the films discussed in this book, none better illustrates the dangers of a premature attempt to read a film as symptomatic of an extracinematic "ideology" that is thought of as determining its form and content.

It is an oddity of the passage quoted above that it singles out *Rebel*'s portrayal of the relationships between parents and children as schematic. The objection to be registered is not that this is false, but that it is strange to cite just this aspect when evaluating a *film* that is crisscrossed with schematic oppositions of a variety of types occurring within a number of narrative and narrational dimensions. For example, if there is an implication that the relations among the teenagers are *not* drawn schematically, then that, for reasons to be explored, is mistaken. Beyond this, the peculiar look and texture of the film are built upon a schematic use of, for example, light and darkness, color, movement and posture, and the pacing of the action. Above all, the variable depiction of space in general and of the individual spaces of the characters' lives underlies the basic narrational schema of the film. The film consistently involves a relatively simplified and diagrammatic rendering of personal relationships, and these renderings are intermixed with, if not subordinated to, a schematization of factors that fall outside the domain of the psychological altogether.

As a result, the film occupies a position of some distance from whatever concrete, detailed individuality its characters might potentially have. Each of the three main teenage characters is introduced primarily as an illustrative sample of the wider social dilemma under analysis. Each such sample is specified with a more or less stereotypical explanatory tag. One of the chief functions of the opening scene at the police station is to provide a setting in which the wanted system of labeling can be laid down at the start with minimal artificiality. Jim, Judy, and Plato are brought upon the scene in such a way that it is hinted that they are all somewhat mysteriously linked together even though they are each to be seen as a separate "case study." They are interrogated, one by one, by an "understanding" juvenile officer who, during the interrogation, sketches in the nature of their distinct disturbances. Jim's father is an inadequate masculine role model; Judy, as she matures, is barred from her father's affections; and Plato is the unhappy product of a broken home. We shall discover that the cryptic implied connection between the three kids serves several purposes. But, at this juncture, the linkage that is most prominent is that their different problems generalize under the rubric "conflict with parents."

The stage-setting explanations that are offered in this scene are never contradicted in the film and are to some extent elaborated. Nevertheless, I have already mentioned some of the properties of this initial treatment of the kids that most demand a satisfactory account. As *Rebel* progressively unfolds, the prelabeled psychological mechanisms are seen to be conditioned and affected by natural laws and forces that are remote from anything the pat psychologizing has put forward. The viewer is therefore faced with the question of placing the explicit psychological explanations within an expanded field of possible explanatory connections. It emerges as a genuine possibility, for example, that the psychological causes that have been explicated by an official voice of authority are not more than very restricted and very distorted manifestations of deeper and more impersonal determinants governing the characters' lives.

It is in this regard that the employment of space and spatial relations in the film assumes its considerable importance, but it will take us a little work to see how this is so. Early in *Rebel*, the teenagers attend a lecture on astronomy at the Griffith Observatory, and there they see, projected on the planetarium's domed ceiling, a vision of the dark infinity of space. The obvious weight that is assigned to this curious and famous scene is hard to grasp on a "straight" viewing of the film. This sweeping perspective of the universe stands in stark, ironic contrast to the views that, up to this scene, we have been given of the characters' environment and daily routines. The cinematic style of the earliest segments of *Rebel* emphasizes the severe constriction and the oppressive clutter of the spaces that these people move within. Although this is a motif that runs through all of the scenes prior to the planetarium episode and through several scenes later on, it defines structures that, once again, the opening scene at the police station is used to diagram.

Specific strategies within the narration depict the adolescents as living lives that are, in Judy's words later, "crushing in upon them." We are shown their confused and explosive energies confined meaninglessly by the narrow, claustrophobic volumes that enclose them. The police station is partitioned into small, glassed-in cubicles that serve as private offices. Judy, Plato, and Jim are taken, in that order, into one or another of these windowed boxes to be examined by a specialist in juvenile misbehavior. During the ensuing exchanges, the kids are pictured as literally "pressed into a corner" with "their backs against the wall" and "trapped" without escape on any side. They are repeatedly shot in medium to full close-ups so that the width of the Cinemascope image encompasses great stretches of the adjacent walls and windows. This device has the effect of flattening out the space that appears in the frame and merging the human figures into the two dimensionality of the plane surfaces behind them. Further, many of the shots in this (and other) interior scene(s) are executed with the camera tilted up from such a low angle that the ceilings of the rooms are visible. Here again, the properties of the Cinemascope image come into play. Its extended horizontal line, combined with the relative verticality of the camera angles of these shots, tends to bring the ceilings down and forward into the frame so that they hover, so to speak, just over the heads of the characters below them. Such stylistic choices help make visible the intense feeling that the kids are being subjected to pressure from everything that surrounds them. The rooms of the station and their furnishings encroach upon their perception and sensibility from every direction. Finally, it is not only the real and apparent constriction of these spaces that generates the unique look of the relevant scenes. There is also the impression that space itself in these regions is an almost palpable medium, which the ensemble of unusual camera setups and abnormally jagged editing has the power to slice and manipulate.

Immersed in this transparent and slightly viscous substance, the adolescents intermittently blow up in rage and frustration. The scene at the police station is one occasion of this. Jim pounds his fists brutally and pointlessly into the side of his interrogator's desk. The incident naturally illustrates the reserves of uncontrollable anger that exist within the boy, and the suffering that is entailed because his anger has no clear-cut object. And yet, perceived from the viewpoint this whole scene has done so much to clarify, it is appropriate that Jim should strike out, no matter how fruitlessly, at the nearest of the surfaces that hem him so closely and completely in.

In the subsequent scene, much of the sense of personal space described above is carried over into the depiction of Jim's domestic circumstances. While they nag, squabble, and provoke one another over every incidental, the family members are shown to have packed themselves into the tiny breakfast nook of their modest middle-class home. Jim's much harassed father, in particular, is so squeezed into his place at the table that he barely has room to set his feet upon the floor. Thus, when Jim looks away from all of this through the window and sees Judy outside—young, lovely, dressed in green—this view is for him, as Charles Barr has pointed out,[3] a visual promise of hope, renewal, and release. However, even this image is qualified by a looming environmental presence. The unattractive neighborhood surrounds and constrains her much as the police station had in the scene before. As the couple walk down the narrow alley and converse, they are framed closely by the fences, walls, and garages that rise up everywhere around them. The monotonous and undistinguished houses of the neighborhood are jammed together but sharply divided by the huge fences on every lot. (It is in this conversation that Judy makes her remark about "life crushing in upon her.") Similarly, at Dawson High, as school begins, a jumbled herd of students crowd, push, and jostle one another up the institution's steps and through its doors. It is emblematic that *Rebel* begins with its three protagonists under arrest, because it is a premise of the whole first segment of the film that they experience their normal activities as a senseless imprisonment.

The first planetarium scene is, in one way, a continuation of this theme. The students, bored and inattentive, sit massed together in the auditorium, gaze upward at the astronomy snow, and listen, at least occasionally, to the accompanying lecture. However, in this scene, the sense of restrictive enclosure is now subordinate to the invocation of its seeming opposite. The part of the lecture that we hear is about "the immensity of the universe," man's insignificant position within that immensity, and the relatively imminent destruction of the earth and all that pertains to man. While images of the vast blackness of space, dotted with stars and galaxies, are projected upon the auditorium dome, the lecturer speaks the following words:

> For many days before the end of our earth, people will look into the night sky and notice a star increasingly bright and increasingly near. As this star approaches us, the weather will change. The great polar fields of the south will rot and divide, and the seas will turn warm. The last of us search the heavens and stand amazed, for the stars will still be moving to their ancient rhythm. The familiar constellations that illuminate our night will seem as they have always seemed, eternal, unchanged, and little moved by the shortness of time between our planet's birth and demise.

The teenagers are not much interested by this introductory statement, and they turn away to engage in horseplay with one another while the speaker begins to catalogue the constellations and their locations in the sky. But all of the horseplay ends suddenly when they are riveted by a renewed and more forceful description of our world's death, a description that introduces a projected enactment of that future catastrophe. The lecturer goes on: "And while the flash of our beginning has not travelled the light years into distance, has not yet been seen by planets deep within the other galaxies, we will disappear into the blackness of space from which we came—destroyed, as we began, in a burst of fire and gas." As these predictions end, the visual show above portrays the blazing finale that the words foretell. A flashing, whirling, pulsating spiral of gas and fire—the earth-destroying star referred to in the lecture—grows larger and larger, descending upon the rapt audience, engulfing them and causing them to cringe back in their seats. Presented with this apocalyptic imagery, they react with primitive dread and horror. They spontaneously huddle closer to one another as though their binding together could protect them from this vision of total annihilation. This explosion of light ends the visual show, and, as the kids begin to reassemble their composure, the lecturer concludes: "The heavens are still and cold once more. In all the immensity of our universe and the galaxies beyond, the earth will not be missed. Through the infinite reaches of space, the problems of man seem trivial and naïve indeed. And man, existing alone, seems himself an episode of little consequence." The lights go on, and the students slowly, uncertainly get up to leave.

I shall try to explain how the visually assisted lecture constitutes the major narrational figure of the film, providing the viewer with the context in terms of which the narrative is to be viewed. To anticipate some later results, I shall argue that this scene at the observatory announces *Rebel's* aim of being a diagrammatic meditation—an essay or itself a kind of lecture—upon what it takes to be the fundamental processes that underlie the epiphenomena of the social issues with which it ostensibly deals. More specifically, there are three related major points that are enunciated in the scene which, for future reference, deserve to be set out. First, the scene introduces the concept of the boundlessness of space in contrast to the sharp impression of the restricted life spaces of the characters. Second, this contrast suggests that the infinity of space should be connected with an ideal of freedom or escape, but the lecture explicitly associates it with oblivion and death—the end of man on earth. What is more, the student viewers seem to be bound still more tightly together in the solidarity of fear. Third, there is a blunt assertion of the mindless, inexorable, and law-governed operations of an indifferent universe and, with this, the insistence, quite odd in a social problem film, upon the triviality of human problems. It is the systematic role of these last two points that need especially to be explored.

It is clear that the scene at the chickie run extends and refines all of these points. This is the scene in which Jim and Buzz, the leader of the high school gang, race cars toward a cliff above the sea in a test of courage. The first to jump to safety will be a "chicken" and this, within the code the teenage males all share, is the worst disgrace that can be incurred. Before the race, the two boys look with awe over the side of the cliff and down at the ocean at its base. Visually, the black waters, marbled with white crests and reflected moonlight, resemble the planetarium depiction of the night sky. While they stand there, contemplating the void in front of them, Buzz states, "This is the edge—this is the end." He means, in the circumstances, that this is the edge of the world, an edge that, if confessed, is the end of life for the person who crosses it. His statement also represents, as things turn out, an unconscious prediction of his fate. For he is accidentally trapped in the car he drives, and he plunges to his death at the foot of the bluff. Indeed, we see the car fall into the ocean, exploding in "a burst of fire and gas" that echoes the image of the earth-destroying star. On the sound track, the music repeats the themes that accompanied the conclusion of the planetarium projection.

The reaction of the teenagers to this new disaster is much the same as their reaction to the earlier vision of final destruction. Peering with horrified disbelief into the world beyond the cliff, they are clustered fearfully together in a confused throng, which has been abruptly dispossessed of its leader. But perhaps the most telling shots occur a moment later. Judy remains frozen at the rim of the bluff longer than the rest, transfixed by the spectacle that she has witnessed. After a brief hesitation,

Jim carefully reaches out his hand to her, and she, without looking away from the site of the crash, slowly and, as it seems, without volition raises her arm until her hand finally meets and clasps his. In the background, Plato, the paradigmatic outsider, watches these apparently automatic actions from beyond the field of forces that is guiding them. It is the effect of binding or being bound together in the face of death, isolation, and sheer nothingness that is so central here, and he is wholly excluded from that effect. This instant at "the edge" seems the instant that really founds the relationship that Jim and Judy go on to develop. But also, it is simply the most prominent and important instance of a human response to death that the movie pictures as primitive and universal. Thus, when, in the film's final scene, Plato is shot down in the fierce lights of the police cars, Jim, with Judy at his side, is once more taken, somewhat passively and ambiguously, under the dubious protection and support of his waiting parents. The ties that he had decisively broken earlier are immediately restored in the wake of Plato's death. We shall return to this later.

However, if unrestricted space is presented as dangerous and threatening, it is also presented, as one would expect in this film, as the terrain of liberation. The tremendous openness of the space at the chickie run *is* the positive opposite of the suffocating enclosures of the kids' homes, neighborhoods, and the institutions that process their lives. The first part of the scene at the cliff gives a dramatic sense of their freedom and exhilaration in this setting. The teenagers are animated vividly by the speed and power of the cars, by the incipient confrontation between Jim and Buzz, and even by the prospective dangers that the confrontation entails. The outpouring of their unchecked energies is conveyed, of course, by the organized exuberance of their behavior, but it is also matched in the narration by the camera's new freedom: its freedom to offer panoramic views of the proceedings over which it presides; its freedom, in extended tracking shots, to follow the movements of the teenagers; and its freedom, assisted by the editing, to assemble both detail and summary in an account of the subtle orderings that thread together the tumultuous range of the group's activities. Here at last in this film is an expanse of space in which the camera can dolly and crane, an expanse without the boundaries that the interior scenes so obtrusively have imposed. Hence, in this sequence, escape from the earlier claustrophobia *and* the threat of extinction are shown as two facets of its open space.

I have underscored, if only in passing, the ordering of the teenagers' actions at the cliff because it is patent that the chickie run is an established and predesigned rite of challenge among these kids. Buzz, as I have indicated, is the acknowledged leader of the high school crowd, and Jim has trespassed into his domain in two ways. The charismatic newcomer has asserted his presence too boldly and too soon after his arrival. Moreover, Judy, who is Buzz's girl, evinces an attraction to Jim, which Buzz detects. In the main hall of the high school, Jim sees a placard promoting Judy for "Queen." Presumably, this is a poster for some school dance or prom, but it assumes an added resonance when we note that the whole ritual of the chickie run is set up as a struggle between the forceful stranger and the already established "King." The ritual concerns, after all, acceptance by the given community, acknowledgment of special honor and courage, and rival claims upon the woman. The trick of exposition, here as in much of the remainder of the film, is to cast a rather distanced and anthropological eye upon the familiar but peculiar practices of contemporary adolescents.

Certainly, the chickie run is governed throughout by rules and known precedents. There are rules about how the trial is to be conducted and about what the consequences of a loss will be. The staging of the action is carefully orchestrated; the positioning of the drivers, the arrangement of their audience, and the starting of the run all have an almost choreographed dimension. Even the drivers' prestart preparations seem to follow a fixed and superstitious procedure. Once the challenge has been accepted, the ordained process sweeps up the teenagers and carries them along. For example, when the time of the test has come, there is no substantial animus between Jim and Buzz. Before the race, they take a friendly walk together to the cliff, shake hands, and share a cigarette. Jim asks, "Why do we do this?" and Buzz replies, "Well, we have to do *something*, don't we?" Jim's intrusion into the group seems to have engaged the gears of a complicated piece of tribal machinery, which has to run though its routine completely even though neither the teenagers nor the film's viewers really grasp its inner workings and its purpose.

It was already a stereotype of the 1950s that adolescents made up a puzzling and troublesome subculture within American society—that their supposedly inscrutable modes of thought and action set them apart as a separate social order. This is another of the popular stereotypes concerning its principal subjects that *Rebel* adopts and, for its special ends, exploits. Throughout the film we are offered examples of codes, ceremonies, ritual gestures, and so forth that the kids seem to employ with some meaning among themselves, but these meanings remain, from the viewer's perspective, cloudy and indistinct.

For example, we learn at the beginning of the film that Plato has been arrested for shooting a litter of puppies. No explanation is ever given of his act, and its significance is left enigmatic. But the shooting seems to have been some sort of perverse and private sacrifice, which, performed on Easter Day, has been conceived as a part of Plato's world of fantasy. More public, less violent, but still undeniably peculiar is the little ceremony that opens the school day at Dawson High. A pair of young men in lettermen's sweaters fire a miniature cannon across the yard, and the firing apparently signals the raising of the flag. This faintly ludicrous procedure starts the students in motion up the school steps, and, as they push their way along, an overhead shot shows that they all rigorously and automatically avoid stepping on the school plaque set in the steps. Jim, who is new to the school, fails to observe the odd taboo and has the proscription stated to him by a brawny athlete while Buzz and his clique look upon the culprit with baleful disapproval. After Buzz has been killed, three of his vengeful lieutenants attempt to call Jim out into another confrontation, and they do so by hanging a live chicken upside down over his front door. The primitive nature of this symbol of humiliation is reinforced by a shot from over Jim's father's shoulder when he opens the door to investigate the disturbance outside. We see, with him, the three boys lounging in the trees and brush on the far side of the lawn, and there they appear like "savages" watching their victim from the veiling foliage. Indeed, the whole pursuit of Jim by the gang's enforcers seems the carrying out of a definite but rather mysterious code of revenge, a restitution called for by their leader's death.

However, along with the chickie run scene, it is the segment that leads up to and includes the knife fight outside the observatory that delineates these considerations most boldly. In this segment, the stylization of the provocation and the ensuing violence is strongly articulated. The interaction between Jim and Buzz's followers is laid out quite formally as a rule-directed pattern of challenge, reply, and counterchallenge, a pattern in which the obscure sense of honor of the antagonists demands, at each stage, a suitably conducted response. Much of the carefully arranged behavior in this scene is rendered with a fracturing abruptness and an insistence upon the strict positionality, within the whole, of each major action. This exposition defines the sequence of action and reaction as a series of moves in a game that occurs down and across a three-dimensional board. Because of Jim's unacceptable intrusion upon the group, its members call upon Buzz, in their phrase, "to bring him down." And this is what literally takes place.

Jim and Plato are standing on one of the planetarium's upper levels when the gang emerges on the drive below them. Its members place themselves in a loose configuration around Jim's car. The girls among them, Judy especially, look up at Jim with ambiguous provocation, both mocking him as a part of the set procedure of challenge and exhibiting a sexual interest in him at the same time. As if he senses and is responding to this unplanned note of sexuality, Buzz intervenes preemptorily by pulling

Judy roughly out of the line of Jim's gaze. He then glances up in warning at Jim, and eventually deflates his tire. This is the act that succeeds in bringing Jim down. As indicated before, there is superimposed upon this behavior a mildly disorienting fragmentation of the various acts of looking, provoking, and responding. These looks and movements are frequently depicted in such a truncated way that, for example, the purpose of a movement or the subject of a look is left without full specification. The point of such an action is given no greater weight than the place it occupies in the charged pattern of confrontation that the editing constructs.

The act that finally moves Jim to overt anger is Buzz's calling him a "chicken." We know from earlier in the film that this appellation is for Jim and, presumably, for the other male youths, the keenest possible insult, the worst aspersion of one's honor. Jim whirls around brandishing his tire iron. The gesture is viewed by Buzz and the others with shock and amazement, because, it seems, a threat in this form lies outside the protocol they accept. Buzz's response is to take up the challenge but to insist, with his friends' agreement, that the fight is to have the format of what they call "the blade game." This is one-on-one battle with switchblades, a "game" whose guidelines are then explained to Jim. During the fight, Buzz points up the ritualized aspect of their combat by comparing it, in his taunts and maneuvers, to a bullfight. Jim is "Toreador," and Buzz will be the bull. The blade game comes to an end when Jim disarms him and, with his knife at Buzz's throat, shoves him back against a guardrail that blocks him, on this occasion, from a fall into the enormous drop beyond. This turn of events, surprising from the gang's point of view, leads directly to the more serious, definitive challenge of the run upon the cliff.

It is in the scenes of violence among the adolescents that the ritualization of their behavior, evident elsewhere, is most pronounced. This observation applies to the episode at "Plato's mansion" when Plato is attacked by Buzz's vengeance-seeking friends. The attack takes place at the bottom of the mansion's emptied swimming pool, where Plato wields a heavy hose, swung over his head and flung out, to ward off the black-clothed enforcers. This fight has the look of a gladitorial combat and thereby hints, as is appropriate to the case, of the persecution of the innocent that this particular struggle involves.

It is possible to summarize the more abstract framework that subsumes many of these narrative and narrational constituents in the following way. The gross stultification of the lives of the middle-class parents—lives that simultaneously are aggravating and moribund—is merely sketched in using the crude lines of diagram and caricature. The assumption is made that the conditions of these lives will be recognized and understood by anyone for whom the film can have real content. And these are the conditions against which the teenagers are in revolt. Further, it is essential that their rebellion has certain distinctive, interrelated properties. First, the rebellion is, in effect, a response of the *community* of adolescents. In ways that I have been recently detailing, they have formed themselves into a clan or tribe, and their activities are deeply regulated by the codes and practices implicit in this social formation. They have, in this fashion, set themselves aside as a unity from their parents' problematic world. Second, the rebellion is predominantly instinctual and unrationalized. This characteristic is partly positive. The rules and forms embedded in their actions permit a much more open and direct expression of sexuality, aggression, fascination with danger, and so forth than do the structures of their parents' repressed and distorted lives. The teenagers have created for themselves a kind of relative freedom, a freedom to release their natural emotions and impulses. Nevertheless, the mindlessness of the rebellion has a more disturbing side. By and large, their revolt against the environment of the adults seems hardly more than an unwilled reaction to the restraint and constriction that they suffer. We are given no evidence that the kids have an articulate sense of the real sources of their frustration and despair. All of them are able, at best, to give half a voice to their grievances against the inadequacies of their individual parents as they perceive them. That the total context of their lives and their parents' lives is impossibly oppressive appears never to be grasped. Equally, there is little or no understanding of the orderings that constitute them as a distinctive culture. They are blind to the powers at work in their dealings with adults *and* among themselves. They are, in short, only blindly in revolt.[4]

One consequence of this is that the rebellion is foundationless and fragile. We are shown that in the face of death and the universal prospect of death and in the forced recognition of their individual isolation and vulnerability, their liberating energy, exuberance, and bravado collapse into helpless terror. They cling to one another either for protection from the vision of oblivion or for shared warmth against its chilling effect or simply for obstruction of the view. But this defines a rigidly dialectical process. The spiritual entombment of mass urban society impells the young to seek some release. Yet this release is dangerous and opens more easily upon a prospect of the void. A glimpse of that prospect impells them back into the safety of the baffled herd. Like their parents, they retreat into the shelter of an enclosure without a view of any kind. In *Rebel*, with this ultra-Hobbesian outlook, these are the fundamental processes that underlie both social cohesion and its resulting tensions. They are presented as processes of nature that are fixed and inexorable in their operation. Their emblem in the film is "the ancient rhythm of the stars."[5]

It is in these terms that the day-long destinies of Jim, Judy, and Plato are to be comprehended. For what happens in the course of their day is that the three of them come to form a "family," which then betrays its own "child." (Or, at least, this is the child's perception of the events in question.) Furthermore, the processes that cause this affiliation and its aftereffects are pictured as having the same iron inevitability as the processes beneath the surface of larger social units. I am thinking, of course, of the first part of the sequence at "Plato's mansion." This is the old, spacious, once elegant but long-abandoned house that Plato has discovered, uses as his asylum from the world, and has earlier in the day, pointed out to Jim from a balcony at the planetarium. Late that night, Jim and Judy come together to this house, and they are joined shortly thereafter by Plato himself. The mansion, through its association with Plato, is marked as a place of fantasy and nighttime desire, and appropriately, the friends almost immediately start up a game of play-acting. At first, Plato pretends to be a real estate agent who is showing the house to Jim and Judy, who pretend, in turn, to be newlyweds in search of a home. As part of the pretense, they imitate their own parents and parody their attitudes, especially what they take the parental attitude to children to be. This act is continued until they arrive at the area that contains the emptied swimming pool, where, as part of the game, the pool is dubbed "the nursery." Further, the dubbing effects a transformation of the game they play. Entering the "nursery," they suddenly begin to act like very small children cavorting with glee and utter unselfconsciousness in and around the pool. The effortless, completely unreflective transition between the two pretenses marks their actual uncertain and unresolved status between childhood and adult life. After the second game has been played out, they settle down to rest, and it is at this juncture that the formation of the mock family is clearly portrayed. Jim lies with his head in Judy's lap, and they adopt the role of the comfortable, settled couple while Plato sprawls happily and childishly at their feet. They chat about a number of topics, including Plato's fantasized conceptions of his absent real family until, at last, Plato is lulled to sleep. Wanting to be alone with each other, Jim and Judy decide to go off and explore the huge house. They gently cover Plato up and retreat to a distant room where they express their love, and each declares that the other realizes what he or she has always been searching for. However, their departure exposes Plato to Buzz's friends, who, having broken into the house, find him alone and asleep. When Plato is awakened to the situation, he sees the newly formed couple's desertion of him for their own private, mutual concerns as the characteristic adult betrayal of a child.

At the very center of these occurrences lies that fact that Jim and Judy are now defining themselves as a pair eligible for marriage, which is potentially the nucleus of a family arising, this time around, within their generation. And this is the culmination of processes that are presented as the predetermined upshot of social, psychological, and biological forces. I have already spoken of that crucial moment in which these two, almost as a kind of reflex, clasp hands at the cliff's edge. This is the act that mysteriously ties them so absolutely together that all of the rest of their interraction, including their behavior at "Plato's mansion," seems to be the working out of that moment after Buzz's death. But, if this is the decisive instant of their relationship, it is an instant that has been prepared for by its antecedents. First, it has been mentioned that there is real attraction on both sides from their first sighting of each other. Because Judy is Buzz's girl, her immediate feeling for Jim is initially unwilling and suppressed, but we have observed that even Buzz appears to detect its existence. Second, the complex of parental problems that Jim, Judy, and Plato have anticipates and leads into the roles that each will adopt in relation to the other two. Jim, whose father can give no guidance whatsoever as to what it is to be both strong and protective, is offered this mock family, which unambiguously calls upon him to perform the masculine function that he seeks. Judy has been turned away by a father who cannot express tenderness and affection to a daughter who is on the verge of womanhood, and she finds in Jim a male figure who can replace her father in the needed ways. And Plato is a lost child whose parents have effectively deserted him, so that he is psychologically triggered to create a new pair of parents out of his friends. In other words, their familiar psychological conflicts are, as the film unfolds, reconceived as effects that arise from factors beyond mere psychology *and* as causes of desires that unconsciously guide their actions throughout the symbolic day.

There is a small and rather obscure motif that should be interpreted, I suspect, along related lines. The first time Plato notices Jim, he sees him reflected in a mirror on Plato's locker door beneath which he has placed a photograph of Alan Ladd. I take it that this signifies that Jim, like Ladd (in *Shane?)* is perceived by Plato as an ideal figure, a compelling persona upon which his lonely wishes for a father and a friend can be projected. It is made manifest in Plato's later words and deeds that this is what takes place. Similarly, when Judy sits on Jim's car during the prelude to the blade game, she looks at herself in a pocket mirror, and then, glancing over it, she sees Jim on the observatory balustrade above her. The sight of Jim and of her reflected self causes her to gasp in momentary surprise. This incident seems to be picked up again when, after Buzz's accident, Jim and Plato take her home. As she gets out of the car, Jim returns a compact of hers he had found earlier at the police station, and he shows her her reflection in its mirror. Once again, she reacts to the reflection with surprise and wonder. It certainly fits well with the present reading of the film that Jim should have the ability to show Judy to herself or, more exactly, to show her what it is she really wants. More generally, it fits well that Jim should serve for his friends as a light-accepting object upon which fantasies are projected and from which the contents of desires are reflected back.

A number of critics who have written on *Rebel Without a Cause* have commented upon the artificiality of forcing the story into a period of one day. For example, Jim and Judy seem soon to forget all about Buzz and his death, and this can seem improbable. Nevertheless, this unquestionable artificiality should be connected with the matters lately under scrutiny. The condensed duration of the film's events makes sense as the product of a use of time that is as schematic as the use of space. The day we watch is the day after Easter, and it carries the connotation that *something* is being re-created and renewed. But that something is not the harbinger of a hopeful rebirth or resurrection. Rather, the predominant significance of the restricted duration lies in a metaphorical association of the domesticating revolution that subdues the rebel with the silent, unshakable revolution of the earth in its orbit. The human changes in the narrative transpire with the same mechanistic regularity and irresistibility with which the day passes, and these changes renew what the film posits as the fundamental forms of human social life. Related to this is the "temporal" image of the smallness of such a transformation within the history of an individual's life. In his early discussion with the juvenile officer, Jim asserts that the one thing he most wants not to be is like his own pathetic father. On the other side, his father repeatedly claims that he was once a young man like Jim with the same troubles and that "in ten years' time" these troubles will be as nothing to him. It is tempting to take the father's statement as mere evasion and excuse. However, by the end of the film, when Jim has paired off with Judy and has already failed his temporary "child," and when he has magically reconciled with his parents, who are themselves magically united in their approval of his final acquiescence, it is necessary to reassess the force of his father's trite predictions. In the scene at the mansion, Jim mentions that he, unlike Plato, has never had any memory of the previous day. What memory then of the day depicted is to be expected from such a person after ten years have elapsed? (And this point thematically rationalizes the "unnatural" forgetting of poor Buzz.) Jim also says to the juvenile officer, "Boy, if—if I had *one* day when I didn't have to feel that I was ashamed of everything—if I felt I belonged some place, you know. . . ." The thought is left incomplete and it is doubtful that the boy has a definite conclusion in mind. But the day that is portrayed appears finally to have, in a strange way, satisfied his wish. A place where he is to belong has now been prepared, and he, shattered into a weakness that even his father can support, should find, as his father demonstrably has, a state of mind in which shame and confusion will be obliterated in a numbed acceptance of his provided space.

In making these claims, I wish to avoid a possible misunderstanding about what I take the tone of the film to be. Despite Jim's blindness to the essence of what is happening to him, and despite the grim resolution of the series of events, neither he nor the other kids is treated with contempt or hostility. On the contrary, the film is, on balance, sympathetic to their youthful sensitivity, vitality, and emotional honesty. The love scenes are typical in this regard. The tenderness, the candid attraction; and the genuinely felt needs are presented with respect. Alone in "Plato's mansion," Judy says, "I love you, Jim. I *really* mean it," and she assuredly does mean what she says. It is less clear, given her immaturity and severely circumscribed vision of the world, just how much, beyond the undoubted feelings of the moment, she has the capacity to mean. It is not that these teenagers are cowards or traitors or liars of some kind. It is simply that they are at the mercy of the hidden causal factors to which the film assigns such crushing weight.

A special sort of sympathy naturally attaches to Plato, who is gunned down on the steps of the observatory. During the attack upon him at the mansion, he has shot one of his attackers and fired at the policemen who arrive upon the scene. He escapes across the wooded hillside to the observatory, hides himself inside the building, and is trapped there by the police. Jim and Judy make their way to him, and he is eventually persuaded by Jim to come back out. But Plato is frightened by the glare of headlights on the planetarium grounds and when, in false alarm, these lights are turned blazingly upon him, he panics, runs, and is shot. Just as Buzz's death was associated with the planetarium images of our globe's destruction by the fiery star, so, in a different way, is Plato's. After Jim enters the planetarium to talk with Plato, he flicks on the switches that start up the visuals for the lecture on astronomy. He even remarks at one point, "Come on, Plato, you've seen this show before." But then, if Jim's action marks the beginning of a projection of that show, Plato's panic on the steps should come roughly at its conclusion. His demise in the overwhelming light should be matched on the domed ceiling inside by the annihilation of the earth in fire and gas. Jim is the new boy in town; but Plato is much more fundamentally a stranger to the world. And thus, it is the unassimilable stranger who is, in the end, eliminated.

Plato's parents have deserted him. He has no friends or social standing at the school. Above all, as his nickname suggests, he is to be seen as a kind of primitive philosopher who lives in thought and dreams. On the one hand, he lives so thoroughly in the imagination that he is clumsily out of touch with immediate circumstances. His loneliness is alleviated only by building fantasies around people such as Jim and movie stars and his real father, to whom he feels some special tie. On the other hand, he is very much in touch with the realities of isolation, emptiness, and death, and these are, in *Rebel*, the basic all-pervading realities of our brief lives. When earlier the lecturer at the planetarium finished his talk, Plato rose from behind the auditorium seats where he had hidden in fear and asked disdainfully, "What does *he* know about 'man alone'?" We are meant to infer that, out of his enigmatic experience, this is what Plato *does* know about, knowing more, perhaps, than the lecture has conveyed.

It is also important that the film hints, as clearly as a fifties Hollywood production could, that Plato's sexual orientation is gay. His being, like Judy, so immediately drawn to Jim presumably has its component of physical attraction too. The importance of this derives primarily from its being still another way in which he is set outside those operations that bring the young couple back into the established structures of family and society. It is because there is no social space for him to occupy that he is eventually destroyed. The mechanisms that assimilate Jim and Judy reject Plato and toss him aside. From this point of view, it is Plato who is, in a sense, the truly intransigent rebel. His rebellion is mostly passive and contemplative, but it is, nonetheless, a rebellion, one that is inevitably struck down at the observatory doors. Jim and Judy, at the mansion, notice and are amused that Plato is wearing one red sock and one of dark navy blue. Color, like space and time, has schematic significance in the film, and, within that scheme, red has its traditional association with rebellion and dark blue with the night sky and all that it has been made, in the movie, to signify. Hence, the pair of mismatched socks symbolizes the schizophrenia of Plato's existence. He is in revolt against the flatness and constriction of "normal life," but his rebellion envisages no worldly change: his eyes are fixed too unswervingly upon the oblivion that surrounds all change of every sort.

In a curious series of shots, occurring after Plato has been killed, Jim and Judy approach his corpse. Jim reaches down and zips up the red jacket that he had given Plato a few moments before, and Judy replaces a shoe that had fallen from Plato's foot. Echoing the earlier images of the temporary "family" the three kids had briefly formed, these actions have the look of an attempt by parents to bundle their child against the cold. The gesture, taken in this way, is pathetic and ironic. Jim's father then bends down and places his jacket on Jim's shoulders. He invites his boy, who is broken by shock and grief, to stand up with him, and he promises, in this context ambiguously, to be "as strong as you [Jim] want me to be." With the red jacket borne away on Plato and with the adult jacket now worn by Jim, an exchange of "uniforms" has been effected. The jacket of rebellion is gone, and, as Jim returns to Judy's side, he wears the token of his new and more acceptable status. As Jim and Judy start to leave together, Jim's parents stare at each other, at first in wonder and then in broad, happy relief. With their arms around each other, they follow the younger man and woman to the waiting police cars.

In the very last shot of the film, the camera cranes slowly up to show the dawn breaking over the observatory. As the assembled crowd disperses and departs, a solitary man (reputedly Nicholas Ray himself) walks up the path toward the planetarium to open it for the new day's work. The standard interpretation of the dawning of another day hardly needs explanation. However, in addition to all the other considerations of this chapter, we should add one terse and wonderfully opaque exchange between Jim and Plato just before the latter is shot. Plato asks, "Jim, do you think that the end of the world will come at nighttime?" and Jim replies simply, "No, at dawn." As far as I can see, Jim's answer does not have an interpretable literal point. What it does is construct an "equation between the coming of dawn and the end of the world. And this equation, especially in the context of this film, potentially cancels out the standard, more positive connotations of the dawn that appears in that final shot. Moreover, for the reasons that I have tried to elucidate, this is not only the end of the world for Plato, but it is likely to be the end of access to an open and living world for the young couple who are enclosed in the black cars that we see moving slowly down the drive.

This treatment of *Rebel Without a Cause* suggests some important ways in which our earlier discussion of cinematic point of view needs to be extended or qualified. For example, this film, like *The Searchers*, satisfies the rough criteria I mentioned for unrestricted narrational authority. For many purposes, this classification of *Rebel* is satisfactory and need not cause confusion. Nevertheless, it is also essential to an understanding of the film that there is a way in which its narration *is* systematically restricted.

It has been argued here that the film, in the first planetarium scene particularly, lays down a set of fairly abstract correspondences between various sorts of spatial and temporal properties and global qualities of the lives and actions of the characters. Furthermore, many of the spatial and temporal properties of the film's image track are themselves guided by or, if one likes, restricted in terms of this set of correspondences. To cite two of the simplest instances of this, I have explicated along these lines the relative constriction or openness of the space in certain scenes and the presentation of the narrative events as occurring in a single day. As I have tried to show, the narration is so elaborately restricted in terms of the relevant correspondences that the film seems to have an essaylike or lecturelike character of its own. It is as if simultaneously the viewer was being given an enunciation of a number of quite general principles and a concrete demonstration of their truth was being enacted on the screen. Unfortunately, however, it is not entirely clear how this *type* of restriction is to be described. Many films set up and operate within a system of, for example, symbolic correspondences, but one would not want to count this as a mode or feature of "point of view." What is special about *Rebel* is that (l) the abstract correspondences concern properties or kinds of properties that are actually instantiated in the narration; that is, the narration and its parts have spatial and temporal properties, and (2) the set of correspondences significantly determines the special way in which these formal properties are instantiated within the shots, scenes, and sequences of the film. Both of these conditions have to be satisfied if we are to think of these correspondences as defining a restriction imposed upon the film's *narrational* strategy. At least, these remarks adumbrate the notion that one would like to capture more rigorously so that its significance as a general possibility could be explored.

I mention this case partly because of its independent interest, but also because it potentially complicates some subordinate topics. Once again, the question can be illustrated in terms of *Rebel*. There are many scenes in the film that seem to invite a reading of the narration as reflecting the subjectivity of the teenagers involved in the action portrayed. That invitation is probably most strongly extended in the scene, after the chickie run episode, when Jim returns home, appeals for help from his parents, and winds up lashing out at their weakness and hypocrisy. (This seems to represent a definitive break with the parents: he tries to kill his father and destroy a portrait of his mother as a younger and lovelier woman.) Early in the scene, Jim is sprawled on the sofa with his head hanging over the edge toward the floor, and, as his mother enters the room, there is a point-of-view shot from his position there during which the camera revolves 180 degrees to capture the subjective effect of his getting up to face the situation. In the segment that follows, the claustrophobia, clutter, and distortion of this domestic space is rendered with almost hallucinatory emphasis. Not only is the space again oppressively confined, with furniture, stairs, and railings arising as barriers between the antagonists, but much of the action, most notably that on the stairs, is framed with the camera tilted to one side or the other so that characters artificially rise and fall in the shots in correlation with their attempts to dominate or to retreat from the course of the argument. Especially with that bizarre shot from Jim's field of vision introducing these events, it is tempting to suppose that the stylistics here are meant to mirror his continuing impressions of the interchange. And, indeed, I am not at all sure that this is incorrect. The problem is that the set of general correspondences operative in the film assigns to many facets of this narration a significance that far outruns anything we can ascribe to Jim's extremely limited perspective. Thus, in this scene, as in others, the use of space may well convey something of the teenager's feeling, but it also bears meaning that he cannot possibly comprehend. Perhaps we can say of this and similar scenes that the subjectivity of a character is reflected *and* it accomplishes more besides. The difficulty with this description is that it is by no means a trivial matter to discriminate the elements that pertain to the subjectivity reflected from the elements that pertain only to the wider conception of the film. Alternatively, "subjective reflection" would have to be redefined to exclude cases with this additional complexity. That task would not prove trivial either.

I have wished to bring out these last considerations without resolving them for the reasons stated at the beginning of this essay. They are typical of the refinement, qualification, and reformulation any vaguely adequate theory of cinematic point of view will, in the long run, have to provide. This suggestion that there is considerable complication lurking just beyond the scope of the discussion here may be discouraging. And yet, the subtlety and complexity of a film such as *Rebel* gives promise that suitable attention to more fine-grained distinctions will yield a satisfactory reward in our heightened appreciation of what the "classical" narrative film can, almost invisibly, achieve.

Notes

1. The screenplay of *Rebel* is credited to Stewart Stern and Irving Shulman, and the story credit is given to Ray himself. However, it is well-known that such divisions of credit can present a misleading idea of the nature of the various actual contributions.

2. This quote is from the entry on *Rebel Without a Cause* in Bawden (581). I chose this quote because it is typical of a common response to the film.

3. Barr's famous essay "Cinemascope: Before and After" is reprinted in Mast and Cohen (140–69).

4. An early working title for *Rebel* was "The Blind Run." Presumably, this was meant to make literal reference to the film's chickie run. However, in the light of the present discussion, it should be clear how the title would have been appropriate to larger thematic concerns as well.

5. It seems to me that Ray's work in the middle to late fifties has a much greater coherence than is generally recognized. *Rebel* was released in 1955. *Bigger Than Life* (1956) deals with a man who, under the influence of cortisone, goes into mad rebellion against the narrowness and constriction of his life. It is made clear that the rebellion, despite the madness, has some genuine justification. *Wind*

Across the Everglades (1958) is about a representative of "civilization" who is thrown up against a group of criminals who have formed their own primitive society in the swamp. His reaction to this confrontation is ambivalent. Finally, *The Savage Innocents* (1959) examines, from an explicitly anthropological perspective, the last of a tribe of Eskimos. The film plainly draws relativistic conclusions about the moral and social codes that order human groups. Many of the concerns in these films could have been predicted from *Rebel.*

Works Cited

Bawden, Liz-Anne, ed. *The Oxford Companion to Film*. New York: Oxford University Press, 1976.

Mast, Gerald, and Marshall Cohen, eds. *Film Theory and Criticism*, second edition. New York: Oxford University Press, 1979.

6

Jon Mitchell

Jim Stark's "Barbaric Yawp"

Rebel Without a Cause and the Cold War Crisis in Masculinity

A suburban explosion characterized the American decade of the 1950s. Eighteen million people made the move to the suburbs between 1950 and 1960, and out of the thirteen million new homes built in these ten years over eleven million of them were in the suburbs.[1] Suburbia became not only a place to live in the 1950s but also a state of mind. For many Americans a suburban home, situated in an idyllic setting and equipped with the newest technological appliances to ease domestic strain, represented the ultimate ideal of postwar life. Social gatherings, such as communal barbecues and religious worship, became commonplace: "The very nature of suburban life encouraged cooperation and volunteerism." William Chafe observes, "from the potluck supper to the local school planning council, the vogue of togetherness . . . reigned supreme."[2] One New York community required all children in grades seven through ten to partake in a "Home and Family Living" course, which featured topics such as "developing school spirit" and "clicking with the crowd."[3] Being a part of the group was an all-important factor for suburban Americans. Regardless of this cult of togetherness, there persisted a restless dissatisfaction at the heart of suburbia evinced in the rise of alcoholism and tranquilizer usage in the period (between 1955 and 1957 tranquilizer sales rose from $2.2 million to $150 million).[4]

Despite the general celebration of prosperity afforded the suburban American in the 1950s, ennui, dissatisfaction, and a feeling that masculinity was in decline surfaced as considerable complaints against this lifestyle. "We abound with all of the things that make us comfortable," noted Louis B. Seltzer. "Yet . . . something is not there that should be—something we once had. . . ."[5]

In 1958 *Look* published a series of articles concerned with the emasculation of the white suburban American man in the immediate postwar decades. To mark the popularity of this series it was published later that same year as a single collection called *Look: The Decline of Masculinity* (1958). During this period, a number of articles bemoaning the same fate appeared in *Playboy*. The majority of these articles from both *Look* and *Playboy*, as well as articles from other disparate and less popular sources, followed in the critical vein of Philip Wylie's *Generation of Vipers*.[6] Wylie held (amongst other important aspects) that America was already in the grip of a matriarchal society to which men had been forced to surrender. He believed that, "the male is an attachment of the female in our civilization. . . . He does most of what he does . . . to supply whatever women have defined as their necessities, comforts, and luxuries."[7]

In these publications the male writers complained about a decline of masculinity, which they felt had been caused by the excessive influence of the feminine on society. For instance, J. Robert Moskin bluntly states that "the American male is now dominated by the American female" and asks, "How did the American male get into this pit of subjection, where even his masculinity is in doubt?"[8] He answers by elucidating the historical factors that he believed transferred power to women:

> The nation's Puritan fathers started it by bringing to America the idea that the body was evil. They gave the new American male a sense of guilt about sex. When the frontier moved westward, women became scarce, and awe and respect were added to guilt . . . [and] "women with guts became more and more acceptable." They first won the right to a college education in Ohio in 1833 and the right to vote in Wyoming in 1869. They started cleaning up the men's world of saloons, brothels and gambling halls.
>
> During World War I, the American woman was called upon to do men's work. . . . In the twenties she "went on a rampage," and . . . jobs for women, "free love," feminine contraception and

> women's suffrage became fair play. Finally, the great depression gave women an economic excuse to introduce their husbands to dirty dishes and diapers . . . Only since the end of World War II has the American woman had a chance to . . . enjoy her now-dominant position. She discovered that she didn't have to imitate men in order to rule. The feminine partner took charge and she did so as a woman.[9]

There is something self-pitying about such an image of oppressed masculinity. Moskin does not consider to any degree what he feels is being lost. Masculinity for him is normalized and ideologically transparent; it is not something for analysis, it simply exists. He views the problem as a struggle between essentials gender types, between the "innocence" and righteousness of American masculinity, and the tyranny of American femininity. He perceives in the latter an intent to bring about the fall of the American man. Therefore, when Jim Stark, in *Rebel Without a Cause* (1955), cries out to his parents, "you're tearing me apart," he acknowledges not only his own conflict and subsequent angst with his domestic life but, more importantly, a greater conflict and angst felt amongst white males in the suburbanized world of mid-twentieth-century America.

The crisis in masculinity, arriving from an ingrained conflict between such binary ideas as "soft" and "hard" men, led many men to retreat to their basements and workshops as the do-it-yourself (DIY) craze heightened. It also pushed them into the woods hunting, fishing, and/or camping. Young American males, however, felt increasingly at odds with such a compromise. As Paul Goodman argues, "we see groups of boys and young men disaffected from the dominant society" and he further warns that "these groups are not small, and they will grow larger."[10] Young males were caught in the cycle of paradox. They enjoyed the luxuries that had benefited them in America's progress, but they suffered, along with their fathers, from this feeling of loss.

The growth of white-collar employment and the suburbanization of America in the 1950s identified the model American male figure as the suburban husband and father. This male paradigm came into direct conflict with the long-established notion of the rugged American male of frontier heritage; that individual male who expressed, to use Walt Whitman's phrase, his "barbaric yawp over the roofs of the world."[11] However, the Cold War climate of paranoia caused parents to fear that an overt commitment to this archetype could lead their children into juvenile delinquency, and subsequently threaten the peaceful order of the 1950s suburban world.[12] Nevertheless, to many males, particularly young males, this archetype of individuality, ingrained into American cultural history by such stories as "Rip Van Winkle" and *The Adventures of Huckleberry Finn* and by the mythologized heroics of Davy Crockett and Daniel Boone, was the only seemingly authentic masculine expression in what they saw as a largely "bland" and feminized world. Caught thus between these two extremes, this crisis in masculinity can be expressed by the following question: when a man acts against conformity, when he puts himself before his subjection to an authority, which side of the line is he on? Is his "barbaric yawp" sounded over the roofs a cry of heroic individuality or the screech of reckless delinquency?

Rebel Without a Cause denotes a concern with this question, and moreover, with the larger question of how to be an "authentic" American man. Jim himself demonstrates this when he pleads to his father, "What can you do when you have to be a man?" Yet Jim also feels torn between the dissatisfaction he feels surrounding his father's model of masculinity, which leads him to rebel, and his wish to conform to an expression of authentic masculinity. His interest in Judy, his need to befriend the "Kids," and his questionable friendship with Plato are all used in the film to demonstrate Jim's sense of conflict. As the film progresses, Jim becomes a figure of compromise, and comes to reflect a balance between these paradigmatic extremes. He is, at once, able to show the heroic determinism of America's frontier heritage, as he battles to be "authentic" in a world of artificial expressions of masculinity, whilst also suppressing this "raw edge" to enable successful adaptation to a suburban America. In short, by the end of the film he becomes a hero who is not too heroic, and paradoxically an individual conformist.

The following discussion will explore how the film moves from Jim Stark's own view of his alienation from society, which he blames unquestionably upon his inadequate father, to his own identification with the benefits of a stable nuclear family, appreciated when he, Judy, and Plato play-act as a family. It will also show how, by taking on the role of a father figure to Plato, Stark gains a greater understanding about his own father, and he thus discovers the "authentic" masculine identity that he had been searching for throughout the film. In other words, he is able to elevate himself above his own delinquency and reacquaint himself with the consensus culture of the 1950s. Overall, the following discussion will attempt to elucidate how the world depicted in *Rebel Without a Cause* acts as a microcosm that reflects the larger significance of the 1950s white masculine culture experiencing a sense of identity crisis. It will also indicate how this crisis and its paradoxical resolution were both a result, and an intricate part, of the pervasive Cold War climate of mid-twentieth-century America.

From the pastoral worlds of Cooper's Leatherstocking Tales, Wister's *The Virginian* (1902), and Schaefer's *Shane* (1948) to the urban pastorals of the Hollywood gangster and the comic book Superhero, the archetype of the American male, defined in 1955 by R. W. B. Lewis as "the hero of the new adventure: an individual standing alone, self reliant and self-propelling, ready to confront whatever awaited him with the aid of his own unique and inherent resources,"[13] has a perennial place in American ideas of masculinity.[14] However, despite the pervasive presence of this archetype in American culture, Michael Kimmel, in his book *Manhood in America*, discusses how masculine identity in America had always been divisive. Kimmel shows how American masculinity is based on an ideological split between two distinctive types with clear links with America's European heritage, the Genteel Patriarch and the Heroic Artisan. He notes of the Genteel Patriarch that at his best he

> represents a dignified aristocratic manhood, committed to the British upper-class code of honor and to well-rounded character, with exquisite tastes and manners and refined sensibilities. To the Genteel Patriarch, manhood meant property ownership and a benevolent patriarchal authority at home . . .[15]

And of the Heroic Artisan,

> Independent, virtuous, and honest, the Heroic Artisan is stiffly formal in his manners with women, stalwart and loyal to his male comrades. On the family farm or in his urban crafts shop, he was an honest toiler, unafraid of hard work, proud of his craftsmanship and self-reliance.[16]

In the opening scene of *Rebel Without a Cause*, Jim lies drunk on the pavement wearing a suit and making a newspaper bed for a toy monkey. His suit represents his attempt to take up the mantle of manhood by the way he dresses, and his fuss over the toy monkey indicates an attitude of patriarchal care, which is further developed when Jim offers his jacket to Plato at the police station. Jim's drunkenness and his playing with the monkey, not to mention his petty annoyance with the imitation of the police siren, reveals the inner infantile state that he attempts to overcome throughout the film. We, as viewers, are immediately alerted to the divisive nature of American masculinity. The major discourse in the film is thus the difference between the epistemology of masculinity and the ontology of masculinity, in other words the difference between the ideals of American masculinity and the realities of being a mid-twentieth-century male. Jim Stark's feelings of conflict represent an America in the throes of maturation; an America attempting to cast off its idealistic past to emerge as a responsible world power.

This move was part of a response to changes over the last half of the nineteenth century and over the first half of the twentieth century that were believed to have destabilized the confidence in the supremacy of white masculinity, and caused men to feel that the male's mastery over both the domestic and political worlds was being questioned. Such changes included the emancipation of slaves, the closing of the frontier, the move toward gender equality achieved by women with the ratification of the nineteenth amendment to the Constitution, along with the economic depression of the 1930s and the resultant escalation in unemployment that called into question the male's breadwinner role. Two World Wars, moreover, had challenged America's place in world politics and had forced them out of their own belief in their isolationist exceptionalism. Following the Second World War, Malcolm Bradbury notes, America became "implicated . . . in the mounting disorders of the modern world . . . unable as she had done in 1918, to withdraw to her own continent and mind her own business."[17] Thus, whilst American masculinity had always been a divided ideal, by the 1950s, this tension had become more acute.

It is also in the opening scene that the narrative issues of the film are contained, as we are introduced to the main characters and their problems. Jim, Judy, and John Crawford (Plato) initially represent a trinity of delinquency. Jim is the rebellious drunken teenager, Judy is the overly independent female, who, as represented in the film, is just looking for something or someone to give her life the proper direction, and Plato is the (sexual) deviant and possible psychopath who has lacked parental guidance. These traits—delinquency, female independence, and deviance—were cast in opposition to the considered "right way" to live as an American, which is encapsulated in the ideal of the stable nuclear family unit, silently held in high esteem in *Rebel.* The film, for instance, attempts to show the problems that occur when this unit becomes deficient and dysfunctional. In *Seeing Is Believing*, Peter Biskind argues that, "it quickly becomes evident that it is not Jim, Judy, or Plato who are the delinquents but their parents."[18] Biskind's reading, however, is only half correct, for whilst there is indeed a warning about neglectful and/or overindulgent parenting, the film is more concerned with Jim's perspective on suburban life, and his own internal conflict with ideals of masculinity, which is abated at the end of the film as he abandons his romantic ideals of authentic masculinity and accepts his father's pragmatic views on life, just as he accepts his father's jacket.

This ideological shift in Jim's perspective begins significantly with the death of Buzz following the chickie run. Already a figure in conflict, Jim's response to the event is to confess his part in the event, whilst his need to confess runs contrary to his parents wishes. It is mainly here that Jim's parents are fully criticized for their attempts to cover up Jim's delinquency. Jim's attempt to confess, and to take responsibility for his actions, is shown in the film to be the right thing to do. It is, moreover, the inability of others to help Jim to do this—his unwilling parents, the disinterested police officers—that leads to an escalation of delinquency at the film's end. Placing Jim's rationale in the context of the House on Un-American Activities Committee (HUAC) hearings, which sought out deviants in American politics and culture believed to be dangerous to the democratic stability of America, his response is indicative of a Cold War America infatuated with fears of a corrupted social morality.

In his article, "The Ideology and Techniques of Repression, 1903–1933," William Preston succinctly sums up the atmosphere that would prevail in the Cold War 1950s, saying that "not only are we afraid of our own shadow, but we also would like to deport it."[19] The shadow America was trying to deport was not simply the shadow of communism, but a conglomeration of what was perceived to be deviant from and/or challenging to mid-twentieth-century American postwar ideology, and thus cast as deviant to mainstream ideals. Instead of simply constituting a political threat, communism became an umbrella term that included the threats of homosexuality, the feminine, sexual promiscuity, radicals, members of, and subscribers to, alternative or conflicting political ideologies, as well as ex-members and ex-subscribers to the aforementioned; in general any and all critics of America at mid-century. This widespread use of branding any critic of America as a communist and therefore on the wrong side of the moral equation supports Donald Pease's argument that "In totalizing the globe into a super opposition between the two superpowers, the Cold War can recast all conflicts anyplace in the world in terms of this pervasive opposition."[20] He further contends that "the Cold War frame manages to control, in advance, all the positions the opposition can occupy," for all such opposition, "can be read in terms of 'our' freedom versus their totalitarianism."[21]

The Cold War frame, however, is multifaceted. It can ultimately be used from a number of angles and can reposition all and any arguments within this framework. Americans cast themselves in the Cold War frame in the role of innocents facing a constant threat from corruption—communists or cocksuckers—whether it is the mainstream facing corruption from communism; men facing it from women; or youths facing it from a perceived suburban apathy. Thus, young males attempted to escape from a society in which they had been cast as totalitarian and, therefore, as threatening to predominant standards of masculinity. This same society, however, cast these same men as a threat to democracy. Subsequently, both sides demonized the other, whilst they believed themselves to be on the side of good. In the end, it creates a constant möbius strip, where the opposition constantly turns back into its counterpart.[22]

Communism, therefore, was not just simply a political enemy; the communist crisis was largely a composite of fears and anxieties that emerged as America realized that it had entered a new phase of development and could no longer simply return to the isolationism of the past. A predominant element of such fears and anxieties was the struggle between the hard and the soft. K. A. Cuordileone comments extensively, for example, on the link between the fear of homosexuality and the fear of communism; how homosexuals were seen to be men of low moral standards, and how such men, employed in governmental roles were open to blackmail and political corruption. This is apparent from the U.S. Senate investigation into homosexuality and sexual deviancy that was instituted during a time when laws were being passed to control loyalty in government positions. The result of this investigation was the report titled *Employment of Homosexuals and Other Sex Perverts in Government.*[23] She further comments on the use of this hysteria by Republicans to discredit the Democrat-led government. She notes how these detractors linked liberals, homosexuals, and communists into an unholy trinity. As a paradigm of this trinity she explores the well-documented case of Whittaker Chambers and his accusations against state official Alger Hiss, concluding that:

> Chambers's self-proclaimed sexual affliction [homosexuality, which he renounced at the same time as renouncing communism] fed the imagination that linked political subversion and "sexual perversion"; his mysterious friendship with Hiss in the 1930s implicated the latter in Chambers's murky past. And although the sexual overtones of the case did not result in explicit accusations that Hiss was a homosexual, he did become the prototypical weak-willed, effete, treasonous eastern establishment liberal, whose softness left him prone to transgressions of a political, moral, and perhaps even of a sexual nature.[24]

Whilst the sexual overtones of the Hiss case remained subtly in the background, Senator Joseph McCarthy, a man not known for curtailing his vulgarities, expressed the following to a group of reporters, "If you want to be against McCarthy, boys, you've got to be either a Communist or a cocksucker."[25] McCarthy's statement makes the link between what is perceived as politically deviant and sexually deviant so explicit as to be beyond doubt.

Plato is a clear representation in the film of the belief in the hidden threat of homosexuality. Plato is doubly cursed: according to essentialist beliefs, his father was absent, thus depriving him of a positive male role model and underscoring his "troubled" sexuality; tellingly, his mother is also vague to him, and the lack of her "civilizing" influence helps to lead to his violent delinquency. Upon his introduction in the film he is, like the other main characters, in the juvenile section of the police station for having shot a couple of puppies with his mother's gun. Plato's homosexuality is never avowed, but his actions and mannerisms throughout the film, as well as the intertextual reference of his nickname, allow for such a reading. An early scene in the film, for instance, shows a picture of Alan Ladd in Plato's school locker. Plato makes a slight glance from Ladd to Jim, which reveals, not only that Plato has found a new object for his hero worship, as Tim Dirks notes, but that he has also found a potential subject for same-sex desire.[26] From his very conception in the film Plato is presented as a morally as well as sexually suspect (and the two were most often linked) character. It is arguable that Plato is a sexual psychopath in the making. The sexual psychopath, given shape by the 1931 German film *M*, which starred Peter Lorre as a former mental patient who killed school girls to assuage his desires, lurked as a formidable threat in the American imagination.[27] This fear, which caused many attempted lynchings, and the call for the sterilization of sex offenders, Estelle B. Freedman contends, also renegotiated the dynamics of sexuality between men and women. The "response to the sexual psychopath," she argues, "evinced a significant departure from the nineteenth-century emphasis on maintaining female purity and a movement toward a modern concern about controlling male violence."[28] Thus his friendship and adoration of Jim represents the influence of a "hypermasculine homosexuality" upon Jim during his time of crisis, and for the film to reach its conclusion, "Plato *has* to die . . . irreconcilable rebellion can not be accommodated within the narrative: it is equated with insanity."[29]

To return to the consideration of the film's opening scenes, when Jim's family arrives at the police station, Jim mocks his own father by offering him the chair as if it were a throne. Jim reveals himself to be a Hamletesque figure who attempts to come to terms with what he believes is the loss of a "legitimate" father figure. For according to Jim's view of the world, his problems are caused by his domestic relationships. Jim yearns for his father to be a better masculine model by standing up to Jim's overdominant mother. He states that if his father "had the guts to knock Mom cold once then maybe she'd be happy and then she'd stop pickin' on him." Jim's view of "authentic" masculinity leads him to perceive his father as being overly domesticated, where he should be rugged and self-reliant. This theme is later emphasized when Jim catches his father wearing his mother's apron, and on his knees picking up the remains of a meal he had dropped on the way to taking it to his wife who had confined herself to bed with sickness. Jim's father does not want his wife to discover his blunder and is frantically cleaning up, much to Jim's disgust at this inversion of the gender role patterns.

In the next scene between them, Jim questions his father on what he should do about the chickie run in which he is supposed to take part, and his father, still wearing the apron, mumbles some inadequate response. Jim then pleads, "What can you do when you have to be a man?" His father attempts to reason with him, telling him to make a list of pros and cons. Hindered by his belief of an essential masculinity—that there is a right and wrong way to be a man—Jim fails to get the response he wants from his father. In Jim's narrow view his father is too domesticated to adequately supply the help he wants, and he is further unable to prevent his son from leaving the house to meet his fate. Consequently, the film subscribes to what has already been seen as the limited vision of presenting the father as the bearer of a highly essentialized masculinity to be passed on to his son. What is presented in the film as the failure of Jim's father to take responsibility for his son, coupled with the effects of his domineering mother, is naïvely shown to lead the son, Jim, toward a "hypermasculine juvenile delinquency."

Jim's father is initially presented as the female-dominated male perceived to be prevalent in mid-twentieth-century America. Abram Kardiner represents such a man as the American stereotype, "Mr. Bumstead," who "assume[s] no responsibility for the female" and is "the submissive breadwinner, while Mrs. Bumstead is the real power in the family." "What kind of masculine ideal," Kardiner asks, "is furnished to the children by a father like this?" His reply is swift, and typical of the period: "The boys of the Bumstead family stand a good chance of developing into homosexuals."[30] This idea is demonstrated in the film by Jim's friendship with Plato.

The poet and spokesman for the later Mythopoetic Men's Movement, Robert Bly, comments extensively in his book *Iron John* (1990) on the loss of the father: "when a father now sits down at the table, he seems weak and insignificant . . . [he] no longer fill[s] as large a space in the room as nineteenth-century fathers did."[31] He extends his argument by questioning the effects of such a father on the son, "In our time, when a father shows up as an object of ridicule . . . or a fit field for suspicion . . . or a bad-tempered fool . . . or a weak puddle of indecision, the son has a problem. How does he imagine his own life as a man?"[32] Bly is an extreme supporter of an essentialized masculine paradigm, similar to the ideal of the archetypal male, which he calls "the Wild Man." He believes in a "natural" masculinity, and provides an essentialist framework of gender relations upon which he bases his analysis.

Whilst believing that the father is meant to be the bearer of a "true" masculinity that he should pass on to his son, it is ironic that, as David Matza and Gresham M. Sykes observe, despite mainstream society working to prevent excessive violence, it paradoxically provides "a persistent support for aggression which manifests itself in the derogatory connotations of labels such as 'sissy' or 'fag.' "[33] Thus, many young males were castigated by the mainstream for their violent behavior while at the same time they were pushed by such derogatory labels into expressing an aggressive masculinity. This is signified when Jim is provoked to action by being called a "chicken," which leads him not only to engage reluctantly in a knife fight, but also in the chickie run. That he becomes embroiled in these events, the film suggests, has to do with the high ideals of masculinity he states to his father about the chickie run, "it's a matter of honor!"

Whilst Jim sees his father as a failed model of masculinity, one might nevertheless read the film as a challenge to Jim's perspective in which his father becomes a model of a caring and encouraging masculine identity. This is a man who is rational, and not quick to lose his temper, a man who has an understanding of the female world, and who attempts to do his share in the domestic sphere. Throughout most of the film, however, Jim yearns for an authority figure who will take responsibility for his actions. After his night of drunken delinquency, for instance, he is eager to conform. This is signified first by his comment to juvenile officer, Ray, where he states, "If I had one day when I didn't feel all confused . . . if I felt as if I belonged some place"; also by his parting words to his parents, "I feel maybe we'll stay awhile"; and finally when he apologies for stepping on the prohibited school motto. The message of the film, however, is that Jim has to take responsibility for himself. This is confirmed in the final scenes of the film. Already commented upon earlier as an example of the failure of parents, they also represent Jim's entrance into manhood.

Feeling a need to confess his part in Buzz's death, Jim finds nobody willing to listen to him. First, he frantically urges his father to stand up for him, and when he does not, Jim goes to the police station, but finds nobody willing to listen to him, either, and the only sympathetic adult, the juvenile cop Ray, absent. Jim attempts to avoid his responsibilities by taking flight with Judy to the abandoned mansion, but his problems follow him, in the "deviancy" represented by Plato as well as the "delinquency" represented by the gang members.

Whilst the film's opening encapsulates the themes recurrent throughout, the ending provides the necessary closing narrative bracket, which concludes the film and provides a neat resolution to Jim's conflict. As the three—Jim, Judy, and Plato—play-act as a family, Jim and Judy come to realize the responsibilities and difficulties of their parents' lives. This leads to a maturation in Jim and Judy's attitudes as they move toward accepting the suburban ideals of the period. They thus abandon Plato and the "deviance" he represents. Shooting the invading gang member, Plato signifies the removal of the temptation of delinquency from Jim, leaving only his homosexual side, represented by Plato. With one form of corruption removed, the film approaches the second form.

The film demonstrates what it believes is the instability of the homosexual deviant by Plato's overly emotional reaction as he runs off and hides in the observatory. His own conflict only partially resolved, Jim goes after Plato, and to show the compromised (not too heroic) hero that Jim is becoming, he does not side with his friend's rebellion against the suburban world; instead, Jim simply removes the bullets from Plato's gun, thus helping to maintain Plato's belief in his rebellion, whilst taking the actual power from it. Biskind refers to this as "the corporate-liberal, manipulative solution."[34] Jim's final, and most symbolic, action is to give Plato his red jacket. The symbolism of this is apparent from the color of the jacket: red, the color associated with communism and thus a derogatory word for a communist within the Cold War frame. When Jim passes his red jacket to Plato the pseudohomosexual, he sheds his rebellion, confirms his place with mainstream society, and basically marks Plato as the communist-like threat as he delivers him into the hands of the authorities. In the climate of the McCarthy's communist "witch hunts" and HUAC, Jim's actions become the visual parallel of naming names. The film shows how Jim has pulled himself from the brink, how he has abandoned his overly idealistic views of masculine individualism, and, as the incident with Plato and the gun suggests, accepted the mainstream view of a compromised masculinity. The final mark of Jim's acceptance of mainstream values is his acceptance of his father's coat. However, just as Jim assuages his deviant urges, his actions spur his father to take on a little more responsibility for his son. Michael DeAngelis, however, by noting that "Jim's efforts to resolve the situation peacefully are undermined by the police officers stationed outside the planetarium who, by reflex reaction, shoot and kill Plato on the first glimpse of a gun in his hand,"[35] hints that, instead of seeing the events as part of Jim's capitulation with the mainstream, they highlight the destructive intolerance of the patriarchal order, represented by the police, that simply destroys those that it cannot assimilate.

He also argues that despite the general culture of twinned fear around delinquency and homosexuality, particularly as emphasized in *Rebel*, James Dean, as both the character Jim Stark and as an actor, offered a fantasy model for gay men of the 1950s to identify with. Indeed, in making such films to warn of the perceived social inerrancies in American society, the film industry brought the issues "out of the closet" and into the public arena for discussion and debate.

Despite such revision, as a 1950s film, *Rebel* nevertheless works to capture the mainstream mood of the period. The film laments the crisis in masculinity, while also representing the fear of taking the archetype too seriously. Jim is redeemed in his manhood by his association with the lead female, Judy. In his moment of temptation in the derelict house, Jim clearly chooses Judy and abandons his infantile innocence when he abandons Plato to explore the house (and, as it transpires, Judy). It is during this period of isolation that the rebellious youth is given the chance to choose between civilization or continued rebellion; to engage with the world or to attempt to remain an innocent.

Rebel demonstrates that to light out for the territories in the 1950s was perceived to be a path not toward the ideal of masculine individualism, but a path leading toward crime, homosexuality, and infantilism, what Kardiner termed "the unholy three of social imbalance."[36] Charles Murray likewise argued that "men who do not support families find other ways to prove that they are men, which tend to take various destructive forms" and his conclusion is that "[without marriage] too many of them remain barbarians."[37] In *Rebel*, the influences of homosexuality and delinquency are overcome, the female is contained in her subservient place, whereby the meaning of her life comes from her relationship with her man, and the film solidifies the importance of the role of the father in the suburban home, all in line with the Cold War standards of mid-twentieth-century America. Jim's rebellion, as the title suggests, was ultimately without a cause, and the film resolves to bring Jim to a state of homeostasis, whereby his "barbaric yawp" is quelled. What the film ultimately argues is the idea that the escapist fantasy, the "flight from masculinity" as Abram Kardiner called it, was no longer an avenue open for the identification with the masculine ideal. In words spoken in the film (by Judy), men "don't run away when you want them!"

It is nevertheless important to understand that despite the overall message of support for mainstream standards in the film, many young males primarily saw Jim Stark as a rebellious character to be identified with and as a model upon which to dress their own anxieties. Commenting on the impact of the film, one 1960s activist noted that "after you saw something like *Rebel Without a Cause*, you felt like going out and breaking a few windshields. And once in a while, you did."[38] Thus, as DeAngelis argues, *Rebel* is problematic.

> [Dean's role] constitute[s] no clearly articulated manifesto of rebellion, yet neither . . . [does it] demonstrate the protagonist's desire to assimilate into the dominant social order and find his place within it. The narratives retain an ambiguity that accommodates readings of the protagonist as either assimilationist or rebellious, and sometimes, paradoxically, as both.[39]

Whilst Jim Stark, therefore, can be seen to have worked to silence his "barbaric yawp," many young males, nevertheless, continued to express theirs and they would insist on placing meaning upon the word "rebel" in the film's title, whilst ignoring the qualifying phrase "without a cause." One such figure was a fan of James Dean, Charles Starkweather, who, with his girlfriend Caril Fugate, went on a murder spree in 1958. Their crimes have been captured in later "rebel films" such as Terrence Malick's *Badlands* (1974), David Lynch's *Wild at Heart*, Quentin Tarantino and Tony Scott's *True Romance* (1993), Dominic Sena's *Kalifornia* (1993), and Oliver Stone's *Natural Born Killers* (1994).

Notes

1. Chafe (117).
2. Chafe (120).
3. Patterson (344–45).
4. Miller (23).
5. Seltzer (20).
6. Such articles include "The Abdicating Male." Moskin; Leonard; Attwood; Schlesinger; and Kardiner.
7. Wylie (218).
8. Moskin (77).
9. Moskin (80).
10. Goodman (21).
11. Whitman (2138).
12. The prevalent fear of juvenile delinquency can be seen by the proliferation of such journal articles as Barron; Rubin; Nye et al.; Matzer and Sykes.
13. Lewis (5).
14. For discussions on the archetypal male in American popular culture, see Madden; Warshow; and Middleton.
15. Kimmel (16).
16. Kimmel (16).
17. Bradbury (126–27).
18. Biskind (201).
19. Preston (260).
20. Pease (389).
21. Pease (390).

22. A Möbius strip is a one-sided surface formed by joining together the two ends of a long rectangular strip, one end being twisted through 180 degrees before the join is made. Thus it has no clearly defined inside or outside. See Barth.

23. Cuordileone (532–33).

24. Cuordileone (534).

25. Cuordileone (521).

26. See Dirks.

27. See Freedman.

28. Freedman (85).

29. McCann (22).

30. Kardiner (29).

31. Bly (98).

32. Bly (99).

33. Matzer and Sykes (717).

34. Biskind (209).

35. DeAngelis (46)

36. Kardiner (19).

37. Murray (128).

38. Cited in Anderson (33).

39. DeAngelis (44).

Works Cited

Anderson, Terry. *The Movement and the Sixties: Protest in America from Greensboro to Wounded Knee*. New York: Oxford University Press, 1994.

Attwood, W. "The American Male: Why Does He Work So Hard?" *Look* (March 4, 1958).

Barron, Milton L. "Juvenile Delinquency and American Values." *American Sociological Review* 16.2 (April 1951).

Barth, John. "Frame Tale." In *Lost in the Funhouse: Fiction for Print, Tape, Live Voice*. London: Penguin Books, 1972. Originally printed in 1968.

Biskind, Peter. *Seeing Is Believing*. London: Bloomsbury, 2001. Originally printed in 1983.

Bly, Robert. *Iron John*. London: Dorset Books, 1990.

Bradbury, Malcolm. *The Modern American Novel*. Oxford: Oxford University Press, 1992. Originally printed in 1983.

Chafe, William. *The Unfinished Journey: America since World War II*. Oxford: Oxford University Press, 1995. Originally printed 1986.

Cuordileone, K. A. " 'Politics in an Age of Anxiety': Cold War Political Culture and the Crisis of American Masculinity, 1949–1960." *Journal of American History* 87.2 (September 2000).

DeAngelis, Michael. *Gay Fandom and Crossover Stardom: James Dean, Mel Gibson, and Keanu Reeves*. London: Duke University Press, 2001.

Dirks, Tim. Review of *Rebel Without a Cause* (1955). http://www.filmsite.org/rebel.html.

Freedman, Estelle B. "'Uncontrolled Desires': The Response to the Sexual Psychopath, 1920–1960." *Journal of American History* 74.1 (June 1987).

Goodman, Paul. *Growing Up Absurd*. London: Sphere Books, 1970. Originally printed 1960.

Kardiner, Abram. "The Flight from Masculinity." In Hendrik M. Ruitenbeek, ed., *The Problem of Homosexuality in Modern Society*. New York: E. P. Dutton, 1963.

Kimmel, Michael S. *Manhood in America: A Cultural History*. New York: The Free Press, 1996.

Leonard, G. B. "The American Male: Why Is He Afraid to Be Different?" *Look* (February 18, 1958).

Lewis, R. W. B. *The American Adam: Innocence, Tragedy, and Tradition in the Nineteenth Century*. Chicago: The University of Chicago Press, 1971. Originally published 1971.

Madden, David. *Tough Guy Writers of the Thirties*. Carbondale and Edwardsville: Southern Illinois University Press, 1968.

Matza, David and Gresham M. Sykes. "Juvenile Delinquency and Subterranean Values." *American Sociological Review* 26.5 (October 1961).

McCann, Graham. *Rebel Males: Clift, Brando and Dean*. London: Hamish Hamilton, 1991.

Middleton, Peter. *The Inward Gaze: Masculinity and Subjectivity in Modern Culture*. London: Routledge, 1992.

Miller, Douglas T. *On Our Own: American in the Sixties*. Lexington, MA: DC Heath and Co., 1996.

Moskin, J. Robert. "The American Male: Why Do Women Dominate Him?" *Look* (February 4, 1958).

Murray, Charles. *Losing Ground: American Social Policy, 1950–1980*. Cited in R. Miles, *The Rites of Man: Love, Sex, and Death in the Making of the Male*. London: Grafton Books, 1991.

Nye, Ivan F. et al. "Socioeconomic Status and Delinquent Behavior." *American Sociological Review* 63.4 (January 1958).

Patterson, James T. "The Middle-Class World of the 1950s." In James Patterson, ed., *America in the Twentieth Century: A History*. 3rd ed. New York: Harcourt Brace Jovanovich, 1989.

Pease, Donald. "Melville and Cultural Persuasion." In Sacvan Bercovitch and Myra Jehlen, eds., *Ideology and Classic American Literature*. New York: Cambridge University Press, 1986.

Preston, William. "The Ideology and Techniques of Repression, 1903–1933." In H. Goldberg, ed., *American Radicals: Some Problems and Personalities*. New York: Modern Reader Paperbacks, 1969. Originally printed in 1957.

Schlesinger, Arthur, Jr. "The Crisis in Masculinity" (1958). In *The Politics of Hope*. London: Eyre & Spottiswoode, 1964.

Seltzer, Louis B. "What Is Wrong with Us? Quoted in John Hellmann, *American Myth and the Legacy of Vietnam*. New York: Columbia University Press, 1986.

"The Abdicating Male and How the Gray Flannel Mind Exploits Him through His Women." *Playboy* (November 1956).

Warshow, Robert. *The Immediate Experience: Movies, Comics, Theater and Other Aspects of Popular Culture*. New York: Atheneum, 1970.

Whitman, Walt. "Song of Myself." *Leaves of Grass* (1855). In Nina Baym et al., eds., *The Norton Anthology of American Literature*, volume 1. New York: W. W. Norton, 1998. Originally printed 1979.

Wylie, Phillip. *Generation of Vipers*. Norman, IL: Dalkey Archive Press, 1996. Originally printed 1942.

James Dean as "Jim Stark."

7

MICK BRODERICK

"Armageddon Without a Cause"

Playing "Chicken" in the Atomic Age

WHEN WE LOOK AT LIFE TODAY, the tensions between peoples, the constant threat of war, the preoccupation with weapons of unequalled power, the universal training of men in the arts of death and destruction, we cannot fail to see in adolescent gang hostility a distorted reflection of the atmosphere of the world itself. The ever more deadly combat of the youngsters, the aimlessness with which they fight, the potency of their weapons, the development of new and atrocious tactics, the wider and wider spread of conflict seem, as in a distorted glass, to mirror the conduct of nations. . . . The shook-up generation is a sub-group of our culture and this is a shook-up age. We live in an era which glorifies violence and we must expect young people to be influenced by their environment. If we are shocked by what happens in the street we should be frantic with anxiety over the conduct of statesmen and nations.

—Harrison E. Salisbury, *The Shook-Up Generation*

In his influential 1958 book *The Shook-Up Generation* Harrison E. Salisbury suggests a significant relationship between the macro events of international cold war belligerency and the 1950s American microcosm of individual, family and community anomie. It's a view Salisbury draws from a leading Californian criminologist of the time, Dr. Marcel Frym, who Salisbury quotes on the relationship between superpower nuclear aggression and its reflection in juvenile rebellion: "The accent on violence is expressed in many ways—the use of atomic power for mass destruction in warfare, over-powerful motor vehicles, acute international tensions implying the threat of war."[1] Such views reflected the postwar sociological and psychological attention being placed on increasing conformism at a time of heightened political sensitivities where McCarthyism was still potent.[2]

Nicholas Ray's 1955 production of *Rebel Without a Cause* alongside Robert Aldrich's masterpiece *Kiss Me Deadly*, released the same year, stands as a potent testament to the apocalyptic sensibility affecting cold war America.[3] Over the years a great deal of attention has been paid to Aldrich's nuclear noir narrative but few critics, if any, have considered the similar thematic and ideological undercurrents latent within Ray's landmark film.[4] Both movies articulate their cinematic "pursuit of the millennium" via secular and nihilistic allegory, employing cataclysmic metaphors to evoke the paranoia and menace of the age, whereby eschaton is palpable and imminent.[5]

This chapter will demonstrate how *Rebel Without a Cause*, a drama centered upon middle-American families in the Eisenhower era, can be read as one of the earliest American films of the cold war to allude to apocalyptic anxieties amongst postwar juveniles.[6] Drawing from the strategic doctrines of deterrence as evinced by the game of "chicken," the psychopathology of "nuclearism" (and "psychic numbing"), and narratives of finitude, three key scenes of *Rebel* will be read closely and discussed in the context of the film's atomic Eisenhower Administration milieu.

Duck's Tails and Cover

At the time of the October 1955 release of *Rebel* the United States had recently conducted the most powerful and controversial atmospheric detonations of the cold war—thermonuclear explosions a thousand times stronger than the "primitive" A-bombs that destroyed Hiroshima and Nagasaki and killed hundreds of thousands of Japanese in the summer of 1945. The "Operation Castle" series of hydrogen bombs ignited over Bikini Atoll shocked the world. In particular, the fifteen megaton "Bravo" test, which was the first to demonstrate that an H-bomb could be a "practical" weapon, deliverable from the air, vaporized an entire island

and sent a 7,000 square mile cloud of lethal fallout across the Pacific, irradiating U.S. observers, Marshallese Islanders, and the crew of a Japanese fishing boat, *The Lucky Dragon*, some of whom died shortly after as a direct result of radiation poisoning.[7]

In the lead-up to these tests America was still at war in Korea. In 1951 and 1953, both Presidents Truman and Eisenhower issued clear warnings that allied forces might employ atomic weapons against North Korean and potentially Chinese forces.[8] Commentators of the time saw a correspondence with biblical prophecy: there were wars and rumors of wars, and some felt the world was heading toward the apocalyptic resolution of history.[9]

After the initial U.S. thermonuclear shots from 1951 to 1953 (e.g., Mike and Ivy) and with the corresponding Soviet tit-for-tat H-bomb blast within only a couple of years of the initial U.S. fusion weapon dominance, the previously held American atomic monopoly and strategic advantage began to wane, at least in the minds of some defense planners and the commander in chief of the time, former five-star general and NATO commander, Dwight Eisenhower, now the thirty-fourth president of the United States of America.

Until the advent of the thermonuclear era, Eisenhower, like many military and political leaders before (and some after) him, conformed to Albert Einstein's adroit and melancholy maxim that the atom age had "changed everything, except man's way of thinking." Indeed, initially horrified by the development of the A-bombs and then deploring their actual use against Japan, Eisenhower quickly found *utility* in the new weapons, particularly for planning their potential deployment in Europe in response to the postwar Iron Curtain separating the West from the East.[10]

Coinciding with America's controversial and accelerated program to develop "the Super," or H-bomb as it later became popularly known, was a long series of domestic atomic explosions being conducted within the continental United States, principally in Nevada at the Yucca Flats testing ground.[11] Ostensibly the purpose was to indoctrinate and prepare U.S. ground forces to fight at close range under battlefield conditions by advancing to Ground Zero, literally within seconds of an atomic explosion. However, both the Atomic Energy Commission and Pentagon recognized the need for public relations to sell the idea of conducting the exercises so close to population centers, small towns, and ranches (Las Vegas, for instance, was less than one hundred miles away and the luminous atomic glow could be seen as far away as Los Angeles).[12] The media were invited and assisted in televising and reporting the atomic spectacles, while AEC consultants assuaged any public fears about fallout and radiation although it has recently been disclosed by the National Cancer

Institute that hundreds of thousands of additional cancers were created by the blasts.[13] Scores of free "public education" motion pictures from the military, the AEC, and atomic contractor industries were distributed to schools, community groups, TV stations, and cinemas, all unequivocally advancing the national security imperative and scientific benefits of the Nevada tests.[14]

Ironically, the Eisenhower administration was also active in a parallel atomic venture, which focused public attention on a greater threat—thermonuclear warfare. Eisenhower publicly championed a robust and coordinated national civil defense program, and initiated a number of urban drills in major cities in order to demonstrate how a mass populace could survive an enemy's atomic holocaust. Hundreds of thousands of citizens—men, women, and children—took part in the drills nationwide, evacuating workplaces, homes, and schools to orderly march into public and private shelters when the air raid sirens wailed. At the all clear, Americans were caught on film and television, cheerily emerging from their subterranean vaults, knowing the simulated apocalypse was being staged as an exercise, reassured by the rhetoric of the time that America would prevail in any such attack.[15] From the government's perspective, any superpower war fought up to, and including, 1954 would significantly favor the United States with its superior atomic arsenal and delivery systems. Indeed, according to the now declassified 1950 National Security Committee Recommendation No. 68, it was *official*—albeit secret—U.S. policy that any point on the globe "which we cannot hold [will be made] the occasion for a global war of annihilation."[16]

However, by 1955, the year of *Rebel*'s scripting, production, and release, the president was having serious misgivings. Once the immensity of the destructive force and spread of fallout from hydrogen weapons began to be comprehended, Eisenhower turned. The world had indeed entered a new era; one of catastrophic potential where antagonistic parties would face—inevitably—mutual assured destruction. Andrew Erdmann has argued in his impressive article " 'War No Longer Has Any Logic': Dwight D. Eisenhower and the Thermonuclear Revolution" that from his inauguration in January 1953 through to the end of 1955 (the time of *Rebel*'s international release), Eisenhower attempted to "integrate nuclear weapons as the preeminent component of American national security policy," while leading the United States through the first three nuclear crises (Korea, Indochina, Formosa) of his administration.[17]

Yet by the time of his famous farewell address of 1961, according to Erdmann, the president's "understanding of 'victory,' defense,' and the dynamics of escalation had been dramatically transformed by the realities of the thermonuclear age."[18]

When it became clear in late 1955 that the Soviet Union had indeed matched the U.S. capacity to deliver hydrogen weapons via intercontinental bombers, the nation's worst case defense scenario had presented itself somewhat in advance of the estimated 1956 to 1960 projection for Soviet "atomic plenty." Only a year earlier, the joint chiefs had been guaranteeing Eisenhower that in either a limited or full-scale war the "outcome for the United States . . . would be successful."[19] But when later faced with "appalling" casualty estimates from differing models of thermonuclear attacks where the United States—regardless of warning and preparedness—would still suffer up to 65 percent population losses, Eisenhower concluded that thermonuclear weapons made war "preposterous." After carefully studying the nuclear war scenarios, the president noted in his personal diary that same night, "It would literally be a business of digging ourselves out of the ashes, starting again."[20]

It is this broad context that informs the first sequence of *Rebel Without a Cause* under special consideration here.

After the opening expository scenes that introduce the three principals of Jim (James Dean), Judy (Natalie Wood), and Plato (Sal Mineo) as teenagers in "trouble" at a local police precinct's juvenile hall, the film shifts attention to the peripatetic Jim's first day at a new senior high school. The following sequence depicts an excursion to the Griffith Park Observatory high above Los Angeles. The core group of teen protagonists inhabiting *Rebel* is shown in attendance, irreverently clowning around during the astronomical lecture. But when impressively violent images projected across the darkened planetarium dome depict the Earth's fiery destruction, the mise-en-scène lingers on the adolescents, both as terrified individuals and as a group, effectively showing a "duck and cover" generation vicariously and collectively experiencing oblivion. Arriving late at the planetarium, Jim notices Judy with her boyfriend and gang leader, Buzz, but Jim's puerile attempts to mimic the gang's earlier lampooning of the lecture backfires, with his new peers ostracizing and alienating rather than encouraging or befriending him. It is at this point the lecturer's ominous delivery is cinematically foregrounded:

> For many days, before the end of our Earth, people would look into the night sky and notice a star, increasingly bright and increasingly near . . . As the star approaches us, the weather will change. The great polar fields of the north and south will rot and divide and the seas will turn warm . . .

Significantly, the astronomer employs the familiar discourse of Judeo-Christian apocalypse, conjuring the poetic imagery of Revelation (celestial harbingers of doom, boiling seas, etc.). His rhetoric is of a planet out of control, where natural phenomena suddenly appear incomprehensible, the narrative evoking the prophetic tone of John of Patmos, whose obtuse and florid vision of the end of the world was recorded two thousand years prior.

The cosmic force described metaphorically by the lecturer—the Sun's eventual "death" by supernova, in which the elementary gases (principally hydrogen) instantly collapse to create a fusion explosion that engulfs and consumes the Earth—has its corollary, as we have seen, in contemporary events.[21] The vivid narrative display is impressive and Ray depicts the students as now listening attentively and watching closely. The lecturer continues:

> And while the flash of our beginning has not yet traveled the light-years into the distance, has not yet been seen by planets deep within the other galaxies, you will disappear into the blackness of the space from which we came—destroyed, as we began, *in a burst of gas and fire!*

The narration effectively mirrors the Atomic Energy Commission's PR rhetoric of the time that was employed to explain the processes of nuclear "fusion" that had been powerfully demonstrated by the U.S. H-bomb detonations in the Pacific in the years prior to *Rebel*, and which was widely discussed in the media. For example, the mass circulation pictorial magazine *Life* devoted its April 19, 1954 full-color cover and a large internal spread to the initial Eniwetok explosion eighteen months earlier, with captions such as "Fireball begins as fusion produces temperatures rivaling those created by collisions of galaxies" and "Expanding gases, heated to 100 million degrees, five times hotter than the sun's center, produce a glowing dome of incandescent air."[22]

The mise-en-scène and cutting in this sequence emphasizes the nuclear metaphor in a surprising but dramatic way. With the narrated "burst of gas and fire," an enormous red explosion erupts across the planetarium's dome, accompanied by a thunderous roar. Suddenly, Plato is shown ducking under his seat. The scene instantly renders Plato as a deeply impressionable teenager. While other adolescents in the audience are depicted cowering and grimacing at the imagery, clearly disturbed by the violent rendering, none are shown as terrified as Plato. By foregrounding Plato's shock and horror, Ray references the popular 1950 civil defense animation *Duck and Cover*, which was screened to tens of millions of American school-age children throughout the cold war, promoting the belief that a school desk, street gutter, or even a picnic blanket would afford protection from the effects of blast and radiation in a nuclear attack.[23] In this regard, Plato's reaction can be read as the automatonlike, conformist, rapid response reflex action *Duck and Cover* demanded of its juvenile audiences—at the first sign of the flash of an atomic explosion, children were encouraged to automatically duck, and cover.

As the high school audience quickly and nervously composes itself, relieved that this demonstration was only a projected simulacrum, the astronomer intones with a dispassionate, existential fatalism:

> The heavens are still and cold once more. In all the immensity of our universe and the galaxies beyond, the earth will not be missed. Through the infinite reaches of space, the problems of man seem trivial and naïve indeed, and man existing alone seems himself an episode of little consequence.

The students hurriedly file out of the building. Jim remains and turns, looking for Plato, who is still cowering under his seat:

> Jim: It's all over, the world ended.

Typologically, this glib comment from Jim returns us to an earlier scene, an exchange between Jim and his new neighbor Judy, who does her best to brush off his chummy, ingratiating banter and attention-seeking with the put-down, "Well, stop the world." Hence, all three lead players are depicted expressing eschatological concerns, whether they are passive witnesses vicariously participating in the apocalyptic moment, or they experience it via ironic and self-reflexive observation and commentary. Similar sentiments will be articulated repeatedly throughout the film, testament to the terminal dread evoked by the atomic age.

Chicken, Deterrence, and Mutual Assured Destruction (MAD)

The next sequence, in which Buzz and his gang outside the observatory challenge Jim to a knife fight, serves to extend the metaphor of terminal violence and nihilism just witnessed. It is a battle, which is ultimately deferred, escalating to a later drag race, one that results in the death of Dean's antagonist while playing "chicken" of the road.

Immediately after the planetarium show, Buzz and his bored gang look for "kicks," deciding to trap Jim, whom they teasingly nickname "Moo" in response to his lame interjection during the lecture. While Jim and Plato look on from the observatory steps, below Buzz pulls a flick-knife and punctures the tires of Jim's car, ostentatiously goading Jim to fight him. But when Jim confronts the gang, pleading that he doesn't want trouble, Buzz and his cronies provocatively make chicken noises, which quickly enrages Jim:

> Jim: Is that meaning *me*? (Louder, specifically addressing Buzz) Is that meaning ME? . . . "Chicken"?
>
> Buzz: Yes.
>
> Jim: You shouldn't have called me that. (Staring at Judy who sits with a girlfriend on Jim's now disabled car.) How about you, huh? Are you always at ringside? No . . . I mean, what do you hang around such *rank* company for?

Buzz rails at the verbal slur, brandishing his flick-knife tauntingly. Again Jim protests and throws away the potentially menacing crowbar he was to use on his car, reiterating that he doesn't want any trouble. One gang member slyly suggests to Buzz, "The 'blade game' huh, Buzz?" and a second switchblade is produced and hurled at Jim's feet.

> Jim: I thought only punks fought with knives?
>
> Buzz: Well who's fighting? I'm not fighting. It's examination time, man. It's a crazy game.

The discourse here suggests the protagonists are fully aware of the rhetorical baiting and brinkmanship of their encounter. Initially Jim chooses to spar verbally in order to counter his armed aggressor's advantage, but his peer credibility is poor (an earlier attempt at humor in the planetarium actually served to target him by the gang). The adolescent joust is, however, more than a harmless display of machismo; it is fueled with a menace barely containing its fatal potential. Metaphorically, this highly stylized, choreographed duel inverts the preceding scene's macrocosmic display of inevitable planetary oblivion by focusing on the microcosmic battle between individuals (Ray's invasive cutaway to the astronomer witnessing the conflict reinforces this link). The scripted action also serves to emphasize the global metaphor of antagonistic cold war parties engaged in games of strategic advantage.

Writing in the 1960s, psychologist Jerome D. Frank assessed the politico-military mindset that embraced mutual assured destruction paralleling it with the game of chicken. Frank's commentary applies as much to the logistics of hostilities depicted between Jim, Buzz, and his gang, as it does to international coercion: "Since in all mutual threat situations the worst thing one side can do is show irresolution or weakness, because this stimulates the other to increase his pressure, each side seeks to intimidate the other while simultaneously demonstrating that it cannot be intimidated."[24]

Consequently, when Buzz and his gang bait Jim, he initially resists the goading, explaining he doesn't want to fight, that is, play the "game." Repeatedly Jim displays equivocation. But when he is pushed and called "chicken" Jim becomes less rational and more aggressive, accepting the weapon, engaging it (literally springing into action), assuming an attack posture (as opposed to his pacifist resignations moments before).

The decade commencing from 1954 is described by Edward Rhodes in his *Power and MADness, the Logic of Nuclear Coercion* as "the golden age of nuclear deterrence theory" during which groundbreaking, canonical studies were conducted. Since there were no perceived precedents for the cold war and its potentially apocalyptic brinkmanship, strategic thinking had to be "made new":

> The workings of deterrence were deduced from basic assumptions about the behavior of individuals and states rather than induced directly from historical case. . . . The principal insight of the period came from the application of the "Chicken" game model to the problem of nuclear deterrence. The "Chicken" analogy led nuclear deterrence theorists to explore notions of denial and punishment and to develop the concepts of commitment, credibility, crisis stability, and arms-race stability.[25]

In the short balletic duel Jim soon disarms Buzz with an unexpected agility, sending his attacker's knife over the edge of the observatory's hillside. With his remaining blade pressed firmly against Buzz's throat, Jim disengages from the fight, having proved his mettle, and demonstrates his nonlethal intent by throwing his own knife away, as he had done earlier with his crowbar. But Jim's withdrawal from aggression is short-lived as is his demonstrable prowess and "rumble" credibility. Buzz immediately escalates the conflict with a challenge to continue at a "chickie run" later that evening. Out of his depth and wishing to save face, Jim accepts, even though we later learn that he has no idea what a chickie run is.

In *The Shook-Up Generation* Salisbury describes the emergence of postwar juvenile delinquents and cites the inevitable escalation of gang fighting from flick-knives to cars: "When switchblades were outlawed they adapted easily to the gravity blade knives put on the market by obliging manufacturers. The automobile, where gang members have access to it, is the most feared weapon. . . . Cars are driven with lethal intent. . . . Survival is sheer luck."[26] Salisbury specifically addresses the milieu of *Rebel* and suggests that what distinguished Los Angeles violence from other large American urban centers of the time was "the use of cars": "Los Angeles is a city of automobiles. It is natural that youngsters bring their cars into their gang warfare. . . . These are the youngsters who employ their automobiles as lethal weapons."[27] In *Rebel*, the link and progression from an abstract and ubiquitous fear of universal death is ultimately reduced to adolescents pursuing potentially suicidal activities "for kicks."

This abstract and sublime narrative trajectory is given powerful cinematic expression within the film by Nicholas Ray's depiction of cars accelerating along vectors of low torque and high velocity, illuminated solely by the spectators' headlights, effectively running the gauntlet of teen peers. During the 1950s chicken became a favored game adopted by nuclear strategists to describe the nuclear arms race in relation to deterrence. Hence, its appropriation from postwar gang culture and theoretical application during the decade by RAND Corporation, the Pentagon, and countless others, expressly underlies the competitive (and sometimes accidental/suicidal) nihilism exhibited by some "atomic age" adolescents. The lemminglike ride at full speed also serves to metaphorically illustrate the precise, temporal logic of Judeo-Christian philosophy's apocalyptic master narrative—history and "progress" as a headlong race along a finite, linear path that accelerates until its anticipated teleological event: collision with the eschatological moment.

Returning home from the excursion, Jim enters into a fruitless discussion with his father (Jim Backus) who seemingly equivocates on every given topic, particularly when Jim needs strong direction and counsel. Disgusted at his father's expedience and evasion, the teenager drives off to meet his destiny, all in the name of "honor." At Miller's Bluff (the name itself connoting chance and gamesmanship) the gang and a host of fellow teens have assembled in the dark for the chickie run. When Jim arrives he and Buzz inspect two stolen cars prior to the race, with Jim trying the driver's door, performing a dry-run jump and roll.[28] Both racers stroll toward the cliff. Like condemned men, they share a cigarette. Peering into oblivion the two gradually move toward a kind of reluctant rapprochement, their resigned exchange recalling the planetarium lecture's apocalyptic rhetoric and existential nihilism.

Buzz: This is the edge. That's the end.

Jim: Yeah. It certainly is.

Buzz: You know something? I like you. You know that?

Jim: Why do we do this?

Buzz: You got to do *something*, now don't you?

The mutual admiration is quickly muted, however, and the cars readied.[29] With Judy acting as "starter girl" for the race, the cars quickly accelerate past her toward the bluff. The race's terminal zone is the vanishing point at the azimuth, but in the dark it is almost impossible to distinguish where the cliff begins and ends since the path is only lit by rows of cars on opposing sides of the track. Ray's montage rapidly cuts between the speeding parallel cars and the banks of onlookers. Approaching the ravine Buzz discovers that the sleeve of his leather jacket is caught on the door handle. Checking his position, Jim makes good his escape, rolling onto the turf. Buzz, however, is trapped, increasingly panicking and unable to jump from the vehicle. Both cars eventually plunge over the edge, exploding on impact, a small symbolic mushroom cloud rising from the ocean rocks below, all rendered in long shot. Only Jim has tumbled out of his car before it goes over the edge.

The fatal plunge of Buzz stuns the crowd and most quickly disperse. Some gang members are inconsolable and threaten reprisals against Jim, who stands at the precipice with Judy and Plato, staring over the edge in silence.

The scene is both stunning and poignant. Significantly, Ray's camera angle, mise en scène, and montage throughout the kinetic race demonstrate that only Buzz is aware of his accidental fate. A careful examination of this sequence demonstrates that neither Judy nor Jim understand exactly what has happened. Equally, the teen bystanders and gang members are unaware of the tragic circumstance that leads to Buzz's death. Everyone is either too far away, otherwise occupied, or from their vantage cannot possibly see inside the compartment to register the mishap that dooms Buzz. From all of their perspectives, Buzz just inexplicably careens over the cliff edge at full throttle. This is an important distinction, since in this game of chicken, the first to jump loses credibility and "honor" by displaying cowardice. Buzz, seemingly, has embraced the chickie run to its logical endgame. Only the cinema audience is privileged with the vantage of witnessing, and cathartically experiencing, the teenager's accidental entrapment/entombment.

Given the film's cold war context it is useful to consider Edward Rhodes's example of chicken to describe the paradox of MAD (Mutual Assured Destruction):

> The heart of the problem of nuclear deterrence in a MAD environment is the difficulty of establishing a credible commitment to an

> effective coercive strategy. . . . The concept of credible commitment thus involves two parts. First, there is the notion of commitment. Second, there is the notion of credibility.[30]

Rhodes suggests that both issues are inextricably linked both in the coercer and coerced's minds, that is, the *perception* of commitment and credibility by both parties. Rationality, or the lack of it, also informs the perception of credible commitment, since it may be irrational to choose to initiate a mutually or self-destructive act.

> In the game of Chicken, for example, an actor may be committed to a strategy of not swerving [to avoid disaster] because: (1) he is rational and prefers death to humiliation; (2) he threw the steering wheel out the window and has no ability to swerve if the other player does not; or (3) although he prefers humiliation to death and still grasps the steering wheel, his mind does not work consistently or effectively enough to ensure that he will swerve at the last minute.[31]

In *Rebel* the game is not about facing each other in a head-to-head impact and winning by being the last to swerve but, rather, racing side-by-side and escaping/ejecting before plummeting to one's death. The distinction here is important. By replacing the concept of deliberate irrational human agency (throwing the steering wheel away) with an accidental loss of vehicle control (Buzz's inability to leave the car) in Rhodes's examples 2 and 3 the effect remains the same. Namely, even in an accidental circumstance, a protagonist can appear (to his adversary and the assembled peer audience) to embrace death before dishonor.

Ray's decision to rework the chickie run, against the head-on gang convention of the time, is significant.[32] The departure suggests a motivation other than maximizing dramatic tension where characters are placed in deadly peril. Ray's preferred title for the project, "The Blind Run," has strong allegorical associations with the atomic age. The film's revised game of chicken reorients narrative emphasis more toward *accidental* death as being, ultimately, immutable if individuals (or nation-states) engage in such posturing and gamesmanship.

In *Rebel*'s chickie run scenario the drama is constructed to have adversaries race alongside each other. This schema enables both drivers to monitor their rival's speed and position. Hence, it's a race analogous to the superpowers' exponential cold war expenditure on nuclear arms and strategic delivery technologies. In *Rebel*'s dramatic strategy parties are expected to tumble from their speeding vehicles moments before being propelled over Miller's Bluff. Both participants are expected to survive, although the inherent risks remain as individual or mutual assured death. By jumping to safety last, the winner maintains the credibility of brinkmanship since his foe has disengaged and withdrawn from the deadly game first—losing face.

Unlike the conventional chicken race, in *Rebel* the technology initiating and facilitating the terminal ride does not survive alongside its driving agent—both cars are trashed and explode in an act of "autogeddon."[33]

But between these two evocative examples of cinematic apocalypse, from the allegorical lecture depicting the Earth's demise by nuclear fire to the terminal arms race metaphor of the chickie run, *Rebel* briefly pauses on an important domestic scene. It is one that brilliantly encapsulates the era's malaise, reflecting a variety of behavioral traits enunciated decades later as "nuclearism."

The Eisenhower Nuclear Family

The term "nuclear family" has become synonymous with the postwar baby-boomer generation, although its sociological coinage and anthropological application has little to do with the nuclear episteme. Frequently confused for the smallest family unit (mother, father, child), the term actually encompasses the microcosmic self-replication of parents via their gendered offspring: mother, daughter, father, and son. It is meant to connote the fundamental atomic attraction and dynamic of the classic familial unit—two children, boy and girl orbiting (like charged particles) the family nucleus of mom and dad.

In *Rebel*, it is not Jim Stark's family that is critiqued for its nuclear paradigm (Jim is an only child, and Plato an orphan). It is Judy's family and its relational model that concerns the filmmakers most at this point.

When Judy (Natalie Wood) returns home from her high school excursion, she twice kisses her father affectionately on the cheek, only to be slapped for her insolence on the second occasion. The scene presents a microcosm of America's emerging nuclear family and the shift in dynamics from those, like Wood and Dean, born into FDR's New Deal and raised throughout World War II, and the precocious baby-boomer generation of the Truman-Eisenhower years. Distraught by her father's repressive, patriarchal wrath, Wood promptly exits the house, leaving behind bewildered parents. The mother tries ineffectually to ease her husband's guilt explaining that their daughter's impulsiveness is due to her "age." At this point, Wood's little brother interjects with "Yeah, it's the ATOMIC Age!" and fires his metallic space rifle that spits out sparks from the barrel across the dining table. It is a marvelous yet seemingly gratuitous aside, which captures the essence of the movie's subtext (and thereby momentarily foregrounds it) of apocalyptic transition from one era to another.

It is worth examining this sequence closely since it is not solely the exchange between father and daughter that is important but the rejoinder by mother and son that contextualizes and retrospectively informs the transgressive moment we have just witnessed.

In the cultural psychology of Robert Lifton we can find an entrée into the troubled Eisenhower era nuclear family. Lifton's close clinical work with A-bomb survivors (*hibakusha*) and other victims of mass trauma has led to a new set of psychological paradigms being proposed. Specifically addressing the psychopathology of "nuclearism," Lifton cites a key component as "psychic numbing":

> What I am calling psychic numbing includes a number of classical psychological defense mechanisms: repression, suppression, isolation, denial, undoing, reaction formation, and projection, among others. But these defense mechanisms overlap greatly around the issue of feeling and not feeling. . . . Psychic numbing has to do with exclusion, most specifically exclusion of feeling.[34]

Lifton and others make the case that for the generations living beneath the "shadow of the bomb"—expecting, planning, and rehearsing for nuclear war, where decades of nuclear testing have rained radioactive fallout across the globe creating untold millions of additional cancers directly attributable to the arms race—that we have all become in effect *hibakusha*.[35]

The scene in which Judy and her family prepare for the evening meal—the verbal exchanges and dynamic interplay—neatly encapsulates the tensions inherent within Lifton's schema for symptoms of psychic numbing as a behavioral signifier of cultural nuclearism. Significantly, the array of "defense mechanisms" Lifton cites are observable in this key sequence and, in particular, "exclusion of feeling" with its associated denial, repression, and projection. Judy, with a desperate need to be loved, is seen in her home asking her father (William Hopper) for a kiss at the meal table after he has returned from work:

> Judy: Daddy? . . . Haven't you forgotten something?
>
> Father: What?

She forces a kiss on him and he mocks her need for affection and humiliates her, embarrassed because she is "too old."

> Father: What's the matter with you? You're getting too old for that kind of stuff, kiddo. You should have stopped doing that long ago.
>
> Judy: I didn't want to stop.

Judy is upset over her father's resistance and persists in trying to kiss him:

> Judy: I guess I just don't understand anything.
>
> Father: I'm tired. (Ignoring Judy and staring straight at his taciturn wife). I'd like to change the subject.
>
> Judy: Why?
>
> Father: I'd just like to, that's all. Girls your age don't do things like that. You need an explanation?!
>
> Judy: Girls don't love their father? Since when? Since I got to be sixteen?
>
> Father: (He swiftly slaps Judy across the face, chiding her) Stop that! Sit down!
>
> Judy: (Addressing her mother, Judy rises to rush off) May I please be excused?
>
> Father: Hey, hey glamour-puss. I'm sorry. We'll break the date. We'll stay home.
>
> Judy: This isn't my home! (She leaves, slamming the door behind her.)
>
> Father: I don't know what to do. All of a sudden, she's, she's a problem.

Judy's mother (Rochelle Hudson) reassures him, also confiding that she too doesn't know how to help their adolescent daughter.

> Mother: She'll outgrow it dear; it's just the age . . .

In a spontaneous and violently ostentatious display (mirroring his father's outburst and slap) Beau squeals joyfully, lifting his friction toy (a disintegrator ray-gun rifle) over the table, firing a burst of noisy sparks.

> Beau: Yeah, it's the ATOMIC Age!
>
> Mother: (Continuing) . . . it's just the age where nothing fits.

This brief sequence serves to illustrate a number of key features that represent middle American life during the cold war Eisenhower years. The confusion articulated by Judy and her parents speaks of familial dysfunction, something vaguely associated with "the age." As a sixteen-year-old in 1955, like most of her adolescent peers (Jim Stark included), Judy belongs to the generation born just prior to the Second World War (later known as the Beats), whereas her parents are associated with the Roaring Twenties or Great Depression. The degree of adult frustration and incomprehension also anticipates and confirms Eisenhower's own generational troubles, as described earlier, in understanding the age in which he was helping to shape. Yet it takes the precocious, postwar baby-boomer son to distill the family drama into a canny metaphor, encapsulating that transformative moment with the marvelous nonsequitur: "it's the *atomic* age!"

Beau's violent expression works on a number of levels. First, it serves as an ironic and self-reflexive comment as précis of the family exchange immediately preceding it ("out of the mouths of babes"!). Second, the spontaneous interjection parallels the shock announcement to the world of the release of atomic energy in the form of the Little Boy atom bomb that obliterated Hiroshima.[36] As such, the blurted remark seemingly comes from nowhere, almost nondiagetically, and appears superficially gratuitous. But its narrative importance can be understood, both structurally and discursively, as a type (or antitype) of apocalyptic rupture in the text—it is a key nodal point that, like the prophesied eschatological moment in Judeo-Christian tradition, comes radically from outside time and space, ushering in a new era.[37] This, in effect, is what the little boy is demonstrating (remonstrating?) to his bewildered family, in both form and content.

Thirdly, the mise-en-scène features the prop/device of an "atomic" ray-gun rifle, popular amongst children at the time. This self-conscious inclusion of pop culture iconography illustrates how, for the *real* nuclear generation (born post-Trinity) the atomic age in part connoted "a Buck Rogers" future replete with atomic guns, nuclear-powered spaceships, and the abundant marvels of atomic energy anticipated to be supplied "too cheap to meter." This aspiration to a new millennial golden age was encompassed by the Eisenhower ideals of his Atoms for Peace program, launched internationally at the United Nations the year prior.[38]

In sum, this scene encompasses a variety of complex cues and motifs now regarded as symptomatic of the atomic age. Nicholas Ray and scriptwriter Irving Shulman's narrative allusion to these themes suggests the discordant generational gap is as much as anything about Beats and Boomers inheriting a future compromised by the confused imaginings of a schizoid nation preparing for nuclear warfare while simultaneously promising a future Eden of atomic plenty.[39]

With a Bang *and* a Whimper

The psychopathology of nuclearism, *Rebel* suggests, is not isolated to 1950s adults. As cited earlier, Jim, Judy, and Plato all articulate expectation of the world ending, just as they manifest similar "symptoms" of atomic age anomie.

Midway through the film Plato confides to Jim about his history as a child of running away from home and being reluctantly returned to his parents. Astonished, Jim says, "How can you remember that? I can't even remember yesterday." Superficially this comment may appear as a glib rejoinder to comfort Plato, but given Jim's own peripatetic background it confirms that he, and other teens, while denying the past, feel trapped in the continuum of the present, unable to see a future (except individual death and/or apocalyptic visions of global or cosmic conflagration).[40]

Ray perhaps best renders the sentiment in the exchange between Jim and Judy after they have been given the brush-off by police while attempting to report Buzz's death. It extends the film's presentation of futility, psychic numbing, and futurelessness, later identified by psychologists as evidence of cold war habituation in children and adolescents.

> Judy: (After hearing the gang's threat over Jim's car radio): They'll be looking for you.
>
> Jim: I didn't chicken. You saw where I jumped. What do I have to do? Kill myself?
>
> Judy: It doesn't matter to them.
>
> Jim: I guess you're still pretty upset, huh?
>
> Judy: I'm just numb.
>
> Jim: You know something? I woke up this morning, you know, and the sun was shining and it was nice and all that type of stuff. Then the first thing—I saw you and, ah, I said: "Boy, this is going to be one terrific day. So you better live it up, 'cause tomorrow you'll be nothing." See? And I almost was . . .

Judy's numbing and Jim's hedonism (as a kind of terminal abandon) recalls Susan Sontag's observation about the science fiction genre, nearly a decade after *Rebel*'s release, as a means of accommodating and negating our perennial human anxiety about death, namely:

> the trauma suffered by everyone in the middle of the twentieth century when it became clear that, from now on to the end of

> human history, every person would spend his individual life under the threat not only of individual death, which is certain, but of something almost insupportable psychologically—collective incineration and extinction which could come at any time, virtually without warning.[41]

Like the adolescent lovers Jim and Judy, Plato also feels the encroaching apocalyptic certainty of the times. In the film's final sequence Plato has fled the gang's attack and pursuing police, firing indiscriminately from his handgun as he retreats into the empty observatory. The police surround the building, using their headlights to illuminate the entrance and appeal over a loudspeaker for Plato to surrender. Secretly Jim sneaks inside only to discover, once again, that Plato is cowering in fear behind rows of seating inside the darkened planetarium. As Jim slowly regains the distraught Plato's trust, their conversation turns to apocalyptic anxiety. In the dim auditorium a dark gulf separates the two interlocutors. It is a distance measured not only in length but personal philosophy:

> Plato: Do you think the end of the world will come at nighttime?
>
> Jim: (Shaking his head) Nup. At dawn.

In the end Jim's reply is prophetic. After negotiating with Plato (and secretly removing the revolver's remaining bullets), he leaves to inform the police of Plato's imminent surrender, but as the other teen emerges, gun in hand, Plato panics when a spotlight is trained on him. Raising his now empty gun, Plato is shot dead. A few moments later the sun begins to rise over the observatory, revealing the dawn of a new day.

By the early to mid-1980s, with renewed superpower tensions, the apocalyptic imagination embodied in a terminal nuclear metaphor had seeped into the very zeitgeist of popular cinema, making some sort of reference or allusion virtually de rigueur.[42] Throughout that decade numerous clinicians reported on a growing, worldwide body of research suggesting a rupture in normative social interaction, implicating as its source decades of adolescent and childhood fears concerning an impending nuclear holocaust.[43]

In this respect, *Rebel Without a Cause* can be appreciated as at the vanguard of modern American cinema in its exploration of generational change and the psychic schism created by the cold war and its association of nuclear Armageddon.

Notes

1. Allied with this, Frym claims that "these developments are reinforced by mass communication media which are more suggestive and impressive than ever before," citing TV programs and motion pictures, "emphasizing and actually glorifying violence as indicative of masculinity." Salisbury (192).

2. According to Erdmann, Eisenhower attempted to strike a balance between the need for rigid social conformism in the 1950s to facilitate the ubiquitous national security apparatus then considered vital to winning the cold war, and the inherent problematic of such security potentially leading to a police state and the abolition of the "American way of life"—personal liberty and the pursuit of happiness.

3. Ray's film inherited the eponymous title from a book by psychologist Dr. Robert M. Lindner, based on World War II case histories of a juvenile, which was optioned by Warner Bros. in 1947. Lindner later wrote on adolescent conformism, around the time of *Rebel*'s development and production. See Kreidl (88–89).

4. One critic, Eugene Archer, in *Film Comment* (No. 1, 1956), drew comparisons between "an increasingly large number of cases of adolescent violence, in contradiction to the generally acknowledged trend toward conservatism in the adult population," suggesting that atomic age conformity was stifling postwar youth. Archer, quoted in Kreidl (69). See also Biskind and Sayre.

5. See Cohn on millennial anxiety.

6. A few films released earlier in the postwar era had youths express their concerns regarding a potential atomic third world war, including *The Best Years of Their Lives* (1946), *The Boy with Green Hair* (1948) and *The Atomic City* (1952), although in each example the boys are prepubescent, not adolescent, as in *Rebel.*

7. Pringle and Spigelman (243–45).

8. Erdmann.

9. See Boyer (1992, 115–26).

10. Erdmann (95).

11. Winkler (91–93).

12. See the photo in *Life* magazine for February 12, 1951, showing the illuminated horizon from Los Angeles's central business district.

13. In 1997 the National Cancer Institute study suggested "a reasonable estimate" of up to 212,000 *additional* U.S. thyroid cancers from the radioisotope Iodine 131 may have resulted from the Nevada tests. This extrapolation is only for one *single* radioisotope produced in atmospheric fission blasts, which often creates scores.

14. MacDonald.

15. Nelson.

16. Quoted in Kovel (64).

17. Erdmann (89).

18. Erdmann (89).

19. Erdmann (105).

20. Eisenhower (23 January 1956).

21. Essentially this narrative is a description of the nuclear fusion that takes place in a hydrogen bomb detonation. It also recalls Truman's famous first attempt to describe the atomic bomb's fission process as "the basic harnessing of the universe."

22. *Life* (April 19, 1954).

23. Three million *Duck and Cover* comics were distributed nationwide to accompany the animated film. See Winkler (115–16).

24. Frank (141).

25. Rhodes (9).

26. Salisbury (50).

27. Salisbury (181).

28. Significantly, Buzz does not attempt a rehearsal. Had he, then the accidental entrapment inside the car may never have occurred.

29. In some cold war films dealing with possible nuclear war, superpower adversaries are sometimes afforded narrative space for similar reflective exchanges. In *Dr. Strangelove*, General Ripper attests with admiration to the fighting skills of the "commies," just as in *Fail-Safe* the two strategic air command chiefs respectively in the Soviet Union and the United States befriend each other over the telephone before the H-bombs fall.

30. Rhodes (107).

31. Rhodes (109).

32. Perhaps the most dynamic films to entertain such head-on vehicle challenges is the *Mad Max* trilogy, but the motif harks back to other genres, such as medieval armored knights on steeds jousting at high speed with spears and clubs.

33. In Western mythology Armageddon is the site of the final battle between the forces of good and evil, hence this neologism appropriately conflates car and holocaust, an association advanced in later films.

34. Lifton (1987, 12).

35. Lifton (49).

36. Truman's announcement invoked the divine, apocalyptically, to contextualize the atomic age: "We thank God that it has come to us instead of our enemies; and we pray that He may guide us to use it in His ways and for His purposes." Quoted in Boyer (1985, 6).

37. Broderick (1999).

38. See Hilgartner (38–54).

39. Significantly, Shulman is also widely credited with crafting the apocalyptic planetarium scene.

40. According to J. E. Mack: "We may find we are raising a generation of young people without a basis for making long-term commitments who are given over, of necessity to doctrines of impulsiveness and immediacy in their personal relationships of choice of behaviours and activity." Mack (1981, 94).

41. Sontag (51).

42. Broderick (1991). For example, nuclear fatalism is overtly expressed in the abject nihilism of *River's Edge* (1987) and its portrayal of modern youth dispossessed of a future, or in other films such as *The Unbelievable Truth* (1988) in

which teenagers articulate kindred sentiments.

43. For example, see Mack (1988, 200).

Works Cited

Alperovitz, Gar. *Atomic Diplomacy: Hiroshima and Potsdam; the Use of the Atomic Bomb in the American Confrontation with Soviet Power*. New York: Simon and Schuster, 1965.

Barnouw, Erik. *Tube of Plenty: The evolution of American Television*. New York: Oxford University Press, 1975.

Biskind, Peter. *Seeing Is Believing: How Hollywood Taught Us to Stop Worrying and Love the Fifties*. London: Pluto Press, 1984.

Boyer, Paul. *By the Bomb's Early Light: American Thought and Culture at the Dawn of the Atomic Age*. New York: Pantheon Books, 1985.

———. *When Time Shall Be No More: Prophecy Belief in Modern American Culture*. Cambridge: Harvard University Press, 1992.

Broderick, Mick. *Nuclear Movies*. Jefferson, NC. McFarland, 1991.

———. "The Apocalyptic Muse: Film, Theory and the Millennial Imagination." University of Technology, Sydney (unpublished PhD dissertation).

Cohn, Norman. *The Pursuit of the Millennium: Revolutionary Millenarians and Mystical Anarchists of the Middle Ages*. London: Paladin, 1970.

Eisenhower, Dwight David. *The Eisenhower Diaries*. Ed. Robert H. Farrell. New York: Norton, 1981.

Erdmann, Andrew. " 'War No Longer Has Any Logic': Dwight D. Eisenhower and the Thermonuclear Revolution.' " In John Lewis Gaddis et al. (eds.) *Cold War Statesmen Confront the Bomb: Nuclear Diplomacy since 1945*. Oxford: Oxford Univesity Press, 1999.

Frank, Jerome D. *Sanity and Survival: Psychological Aspects of War and Peace*. London: Barrie and Rockliff, 1967.

Hilgartner, Stephen, Richard C. Bell, and Rory O'Connor. *Nukespeak: The Selling of Nuclear Technology in America*. New York: Penguin, 1982.

Kovel, Joel. *Against the State of Nuclear Terror*. London: Pan 1983.

Kreidl, John F. *Nicholas Ray*. Boston: Twayne Publishers, 1977.

Lifton, Robert J. and Richard Falk. "On Numbing and Feeling." In Ralph K. White, ed., *Psychology and the Prevention of Nuclear War*. New York: New York University Press, 1987.

MacDonald, J. Fred. *Television and the Red Menace: The Video Road to Vietnam*. New York: Praeger, 1985.

Mack, J. E. "Psychosocial Trauma." In Ruth Adams and Susan Cullen, eds., *The Final Epidemic: Physicians and Scientists on Nuclear War*. Chicago: EFNS, 1981.

———. "The Threat of Nuclear War in Clinical Work." In Howard B. Levine et al., eds., *Psychoanalysis and the Nuclear Threat: Clinical and Theoretical Studies*. London: Analytic Press, 1988.

National Cancer Institute. *Calculation of the Estimated Lifetime Risk of Radiation-Related Thyroid Cancer in the United States from the Nevada Test Site Fallout*. Washington, DC, 1997.

Nelson, Joyce. *The Perfect Machine: Television and the Bomb*. Philadelphia: New Society, 1992.

Pringle, Peter and James Spigelman. *The Nuclear Barons*. New York: Holt, Reinhart and Winston, 1981.

Rhodes, Edward. *Power and MADness: The Logic of Nuclear Coercion*. New York: Columbia University Press, 1989.

Rhodes, Richard. *The Making of the Atomic Bomb*. New York: Simon and Schuster, 1986.

Salisbury, Harrison E. *The Shook Up Generation*. London: Joseph and Sons, 1958.

Sayre, Nora. *Running Time: Films of the Cold War*. New York: Dial Press, 1982.

Sontag, Susan. "The Imagination of Disaster." In Mick Broderick, ed., *Hibakusha Cinema: Hiroshima, Nagasaki and the Nuclear Image in Japanese Film*. London: Kegan Paul International, 1996.

Weart, Spencer R. *Nuclear Fear, A History of Images*. Cambridge: Harvard University Press, 1988.

Winkler, Allan M. *Life Under a Cloud: American Anxiety about the Atom*. Chicago: University of Illinois Press, 1999.

8

Daniel Biltereyst

Youth, Moral Panics, and the End of Cinema

On the Reception of *Rebel Without a Cause* in Europe

> La jeunesse est un temps pendant lequel les conventions sont et doivent être mal comprises.
>
> —Paul Valéry, *Monsieur Teste*

Introduction

In his groundbreaking study *The Stars* (1960),[1] French philosopher Edgar Morin argues that James Dean has been a key figure in the reconfiguration of cinema, the star system, and youth culture. Following Morin, Dean incorporated the ultimate modern adolescent film star. But his death also opened an era (between 1957 and 1962) where youth culture moved away from cinema. Dean's angst-laden movies had shown a model for tormented young heroes, which was picked up and developed further on by rock 'n' roll music and French "chanson"' or dance. Dean's movies were historically important for crystallizing a new form of youth culture, including forms of counterculture and a further dissociation from adults' entertainment. Cinema continued to be a juvenile attraction, but, according to Morin, the film industry was less successful in inspiring adolescents' search for pungent role models. According to young film critic François Truffaut,[2] who wrote a commemorative article one year after Dean's tragic death, *Rebel Without a Cause* had been one of the last truly influential films where contemporary (French) youth found itself.

Enjoying an outstanding success at the box office throughout Europe, *Rebel Without a Cause* has also been a controversial movie. Though the historical reception of Nicholas Ray's successful picture was sensitively influenced by Dean's death (September 30, 1955), it was far from recognized as a milestone in film and youth culture history. On the contrary, as we will indicate, when the movie was distributed in Europe (at the end of 1955 and in 1956), it was rather seen as an exploitation movie explicitly dealing with contemporary problems of adolescent crime.[3] Framed as another juvenile delinquency movie from the United States, *Rebel Without a Cause* helped to whip up public debate on these issues.

This chapter deals with this public controversy around *Rebel Without a Cause*, concentrating on how the movie was received in various Western European countries including France, Germany, and the United Kingdom. Inspired by a materialist approach in relation to historical reception analysis,[4] we try to understand the different social meaning(s) of *Rebel Without a Cause*, including the struggle around those meanings. The distribution of the movie being a well-publicized event, *Rebel* quickly became the target of intense debate, (external) pressures, and censorship. We argue that in various countries the movie as it was shown to the audience lost much of its original critical edge due to the operations by the industry, the press, national censorship boards, and religious interest groups. In order to understand the controversy and pressures upon the movie, we first need to locate *Rebel Without a Cause* in the context of the wider public debate and even the moral panic about youth crime and the representation of it through juvenile delinquency movies.

Moral Panics, Youth Culture, and Juvenile Delinquency Movies

When European audiences, critics, and censors first saw *Rebel Without a Cause*, there had been a longer public anxiety about violence committed by adolescents. At the end of the 1940s and in the 1950s, the national press in various European countries had put juvenile street gang violence, the teddy boys and rockers phenomenon, high on the agenda. One could even claim that the popular media had fuelled a wider panic around adolescents, crime, and their lack of respect for different forms of authority. Mainly through a process of stigmatization and exaggeration, the popular media identified this type of youth violence as a threat to key moral and social values (e.g., violence, risk, security, parental and other forms of authority, solidarity among generations). The new deviant "folk devils" became the object of a spiraling debate, which was later on identified from a critical sociological perspective as a moral panic.

Referring to moral panics theories and the role of the media,[5] the latter are often identified as important catalysts in whipping up the controversy among intellectuals, journalists, public opinion, as well as interest, religious, and other groups in society (e.g., parents' organizations). Following moral panic theories, this debate and the media representation of the folk devils ultimately influence the wider perception of the issue by these and other key social institutions (e.g., politicians, courts), often identified as moral guardians. In some cases, a moral panic even may lead to concrete actions by state institutions, such as in the United States where in 1955 a Senate Judiciary Subcommittee reacted upon wider public anxiety and decided to investigate juvenile delinquency and the role played by certain popular entertainment media.[6]

From this moral panic perspective it is not difficult to look at film criticism and censorship boards as "moral guardians," or as social institutions reacting upon a wider debate on moral and social values. When the issue of juvenile delinquency was picked up by the film industry, European censorship and classification boards were more sensitive than ever to an ongoing debate and to the representation of crime committed by young people. Not only in Hollywood,[7] but also in Europe and elsewhere youth violence was heavily explored (for some: exploited) through such films as *Sciuscia* (de Sica, Italy, 1946), *Los Olvidados* (Buñuel, Mexico, 1950), "I Vitelloni" (Fellini, Italy, 1953), and *Avant le Déluge* (Cayatte, France, 1953). However, when the American juvenile delinquency movies came to be perceived from 1954 onward as an identifiable wave of straight violent movies, film censors and critics reacted strongly.

The controversy around *Rebel Without a Cause* in 1955 and 1956 cannot be understood without the problematic career and historical reception of some earlier American movies, including *The Wild One* (Benedek, U.S., 1953) and *Blackboard Jungle* (Brooks, U.S., 1955) in particular. In the United Kingdom, Benedek's motorcycle picture with Marlon Brando was rejected several times by the British Board of Film Censors (BBFC).

Referring to the "present widespread concern about the increase in juvenile crime," the Board claimed in January 1954 that they were not prepared to pass *The Wild One*, "even with an 'X' certificate" given the "unbridled hooliganism."[8] *The Wild One* was rejected "because it was feared that the film might encourage the growth of motorcycle gangs in the country."[9] Columbia's London office unsuccessfully offered a new, heavily cut version of the movie, but again *The Wild One* was banned twice in 1955 and once more in 1959. In the meantime, the juvenile delinquency movie cycle from the United States had increased with dozens of other titles,[10] while in the United Kingdom violent incidents committed by adolescents gangs had received more publicity than ever.[11] Only in November 1967 did the BBFC finally agreed to award an X certificate to the movie.

The picture, which set the tone for the reception of *Rebel Without a Cause*, was the tough school juvenile delinquency movie *Blackboard Jungle*. In the United States, Brooks's motion picture had already created wide controversy, while the picture was even mentioned by the Senate Committee's report Motion Pictures and Juvenile Delinquency in March 1956 as a movie "that will have effects on youth other than the beneficial ones described by its producers."[12] When the movie was first presented to the British censors in March 1955, the BBFC rejected the film immediately, claiming that this "spectacle of youth out of control" would "have the most damaging and harmful effect on such young people, particularly those between the ages of 16 and 18."[13] On MGM's request new viewing sessions were organized and cuttings made, but the BBFC continued to be extremely sensitive to the fact that "scenes of unbridled, revolting hooliganism would, if shown in this country, provoke the strongest criticism from parents and all citizens concerned with the welfare of our young people."[14] Even after some cuttings and heated conversations with MGM executives,[15] the British censors refused to pass the film even with an X rating, which "should have exposed ourselves to serious public criticism."[16] Only after additional cuttings proposed by the Board, the movie received an X certificate in August 1955.[17] However, *Blackboard Jungle* continued to be controversial even before the movie was released in Britain in September 1955. At the Venice film festival in late August, the American ambassador claimed that *Blackboard Jungle* offended U.S. society and she requested the withdrawal of the movie. This incident was widely reported in the European press, while MGM even used it in various European countries as a publicity tool.[18] It was clear that this all only increased the motion picture's controversial (market) value. When *Blackboard Jungle* was shown in the British theaters, the press highlighted stories again about the euphoric and cynical reception of the picture by local teddy boys.[19]

In other European countries both *The Wild One* and *Blackboard Jungle* received certificates, which underlined similar public anxieties about the possible impact of violent adolescents movies. In most countries children were not allowed to see the movies. In France and Belgium for instance, *Blackboard Jungle*, released in December 1955 as *Graine de Violence (Seed of Violence)*, was not allowed for minors under the age of sixteen. Even in 1963, when the movie was examined again by the French Commission de Classification, the movie's initial category didn't change.[20] Also in other countries such as the northern and Scandinavian countries, national censorship boards prevented people under sixteen or eighteen years old to see the movie. Still however, the *Blackboard Jungle* case exemplified an important shift in the historical reception of American imported juvenile delinquency movies of the fifties—announcing in some sense *Rebel Without a Cause*. What is interesting with this movie is the shift into a more positive critical attention. Among some leading French film critics for instance, Brooks was considered at the time to be a leading figure within the new generation of American filmmakers. This attitude at least opened a greater willingness to read *Blackboard Jungle* as an important manifesto or even as a courageous "sociological" study of contemporary problems with youth and violence.[21]

By this time, there had been a wider academic sociological interest in the juvenile gang and delinquency phenomenon too, mainly as part of the study of youth subcultures. During the 1950s, the teddy boys and rockers phenomenon had inspired academic research, which looked at the compensatory function of and the value system within juvenile gangs. In the United Kingdom some researchers began to link juvenile delinquency and class, as well as gang and parent culture. In his authoritative book on U.K. postwar youth culture, *Subculture*, Dick Hebdige summarized some of this early research on juvenile gangs:

> . . . working-class adolescents who under-achieved at school joined gangs in their leisure time in order to develop alternative sources of self-esteem. In the gang, core values of the straight world—sobriety, ambition, conformity, etc.—were replaced by their opposites: hedonism, defiance of authority and the quest of "kicks." . . . It was left to Phil Cohen to explore in detail the ways in which class-specific experience was encoded in leisure styles. . . . Cohen was interested in the links between youth and parent cultures. . . . He defined subculture as a "compromise solution between two contradictory needs: the need to create and express autonomy and difference from parents . . . and the need to maintain the parental identifications."[22]

In retrospect, these sociological descriptions of the juvenile delinquency and youth culture phenomenon in the 1950s and 1960s seem to be strongly reflected in U.S. movies on these issues. While gang violence in *The Wild One* and *Blackboard Jungle* could easily be explained by arguments based on the working-class background of the juveniles, *Rebel Without a Cause* much more exemplified Cohen's shift in understanding the phenomenon. Ray's movie went further than the class aspect and focused much more upon the subtle idea of the contradictory needs in terms of identity politics. Ray offered a more universally identifiable adolescent role model, which searched for autonomy and difference, but also maintained a hybrid relation with parent culture. This in part explains why *Rebel Without a Cause* was not only attacked on the basis of hooliganism and violence, but also for its raw depiction of the traditional values of parent culture.

Denominating, Flattening Out, and Censoring *Rebel Without a Cause*

In a critical evaluation of *Rebel Without a Cause*, George M. Wilson looked at Ray's movie as a "fundamentally reassuring contemporary morality play."[23] According to Wilson, *Rebel* operated as a classical American social problem film, ultimately rejecting the social message it seems to proclaim openly:

> The social problem in *Rebel Without a Cause* is, of course, juvenile delinquency. . . . The teenagers in this 1955 film are presented as rebelling against their parents and their way of life, but, as the title suggests, not out of any identifiable cause or counterideology. . . . The film thus invokes the perception, widespread at the time, that the issue of teenage rebelliousness had an especially enigmatic character. . . . the story, at the time, hastens to dissipate any possible sense of paradox. . . . Moreover, it is designed not to be too provocative in relation to the failures of the parents.[24]

Wilson recognized that Ray did call up notions of rebellion and a clash with parents, but *Rebel* finally analyzed the problem according to "conceptions common in the period." What appeared to be a "serious reaction to the ongoing social order is revealed to be nothing more than remediable psychological maladjustments within the family."[25]

Looking at the historical reception of *Rebel Without a Cause* in the mid-1950s in some Western European countries, it seems that censors, film critics, and other groups in society did not consider the movie to be a "schematic," "simplified," or reassuring morality play.[26] On the contrary,

Rebel was, more than any other juvenile delinquency movie, able to whip up a lively debate about the social problems the movie invoked, while official film censors and religious groups active in film classification heavily indicated their anxiety about the possible impact of the movie. In some cases the latter succeeded in cutting hard into the film text in order to flatten out the movie's critical analysis of youth violence, adolescents' search for autonomy, and their estrangement with their parents' culture.

Even the translation of Ray's original provocative title for the movie, to which Wilson was referring, often lacked any sense of paradox. Looking at the European titles for *Rebel Without a Cause*, we may perceive a double move. First, in most countries the Warner's local office underlined the violence in the movie and tried to resolve the paradox of the mixed responsibility by laying it firmly on the youth's shoulders. Second, this move clearly went into moralizing the movie's content. In the Netherlands and the Flemish part of Belgium, the movie was called *Botsende Jeugd* (*Clashing Youth*), while in Italy the movie was released as *Gioventù bruciata* (*Spent Youth*).[27] In northern countries similar titles appeared, such as in Denmark where the movie was called *Vildt Blod* (*Wild Blood*). The French title, *La Fureur de vivre (Fever/Will to Live)*, was heavily attacked by many film critics for just lacking the titillating, thoughtful paradox in Ray's original title.[28] A clear example of moralizing youth violence has been the German-language title (*. . . denn sie wissen nicht, was sie tun*, or *. . . forgive them, for they know not what they do*, [Luke 23:34]), which contains a clear biblical reference. A German film critic at the time noted that this title contained a clear weakening of the movie's critical content, while at the same time it already incorporated an "excuse" and a "forgiveness" of the youth's responsibility.[29]

Religious Interests

A crucial step in softening the movie's message was informing parents about the dangers of watching the picture (through classification, information, and influence on film critics), prohibiting young people to watch the movie, as well as straight cutting (censorship). Before turning to official censorship, it is worth indicating that, in various European countries, the local Catholic church leaders and organizations were still very active in the film sector of the 1950s. Inspired by the American Legion of Decency, these film organizations aimed at influencing the Catholic press in their film coverage as well as putting more pressure on commercial cinemas to prohibit the programming of "unhealthy" movies. Supported by local bishops, the Catholic film organizations also installed classification boards. In general, these boards were critical toward U.S. juvenile crime movies, including *Rebel Without a Cause*. In most countries, the local Catholic boards found the movie unsuitable for adolescents and marked the movie with the category "only for adults, with strong reservations."[30] For the Catholic boards, the major problem was not only the issue of delinquent youth, but also the movie's stress on "the failure of family life, as well as the responsibility of the parents and of the educational system"—fields where the Catholic church tried to maintain its power in the 1950s.[31] Most boards had not only problems with the "extreme violent scenes," but they severely attacked the movie on the basis of how the problem of the failing parents and school system was developed, that is, "in an incomplete and rather artificial form." In the movie's file description by the German Catholic film movement, the critic claimed that *Rebel* could be interesting material for local discussions, but finally the "German title reminds us that . . . the movie lacks a Christian answer" to the problems it portrays.[32]

Official Censorship

Although in most European countries there were no close ties between these classification boards and official censorship, the latter was often congruent in its final decisions. Similar to what happened with other juvenile delinquency movies, *Rebel Without a Cause* received in most European countries the harsh verdict of no children allowed under sixteen or eighteen years (e.g., in Belgium, Denmark, Finland, the Netherlands, Norway, Sweden).[33] In Germany, the censorship board (the Freiwillige Selbstkontrolle der Filmwirtschaft, or the film industry's voluntary self-control) stated that both the movie and the trailer could not be shown to children under sixteen. In 1972 and again in 1989 a similar decision was made, while only in 1996 was the age category lowered to twelve years.[34]

The official censors' power however went further than just imposing age categories. It also included the possibility to cut movies or, more elegantly formulated, to suggest cuttings. The Swedish censors decided only to award a "16 years" certificate by cutting five meters, while in Finland forty-five meters had to be removed.[35] The French national control commission (*Commission de Classification—CNC*) decided to grant a license for adolescents and adults (over sixteen years) only if Warners removed some minor scenes.[36] In the commission's argumentation, no references were made to the parents' culture or responsibility, but it only mentioned the "particularly violent scenes (knife fight, murders committed by adolescents, etc.)."[37] Some film critics supported this decision,[38] while others who were in favour of the movie such as Jean de Baroncelli in *Le Monde*, claimed that censors were wrong and that "parents and people who love great movies should not miss this work."[39] This point of debate within the French film press came back in 1962, when the control commission reaffirmed its original decision.[40] One decade later (October 1973) the movie was finally open for all audiences. In a letter to the local distributor, the commission's president claimed that "the motifs which could have legitimated in 1956 a restrictive measure for minors, were certainly justified at that time given the suggestive and new character of the subjects treated in the movie," but that now the commission had "decided unanimously that these motifs were no longer justified."[41]

Referring to the censorship and release history of *The Wild One* and *Blackboard Jungle* in the United Kingdom, it is no surprise that Warners faced the BBFC with apprehension. Watching *Rebel Without a Cause* for the first time on October 14, 1955, the British censors estimated in an internal note that this "is another story involving delinquency in an American high school, this time with the accent on the sins of neglectful and quarrelling parents."[42] In the same note, the examiners claimed that they "did not like the film on censorship grounds and thought it would be no loss from the artistic point of view." Hereby they explicitly referred to *Blackboard Jungle*, "a better, but also a more violent film." In a letter to Warners, the BBFC secretary Arthur Watkins defended its policy of rejection in the following terms:

> I do not have to tell you the serious view which the Board takes about any film dealing with juvenile delinquency, especially in these times when there is such widespread public anxiety about the problem. Before the Board can certificate that the moral values are sufficiently firmly presented to outweigh any harmful influence which the film might otherwise have on young and impressionable members of the cinema audience.[43]

Watkins claimed that the film should be resubmitted and could only receive a certificate when some "primary and essential cuts have been made." And then a long list of suggestions was formulated, mostly referring to vulgar speech, acts of violence, and the representation of the parents. In the first reel all shots of Jim (James Dean) punching and kicking the desk should be removed. In the third reel the BBFC suggested that it would be good to remove the knife fight altogether "if a way can be found . . . from the technical point of view." The cliff top sequence was referred to as: "the less we have of this whole unpleasant idea of young people meeting together to witness a contest which could end in the death of one of the participants, the better." Also the shots of Jim "trying to throttle his father" were asked to be removed.

Warners agreed to proceed to voluntary cuttings, including the punching and kicking scenes, the slashing of tires, as well as big parts of the knife fight. In a letter to the BBFC, a Warners representative tried to appease the censors by explaining and defending his cuttings.[44] With regard to the fight with knives, he claimed that "I have rendered this absolutely innocuous, having taken out every inch of the fight and at no time do you see knives, except a brief shot at the end when Buzz holds the handles towards Jim." The car contest scene, too, was heavily cut, reducing "Judy's actions showing unrestrained excitement down to an absolute minimum," as well as the "scene and scream of Buzz going over the cliff and the shot of the car actually crashing on the rocks below." Finally, the scene where Jim was trying to throttle his father was also removed.

However, the BBFC did not follow Warners' request for an A certificate. The new, heavily damaged version of *Rebel Without a Cause* did not yet satisfy the examiners, who continued to have problems with the depiction of the parents' shortcomings, and scenes of drunkenness and hooliganism. On November 3, 1955, the movie finally received an X rating.[45] Warners' managing director Arthur S. Abeles could not hide his disillusion and anger, and in a new letter to Watkins he wrote that "this is the first time that such a thing has happened with a Warners' film," asking him to reconsider the classification in order not to force the company "to cater to the morbid element of the population by branding it with an X."[46] Defending an A certificate, Abeles argued that Warners not only agreed to fulfill all cuttings requests, but also that the company had put in something praiseworthy ("a line of dialogue in which the hero refuses to fight with knifes").

However, again, the BBFC examiners, including Watkins and his successor John Trevelyan, were not impressed by Abeles's "naïve arguments."[47] In an internal document they claimed that they "still have a rather uncomfortable feeling that an 'X' may be heavy weather for this film as cut."[48] Again they proposed a rather long catalogue of cuts that should be made in order to "tip it over the border line into 'A.' " Some of those new suggestions were related to complete scenes (e.g., a reduction of Jim's drunkenness scene), single lines (e.g., Jim's speech beginning with "That's a Zoo"), and concrete actions (e.g., Judy's face being slapped by her father; the deletion of the shot of the mass of cars driving away from the cliff top; the kiss between Jim and Judy). The internal document did not hide the examiners' personal appreciation of the movie as "rubbish" and "stuff for the teddy inclined adolescent."

In the meantime, Nicholas Ray was also involved in the British censorship affair. Following different sources, it is clear that Ray came over to London in order to try to work out a solution and to make the film acceptable.[49] Watkins continued to have problems with "the behaviour of the parents in the film" and with "the irresponsible behaviour of the teenagers themselves."[50] In an interview with *Variety*, Watkins referred to the problems that Britain had with teddy boys, "delinquents who wear zoot-suits, carry razors and knives, etc."[51]

For Warners's managing director in Britain the game was clearly over now. Abeles surrendered by claiming that "the cuts you suggest . . . would reduce the film to nonsense":

> If we don't show the weakness of the parents we have no motivation for the unhappiness and loneliness of the adolescents. Although we are accepting an "X" for the picture, I should like to repeat that I honestly feel the way the film now stands it deserves an "A."[52]

By December 1, 1955, *Rebel Without a Cause* finally got its X certificate, followed by three additional cuttings in the trailer (e.g., removal of Judy's father slapping his daughter's face). This crude, at times hilarious, censorship history stresses not only the censors' power in influencing the textual meaning and reducing the movie's critical edge. Even in such a manner that we understand a British film critic's comment indicating that "the knife fight has been dramatically curtailed . . . and becomes momentarily incomprehensible."[53]

But the history also indicates that the censors in some sense react upon a wider society's anxiety, even if their evaluations seem to be highly subjective. When censors (over)react to a perceived moral panic within society, they can be seen as acting as "moral guardians." Just calling them paternalistic is not very productive. The *Rebel* case indicates that censorship problems around troubling images are not only due to pretentious or old-fashioned censors. We might also look at the British case (as well as those in other European countries) as examples of how censorship files may be considered thoughtful indicators of shifts in core societal and moral values being (or being perceived by dominant elites as) threatened. From this moral panic perspective, it is interesting how former examiners in later writings agree upon their extreme reaction at the time. Talking about the British censorship approach to *Rebel Without a Cause*, Enid Wistrich claimed:

> Possibly films which deal with disturbing social and political themes are only acceptable once the danger is felt to be past. The recent decision of the censor to reclassify for adolescent audiences without cuts *Rebel Without a Cause* . . . is a case in point. The film was cut and banned to teenagers because it was thought to sanction and

> thus encourage the anti-social and rebellious behaviour of the young hero. . . . Certainly the censor was happy to reclassify the James Dean saga in 1976, but if a modern version with a different message was as challenging in the 1970s as the Dean film was in the 1950s were to appear, would the decision be any different?[54]

When the movie finally got an "Adults" category without cuts in April 1976, the examiners wrote in a similar sense that earlier on the film caused the BBFC "some anxiety because of its apparent challenge to parental authority and its possible effect on the increase of juvenile delinquency." But reviewing it all these years later, the censors now "felt that it tells a moral tale."[55]

Critical Disagreements

When *Rebel Without a Cause* was finally released in Britain at the beginning of 1956, the censors were surprised by the praise from many of the critics.[56] Also in other countries, the specialized film press and other critics were not unanimous in attacking Ray's movie. In the United Kingdom for instance, some critical remarks did run through many reviews such as those on the sensationalist and violent character of the movie,[57] the negative image of the United States,[58] as well as the ambiguous portrayal of the parents and the delinquent youth. The *Times*, for instance, talked about a "routine of blaming the parents for the sins of the children" and a "suspect doctrine" that the last person to be held responsible for delinquent behavior was the delinquent himself. But the reviewer immediately admitted that *Rebel* was a "brilliant piece of work" and "an excitingly intelligent exploration of the adolescent mind."[59] In *Sight and Sound*, Penelope Huston developed a fine analysis of recent U.S. juvenile delinquency movies, calling *Rebel* a social document, touching society "in its most elementary aspect, the individual's own adjustment to the world he has to live in." For Huston, the movie's "basic sense of insecurity" and the "malaise" call into question the American dream.[60]

In France, *La Fureur de vivre* caused a more vivid, polemical debate among critics. This had, on the one hand, to do with the success of the Catholic film organization and its classification board in influencing a more negative opinion within the conservative and religiously affiliated press. On the other hand, a group of young film critics had been admiring and defending Ray as one of the leading figures in American cinema. Calling Ray one of the major new auteurs, *Cahiers du Cinéma* critics such as Truffaut and Eric Rohmer played a key role in sanctifying *Rebel Without a Cause*. Their intellectual mentor André Bazin, who devoted several reviews to the movie, wrote that he could not always "follow his young friends in all their admirations, even if we take into considerations the polemical margin of their actions." But Bazin immediately confirmed that "in relation to Nicholas Ray they were clearly right."[61] This canonizing *Cahiers* attitude was strongly countered by more leftist critics, exemplified by the one of the rival film journal *Positif*.

So, at least three sorts of reviews can be identified in the French debate. One of the first articles to appear exemplified the Catholic conservative voice. In the newspaper *France Catholique* the reviewer denounced Ray's picture in often provocative terms, calling upon parents (readers) to advise their children not to go watch this a-religious thesis film.[62] The movie was attacked on the basis of its false moral tone, its weak script (mainly the second part), while it lacked any psychological depth in its portrayal of both parents and adolescents.[63]

This type of criticism was quickly countered by an article in *Arts* by François Truffaut, who opened another register in the debate.[64] Rereading Truffaut's review nearly half a century later, it is astonishing how the future New Wave filmmaker did not go into the usual criticism (i.e., the portrayal of violence, youth, parents' culture) or defend Ray in terms of his daring analysis of the social issues treated in the movie. Instead, one is struck by how Truffaut denied the political engagement in Ray's movie, as well as the conservative and moralistic tone of his article. Truffaut's praise was based on Ray's power as a cinematographic "poet," calling Benedek a "sociologist" and Brooks a (revolutionary) "reformer." The central reason for glorifying Ray as one of the major auteurs in Hollywood lay in his cinematographic power: he does not use a "scriptwriter's script," but a "scenario de metteur en scène"; Ray's realistic style glimmers through staging, editing, use of color and Cinemascope, and acting.

Other *Cahiers* critics treated *Rebel Without a Cause* in similar terms, where the articles by Bazin go even further in denying the sociological and political force of *Rebel* and in underlining Ray's cinematographic, poetic, and spiritual power.[65] Calling *Rebel* soon one of the postwar classical movies, Bazin looked at it as a "moral drama" too and he did not stop to locate Ray and his movie within the history of art, literature, and cinema. Completely in line with the auteur theory, he tried to compare Ray's mood with that of Cocteau and Rimbaud, his style reminiscent of Rossellini and Renoir: "Similar to Jean Renoir for instance, the reality in the movie lies above a superficial level, it resides in what I would call the spirit of the scene ("l'âme de la scène"), or better perhaps, in its moral poetry, or at least in its lyricism."[66] A third important *Cahiers* critic, the future filmmaker Eric Rohmer, also looked at Ray's movie as pure moral poetry. It would be too much of a digression to analyze Rohmer's article in *Cahiers du Cinéma*, but he basically went on to compare the movie with the dramatic power and moral tone of ancient Greek drama. Not only the structure of the movie, but also its mood was remarkably similar to the one in Greek tragedies. For Rohmer violence is no longer to be explained as a societal phenomenon, but as a physical result of hubris and honor.

This type of analysis was strongly countered by more leftist voices. The clearest example was a review in *Positif*.[67] Inspired by the harsh (ideologically inspired) rivalry, most of the *Cahiers* critics' praise was reversed. For the *Positif* reviewer Ray's oeuvre bantered in tasteless moralistic "pathos." Openly preferring Brooks's approach, *Positif* tackled Ray's social problem analysis: "(For) Ray the key to the Problem of Juvenile Delinquency . . . : his heroes are adolescents-who-fight-to-become-men; their crisis is nothing more than the passage from childhood to adulthood."[68] In the review, Ray's style was also severely attacked, calling him an unoriginal filmmaker, whose poetry resides often in cheap effects. This extremely critical approach to the movie, however, is—as the reviewer himself indicated—highly inspired by the specific position of the *Positif* journal within the French film criticism at that time, while it is not completely representative for how the left press looked at *Rebel Without a Cause*. Similar to what happened in other countries, where quite similar conservative, religiously inspired and leftist voices were present in film criticism, in France communist and leftist newspapers saw and—sometimes lauded—Ray's critical portrayal of American capitalist society.[69]

Conclusion: Loosening Authority, Americanism, and Modernization

In 1956 *Rebel Without a Cause* had been among the most popular films at the box office, while many critics choose it as one of the best movies of the year.[70] This had much to do with the Dean cult, which in Europe might have been less spectacular than in the United States, but whose long-term influence on youth culture cannot be underestimated.[71] It remains difficult to speculate about the influence of one single cultural product or a star, certainly upon the audience. But it is astounding how the movie has been successfully released in the 1960s, and again in the 1970s, while Dean's mood and attributes (jeans, "blousons rouges," t-shirt, boots) were largely taken up—as well as commercially exploited.

An alternative approach in locating the movie's influence is to put it into a wider flow of cultural products. If we look at the European cultural debate of the 1950s (and later), it is astonishing how important the trope of America has been. Dean's attributes—as portrayed in its purest form in *Rebel Without a Cause*—were often identified as another clear example of the further Americanization of Europe.

In the twentieth century, America played a key role in European cultural criticism and in its theoretical mapping of art, popular culture, and modernity. Exemplifying the wider American cultural industry, Hollywood embodied ever since the 1920s the "America-as-threat" paradigm. In many European countries, intellectuals, politicians, and cultural critics from different ideological origins were unanimous in their negative consensus around the influence of American mass culture. This debate was intensified after the Second World War and into the 1950s, when the reconstruction of Europe was accompanied by an increasing flow of U.S. movies and other cultural products and symbols.

However, in the postwar cultural debate on Americanization, some dissenting voices were raised. The latter strongly denounced the pejorative and ideologically inflected character of the traditional elitist views upon American popular culture, while for many young working-class people (and critics), American culture represented a "force of liberation against the grey certainties of (British) cultural life."[72] Writing about the postwar cultural development of Italy, David Forgacs argued that "from the mid-1950s rock'n'roll music . . . and films like *Rebel Without a Cause* . . . helped give shape to a new model of youth autonomy and rebellion."[73] Among young people cultural symbols of Americanism were increasingly associated with modernity and a loosening of traditional authority, hence underlining its potential for models of resistance.

From this perspective, it remains interesting that throughout Western Europe, this type of controversial material from the U.S. was able to whip up a vivid debate. Not only on American social and moral issues, but also on local forms of—in this case—delinquency, juvenile rebellion, and so on. Although official censors, religious classifiers and conservative parts of the press tried to resolve the ambiguity or to flatten out the critical engagement in Ray's movie, one is struck by the persistence of countervoices in the public debate—defending *Rebel Without a Cause* in its mood and analysis of youth's existential rebellion and identity crisis.

It also remains astonishing how mainly European filmmakers later claimed to be influenced by this type of American movie, *Rebel Without a Cause* in particular. Especially in France, where anti-American feelings have been so high on the cultural and political agenda—sadly, up till today—it is hard to underestimate the importance of Ray's movie. Dean's performance in *Rebel Without a Cause* can still be admired through French popular culture such as Johnny Halliday, still France's most popular rock 'n' roll star (Chateau). But its most truthful influence has been on French cinema itself, where the young film critics were mentally becoming filmmakers. New Wave cineastes such as Truffaut, Godard, and Rivette saw in *Rebel Without a Cause* a model for their own quest for a fresh and unspoiled contemporary cinema in which adolescents' complex "vision du monde" could play a major part.

Abbreviations

BBFC	British Board of Film Censors
CCC	Commission Catholique de Cinéma (Belgium)
CNC	Centre National de la Cinématographie (France)
FSK	Freiwillige Selbstkontrolle der Filmwirtschaft (Germany)
KFA	Katholieke Filmactic (Catholic Film Action, Belgium)
OCIC	Organisation Catholique Internationale du Cinéma

Notes

The author would like to thank David Barrett, Laura Bezerra, Susanne Boe, Ib Bondebjerg, Joël Cammas, Pierre Chaintreuil, Michael Isaksen, Rüdiger Koschnitzki, Philippe Meers, and Hilde Van Liempt for their help in searching original material for this chapter. A first version of this chapter was presented during my stay at the Department of Film and Media Studies of the Copenhagen University in November 2002. Thanks also to my friends and members of the Working Group for Film and Television Studies, Ghent University.

1. *Les Stars* was first published in 1957, but Morin extended his manuscript for later reprints such as one in 1962 and another in 1972. We draw upon the latter version, published by Seuil.
2. François Truffaut. "James Dean," *Arts* (September 29, 1956). Quoted in Morin (141).
3. See Doherty.
4. See Staiger.
5. See Cohen; and Springhall.
6. Doherty (117).
7. Doherty.
8. BBFC file on *The Wild One*, quoted in Robertson (105).
9. Phelps (120).
10. Doherty (119).
11. See Robertson (107–8) and Matthews (128–29).
12. Doherty (117, 118).
13. Robertson (114).
14. Letter Watkins (BBFC) to Ayres (MGM executive), March 24, 1955, BBFC file on *Blackboard Jungle*.
15. Robertson (115).
16. Letter Harris (BBFC) to Eckman (MGM junior executive), July 18, 1955.
17. Trevelyan (1957).

18. At least in Belgium and France, MGM used the slogan: "Le film qui a provoqué un incident diplomatique" ("The movie that caused a diplomatic incident"). See Doniol-Valcroze.

19. Matthews (131–32).

20. CNC—Commission de Classification file on *Graine de Violence*.

21. See, for example, Mauriac.

22. Hebdige (76–77).

23. Wilson (111; reprinted in this volume as chapter 5).

24. Wilson (110–11; reprinted in this volume as chapter 5).

25. Wilson (111; reprinted in this volume as chapter 5).

26. Wilson (111–12; reprinted in this volume as chapter 5).

27. Also David Fogacs (311) indicates that in Italy *Rebel Without a Cause* received a "more moralistic title."

28. Jean de Baroncelli, for example, even opened his review with: "*La Fureur de vivre* (is a) stupid title that completely ignores the deeper sense of the movie and that does not correspond to the American title . . ." (my translation). See de Baroncelli (81).

29. See Ruppert. See also the comments by I. W.

30. For data on Belgium, France, Germany, Italy, the Netherlands, Spain, and Switzerland, see OCIC file on *Rebel Without a Cause/Fureur de vivre*.

31. See KFA/CCC file number 5843 on *Botsend Jeugd/Fureur de vivre*.

32. See: K. B. (127).

33. For the Nordic and Scandinavian countries, see Statens Filmcensur, Copenhagen, file 61469 on *Vildt Blod/Rebel Without a Cause*.

34. See FSK file number 11405 (a, b, c, and d) and file number 11755 on . . . *denn sie wissen nicht, was sie tun*.

35. See Statens Filmcensur file 61469 on *Vildt Blod/Rebel Without a Cause*.

36. Internal note, January 25, 1956, CNC—Commission de Classification file on *Graine de Violence*.

37. Ibid., letter Flaud (CNC) to Warners, February 24, 1956, as well as an official CNC document, March 14, 1956.

38. See Magan.

39. De Baroncelli.

40. Letter CNC to Warners, October 9, 1962, CNC—Commission de Classification file on *Graine de Violence*.

41. Ibid., internal document, October 4, 1973.

42. Internal document, October 14, 1955, BBFC file on *Rebel Without a Cause*.

43. Ibid., letter Watkins (BBFC Secretary) to Abeles (Warner London), October 17, 1955.

44. Ibid., letter Wackett (Warner) to Watkins (BBFC), October 25, 1955.

45. Ibid., letter Watkins (BBFC) to Abeles (Warners), November 4, 1955.

46. Ibid., letter Abeles (Warners) to Watkins (BBFC), November 8, 1955.

47. Robertson (3).

48. BBFC file on *Rebel Without a Cause*, internal document AW/JT, November 21, 1955.

49. See: "Cuts." See also, letter Ray to Watkins (BBFC), December 10, 1955, BBFC file on *Rebel Without a Cause* and Watkins's letter in response in which he thanks Ray for the "co-operative attitude which you showed when you were over here," Ibid., letter Watkins to Ray, December 15, 1955.

50. Ibid., letter Watkins (BBFC) to Abeles (Warners), November 24, 1955.

51. "Cuts."

52. Letter Abeles (Warners) to Watkins (BBFC), November 30, 1955, BBFC file on *Rebel Without a Cause*.

53. G. L. (17).

54. Wistrich (117–18).

55. Internal document NKB/RAS, April 12, 1976, BBFC file on *Rebel Without a Cause*.

56. Ibid., letter Watkins (BBFC) to Mirams (film censor, New Zealand), February 1956.

57. See, for instance, Majdalany.

58. See Lejeune.

59. "The Juvenile Delinquent."

60. Huston.

61. See Bazin.

62. "La Fureur de vivre." *France Catholique* (March 30, 1956).

63. For instance, Magan. Also, "Le Malheur d'avoir de la lecture. " *Carrefour* (April 11, 1956).

64. Truffaut.

65. Bazin (April 15, 1956; 44) and Bazin (May 17, 1956).

66. Bazin (April 6, 1956).

67. R. T. (38–41).

68. R. T. (39).

70. For the United Kingdom, see Thumin.

71. Devillers (74–75); Howlett (193–97).

72. Storey (12).

73. Forgacs (311–12).

Works Cited

Bazin, André. "La Fureur de vivre." *France-Observateur* (April 6, 1956).

———. "La Fureur de vivre." *Radio-Cinéma-Television* (326) (April 15, 1956).

———. "La Fureur de vivre." *Education Nationale* (May 17, 1956).

Chabaud, Charles. "La Fureur de vivre." *Cinéma* 56 (May 1956).

Cohen, Stanley. *Folk Devils and Moral Panics*. London: MacGibbon and Kee, 1972.

"Cuts Ease Way in Britain for *Rebel*." *Variety* (November 23, 1955).

de Baroncelli Jean. "Fureur de vivre." *Le Monde* (May 7, 1956).

Devillers, Marceau. *James Dean*. Paris: Pygmalion, 1985.

Doherty, Thomas. *Teenagers and Teenpics: The Juvenilization of American Movies in the 1950s*. London: Hyman, 1988.

Doniol-Valcroze, Jacques. "Richard Brooks aux écoutes." *France Observateur* (December 1, 1955).

Forgacs, David. "Twentieth-century Culture." In *The Oxford Illustrated History of Italy*. Oxford: Oxford University Press, 1997, 291–319.

G. L. "Rebel Without a Cause." *Monthly Film Bulletin* (January 1956).

Hebdige, Dick. *Subculture: The Meaning of Style*. London: Routledge, 1998. Originally published in 1979.

Howlett, John. *James Dean: A Biography*. London: Plexus, 1975.

Huston, Penelope. "Rebels without Causes." *Sight and Sound* 25(4).

I. W. "Filme in Freiburg." *Badische Zeitung* (August 15, 1956).

K. B. ". . . denn sie wissen nicht, was sie tun." *Filmdienst* (April 12, 1956).

Lejeune, C. A. "Homes Unblessed." *The Observer* (January 22, 1956).

Magan, Henry. "La Fureur de vivre. Un témoignage accablant." *Lettres Françaises* (April 4, 1956).

Majdalany, Fred. "But Does This Do One Any?" *Daily Mail* (January 1, 1956).

Matthews, James D. *Censored! What They Didn't Allow You to See and Why: The Story of Film Censorship in Britain*. London: Chatto, 1994.

Mauriac, Claude. "Edifiante Audace." *Figaro Littéraire* (December 3, 1955).

Maze, Lucien. "La Fureur de vivre." *Monde Ouvrier* (May 5, 1956).

Morin, Edgar. *Les Stars*. Paris: Seuil, 1972. (English version: Morin, Edgar. *The Stars*. London: William Morrow, 1960.)

Phelps, Guy. *Film Censorship*. Letchwork: Garden City Press, 1975.

Rohmer, Eric. "Ajax ou Le cid?" *Cahiers du cinéma* 59 (May 1956): 32–36.

Robertson, James C. *The Hidden Camera: British Film Censorship in Action. 1913–1976*. London: Routledge, 1989.

R. T. "La Fureur de vivre. Les causes et les effets." *Positif* 17 (June/July 1956).

Ruppert, Martin. "Mörder aus gutem Hause." *Frankfurter Allgemeine Zeitung* (March 21, 1956).

Springhall, John. *Youth, Popular Culture and Moral Panics: Penny Gaffs to Gangsta Rap, 1830–1996*. London: Macmillan, 1998.

Staiger, Janet. *Interpreting Films. Studies in the Historical Reception of American Cinema*. Princeton: Princeton University Press, 1992.

Storey, John. *Cultural Theory and Popular Culture*. London: Prentice Hall, 1997.

"The Juvenile Delinquent on the Screen." *The Times* (January 23, 1956).

Thumin, Janet. "The 'Popular,' Cash, and Culture in the Postwar British Cinema Industry." *Screen* 32(3) (1991): 245–71.

Trevelyan, John. *What the Censors Saw*. London: Michael Joseph, 1973.

Truffaut, François. "La Fureur de vivre." *Arts* (April 4, 1956).

Wilson, George M. "Nicholas Ray's *Rebel Without a Cause*." In *Narration in Light: Studies in Cinematic Point of View*. Baltimore: Johns Hopkins University Press, 1986. Also reprinted as chapter 5 in this volume.

Wistrich, Enid. *"I don't mind the sex, it's the violence." Film Censorship Explored*. London: Marion Boyars, 1978.

James Dean as Jim Stark in *Rebel Without a Cause*. *(Courtesy of Photofest)*

9

ELENA LOIZIDOU

Rebellion and Citizenship

Hannah Arendt, Jim Stark, and American Public Life in the 1950s

What is a rebel? A man who says no: but whose refusal does not imply a renunciation.

—Albert Camus, *The Rebel*

THERE IS NOTHING PARTICULARLY unique in writing about the figure of the rebel or the practice/idea of rebellion. Both the figure of the rebel and the practice/idea of rebellion have been featured in a variety of intellectual writings. Albert Camus's influential book *The Rebel* and Hannah Arendt's equally famous political philosophical study *On Revolution* are illustrative works that discuss and analyze the practice/concept of rebellion as well as the figure of the rebel. Both Camus and Arendt draw on the terms "rebel" and "rebellion" as they emerged sociohistorically. Camus's book, written in 1951 and appearing in English translation in the United States in 1954, paints a humanist account of the figure of the rebel and draws chiefly upon the French Revolution of 1789 and the Russian Revolution of 1917, as well as previous philosophical writings and experiences. Arendt's 1963 study, as its title suggests, is concerned with establishing the meaning of revolution, and does so by drawing upon post-medieval rebellions, principally the American and French Revolutions. However, the figure of the rebel and the concept/practice of rebellion have not only been read through and in relation to the concept and practice of revolution.[1] Rebellion and the rebel have also been the focus of cultural analysts and thinkers, whose readings are not of historical phenomena (though each might be historically located) but rather as private modes of expressing individuality and responding to the state of affairs or the status quo. In their *Cool Rules: An Anatomy of an Attitude*, Dick Pountain and David Robins accordingly trace the rebel or rebellion through the phenomenon of "cool," which can be located in artistic movements, youth culture, celebrated figures, and generally in popular culture, and point out that cool "can be seen as a permanent state of private rebellion."[2] Besides their potential relation to historical conditions, in other words, the figure of the rebel and the concept of rebellion can thus be discussed in relation to their cultural location.

This chapter ponders the figure of the rebel, along with the concept/practice of rebellion, through and beyond historical contingency—history, in this particular context, making reference to grand "history" or the history of grand events. This is not to suggest that the rebel should be discussed, as Pountain and Robins might have us believe, as a private figure whose individuality is reflected through the act of rebellion. Rather, the argument here will be to read the figure of the rebel and his/her act of rebellion through Arendt's ideas and how the very public act of rebellion tells a story about citizenship. The rebel and rebellion will thus be read as indices of alternative and possible citizenship. By "alternative," of course, is not meant "ultimate." The argument here will instead be made, first, by scrutinizing both the way by which Arendt gives meaning to these terms and the meaning she ascribes to them and, second, by reading how the figure of the rebel is articulated and depicted in Ray's film *Rebel Without a Cause*.

As a legal academic writing about law and film, I am using *Rebel Without a Cause* to talk about a subject that is of particular interest to lawyers and legal scholarship: the rebel as figure that can tell an alternative story about citizenship.[3] *Rebel Without a Cause* therefore potentially becomes a film that is paradigmatic of a series of discourses in the 1950s that question and represent the American teenager and the social demands on and of that group.[4] An esteemed feminist academic has suggested that another film might more effectively make that point: for despite its ostensible attention to "rebellion," she observed, *Rebel Without a Cause* is a very conservative and misogynist film, a popular and ordinary film. Critic Lauren Berlant's words about "ordinariness" of popular cultural production are pertinent here in countering that suggestion: "Its very popularity or its effects on everyday life or its expression of emblematic knowledge makes it important. Its very ordinariness requires reflecting on what is merely undramatically explicit."[5] Such, precisely, is the goal here in approaching Nicholas Ray's *Rebel Without a Cause*—first, through a historical and cultural analysis of the 1950s and the context in which the film and its central figures of rebellious youth emerge; and second, a critical analysis of the way Arendt reads rebellion and the rebel; and, third, using Arendt's critical perspective to read the film. The main aim here is to view *Rebel Without a Cause* not as simply or even primarily as the story of juvenile delinquency or youth rebellion in suburban America during the 1950s, but rather as a story of youth's demand for recognition of their individuality and their political citizenship.

An American Context: Individuality and Citizenship

Rebel Without a Cause takes place in the mid-1950s in a Los Angeles suburb. The director, Nicholas Ray, and the scriptwriter, Stewart Stern, set off to portray the life of the contemporary American teenager. The story is organized around Jim Stark (James Dean), recently arrived with his parents in the hope that their son will conform and lose his rebellious streak and take "a right step in the right direction."[6] But Jim manages to get into trouble quickly. After being challenged by Buzz, the popular kid in town, to a "chickie run" (two drivers of stolen vehicles drive toward a cliff; the one that jumps out first is considered to be a chicken i.e., a coward or not a man), Jim finds himself surviving while Buzz plunges off the cliff and dies. Against his parents' advice, Jim goes to the police to report the event, but, not finding Ray, the sympathetic officer he knows, he leaves. At the same time, Buzz's friends fear that Jim has reported the event to the police and pursue him. Jim hides in a deserted mansion with Judy (Natalie Wood)—who had been Buzz's girl but couples with Jim after the chickie run—and Plato (Sal Mineo), a younger marginalized teen. Running toward the safe haven turns out badly. When Buzz's friends and the police discover the three, Plato shoots and injures one of Buzz's friends before running to the planetarium to hide, fearing that the police will shoot him. Jim and Judy run after him, and the police surround the planetarium. Jim convinces Plato to walk out and also negotiates with the police a peaceful "arrest" of his friend Plato. Despite this, Plato panics and, holding his bulletless gun, runs out and is shot dead by the police. The film ends with Jim and his parents mourning this loss and reconciling their differences.[7]

The story that Nicholas Ray and Stewart Stern narrate at some level is a story of discontented teenagers and fractured families, of youth rebelling against "the suffocating web of family ties, school, suburban respectability and labour discipline that the new 'mass society' imposed."[8] In doing so, the film offers a startling counter to much post-World War II political rhetoric, which depicted the United States as a nation prosperous, homogeneous, and bereft of social conflict. During these years, the United States underwent transformations in the social, economic, political, and military domains. The effects, both immediate and long-term, of the dropping of atomic bombs by the United States in Hiroshima and Nagasaki made President Truman and his administration realize that the existence of nations and their populations were fundamentally at risk and could be destroyed or vanish in an instant.[9] With the fear of the USSR and the realization that the United States could not be assured of defending itself, the United States resumed an aggressive production of arms in what was described as the arms race.[10] The economic effects of the arms race were remarkable. For Hugh Brogan, the huge expenditure on new weapons:

> . . . re-made the industrial map of the United States. . . . Defence establishment of all kinds were allocated to regions which private enterprise might have left to stagnate: for example, the committees of Congress being usually dominated by elderly veterans of the Democratic South, their states and districts got the larger part of the federal largesse and that was now flowing. Georgia, Texas and Florida began to bloom under the rain of dollars. . . . Where defence went, other industries and private investments followed: soon the economic gap between the South and the rest of the Union, which had endured since the Civil War, began to close and the South-West became the most rapidly growing part of the country . . . California was the chief beneficiary of this new movement.[11]

The arms race rejuvenated the American economy, and Americans found themselves enjoying secure employment and earning steady salaries.[12] As Andrew Hurley suggests, this outcome was "celebrated by going into a consumer binge."[13] Hurley's statistical information is telling:

> In just the four years following the end of the war, Americans purchased 21.4 million cars, 20 million refrigerators, 5.5 million stoves, and 11.6 million television sets. During the late 1940s and 1950s,

> annual expenditures on jewelry, toys, and kitchen appliances were twice what they had been in the immediate pre-war era.[14]

In the post-World War II period, the purchase of goods such as cars and televisions became a way of expressing Americans' aspirations and celebrating the repudiation of their fears of a recession after the war.[15] This economic growth permeated the whole of society. Blue-collar workers were earning as much as white-collar workers; they found themselves for the first time being able to afford the goods that the wealthy had long wanted to enjoy. On the basis of purchasing power, the rift between the working and middle classes became smaller during this period.[16] During the 1950s the rift between working classes and middle classes narrowed and the shape and behaviors of the middle class stabilized. This new middle class was characterized by family life in the suburbs and the purchasing power of domestic family goods.

The "American way of life," a popular cliché of the time, was extended by consumer culture. This notion of Americanism was supported by the predominant political and financial institutions of the time. Again, Hurley helpfully suggests that:

> Indeed, the premise became a kind of party line among nationalistic pundits who sought to distinguish the United States from its communist rivals. A consumer culture that denied class distinctions evinced proof of the nation's enduring democratic culture. Its ability to absorb people from working-class backgrounds and foreign ancestries testified to the superiority of the American way, namely free-market economy.[17]

Without class as its explicit guide for either the production or advertising of goods, the purportedly "classless" American society emerging in the 1950s also forced manufacturers and advertisers to search for new markets and target new consumer groups. Suburban family life and domestication became the focus of production and advertising. Hurley writes:

> The lure of the suburban middle majority market, however, catapulted family fetishism to the heights of absurdity after the war. This was, after all, the era of the family car, the family room, the family film, the family vacation, and the family-size carton. Products and service that could be shared and experienced by entire families gained a special legitimacy as well as a practical competitive advantage in the market place.[18]

Manufacturers and advertisers found a way to exploit and capitalize on not only the institution of family and its attendant moral values but also members of the family who previously were not considered consumers or individuals with dispensable incomes or consumer desires. Women and teenagers became the focus of advertising and product campaigns. Advertisers and manufacturers "positioned themselves as surrogate families" and "encouraged men, women, and children to find fulfilment and pleasure beyond the family circle."[19] A good example of this commercial encouragement was the production of cars. Housewives were encouraged by advertisers to develop activities outside the home (including buying of other products). To carry out these activities, they had to have their own car. Teenagers were likewise encouraged to develop their own individuality; manufacturers and advertisers rewarded them with low-frame, fast cars.[20] Commercial industries, however, did not encourage the development of individuality entirely outside the institution of the family. Importantly, while encouraging housewives and teenagers to become more independent and mobile, predominant commercial and political discourses nevertheless continued to support the homogeneous and respectable idea of the family with the father being the clear authority in this central social institution.

While growing economically and enriching many of its citizens, the post-World War II United States was not bereft of social problems. One, the growth in juvenile delinquency, became an increasing subject of analysis for criminologists and sociologists. Clifford Shaw and Henry McKay, for example, suggested that crime was related to the geographical transition of spaces.[21] While economic prosperity stabilized city areas and increased the value of property and the cost of living, they explained, populations moved into new areas in order to maintain a better standard of living. These new areas were characterized by Shaw and McKay as disorganized spaces that gave rise to very little community cohesion, a sense of temporality, and the erosion of family ties. This translated into individual dissatisfaction and loss of moral direction, which, in turn, led to conflicting moral and social values that encouraged lawbreaking and delinquency. Other theorists have proposed that the lawbreaking acts of juvenile youths reflected a normal response to abnormal societal or personal circumstances: juvenile crime is seen in this way to be caused by an overall failure of society. Robert Merton thus argued that juvenile crime represented the failure of the social system to legitimate material success for young people, and Albert Cohen explored delinquency as a reaction to status formation that was resolved through the formation of youth gangs. Middle-class values are inverted in the models to form the violent and indulgent values of the youth gangs.

Ray's *Rebel Without a Cause* can be viewed to convey a mid-1950s representation of youth gangs, youth discontent, and a critique of family cohesion, suburban affluence. One can read the character of Jim Stark (James Dean) and his actions either according to Shaw and McKay, that is, as a response to a system that could not provide him with material recognition, or to Cohen, as a reaction against status formation and the resultant forming of a youth gang. Yet neither of these modes of analysis provides us with a full description of Jim, whose material desires appear fully provided by his parents. (At the beginning of the film, when asking why his son is breaking the law, the father can imagine no excuse, since the parents provide him with "everything.") Cohen's analysis likewise does not account for Jim's rebellion against family and status quo, which is an insular rebellion rather than one associated with the formation of a gang. While criminologists propose to understand the causes of crime such as juvenile crime, their understanding of crime tends specifically to interpret the discontent in negative terms—even if the rebellious actions are read as understandable reactions to an abnormal society (as Merton does). The negativity arising from these actions stems from their being seen as lawbreaking or norm-breaking rather than as potentially positive actions capable of giving rise to a youth citizenship, or at least a demand for youth citizenship, to be recognized by prevailing social and political structures.

The point here is not to examine what specifically brought about Jim's "rebellious" stride, though Hurley's suggestion of the growing sense of young men and women of the emptiness of the consumer culture and conformism is compelling. Indeed, Jim's "rebelliousness" might be read as an early critique of consumer culture, which itself is linked to various other criminological or sociological explanations: lack of cohesive community, competing moral values, general dissatisfaction with the social mores. Rather than the etiology of rebellion, my greater interest here is in reading how either rebellion or the figure of the rebel *affects* the social and political arena. The following critical analysis of Arendt's work on revolutions demonstrates why it is important to adopt such an affective reading to events or characters.

What Is a Rebellion, Who Is a Rebel?

Hannah Arendt's *On Revolution* offers both sociological and philosophical analyses of the modern phenomenon of revolution. Arendt looks into the principles that underlie the concept/practice of revolutions and how they developed since the French Revolution (1789) and the American Revolution (1776). The book is mostly preoccupied with how we are to understand the concept/practice of revolution. Arendt therefore engages in writing that allows her to differentiate and "purify" the concept/practice of revolution from other, similar concepts/practices of rebellion, resistance, and struggle. Through this process of "purification," Arendt establishes both the concept/practice of revolution as a unique modern phenomenon (i.e., located since the latter part of the eighteenth century) *and* as different from rebellion, war, the birth of Christianity, and the concept of revolution developed in the natural sciences.

While important to note that Arendt distinguishes the concept/practice of revolution from these other terms, the priority here is to focus on the way she differentiates revolution from rebellion. For her, the modern concept of revolution is inextricably linked with two ideas: the idea of novelty and the idea of freedom. For a revolution to have taken place, she submits, these two ideas must coincide. Of novelty, Arendt writes, "The modern concept of revolution, inextricably bound up with the notion that the course of history suddenly begins anew, that an entirely new story, a story never known, or told before is about to unfold, was unknown prior to the two great revolutions at the end of the eighteenth century."[24] Revolutions uproot the foundations of the old or ancient regime and bring into effect something else, and write in its place their own history. Revolutions transform the sociosymbolic system to such an extent that it becomes unfamiliar, anew, a new story. It is in this sense that modern revolutions are seen to be affecting something novel.

"Crucial . . . to any understanding of revolutions in the modern age," Arendt also asserts, "is that the idea of freedom and the experience of a new beginning should coincide."[25] Freedom, she writes, should not be understood as being synonymous with liberty or liberation, which "may be the condition of freedom but by no means leads automatically to it."[26] Put differently, the idea of liberation or liberty leads to the formation of civil liberties and constitutional governments, but neither can "capture" the "desire for freedom."[27] It is this "desire for freedom" that leads to doing and making something new. The institutionalization of civil liberties at the end of the French Revolution and the American War for Independence "meant no more than freedom from unjustified restraint."[28] What those revolutions effectively did was to bring into being something that was already there, rights that were not new but rather were preexistent. Illustrating her argument, Arendt points out that the core idea supporting civil rights is that of "freedom from unjustified restraint." She suggests that one can trace the origin of this idea to eighteenth-century legal theorist William Blackstone's idea of personal liberty consisting in the "power of locomotion . . . without imprisonment or restraint, unless by due course of law."[29] If revolutions were only aimed at guaranteeing civil liberties, she argues, they would have as their goal the control of governments that violated "well-established rights."[30] The idea of freedom as a way of political life means access to the public arena and meaningful participation in public affairs.[31] This understanding of freedom was not entirely unprecedented in the modern era: she points out, for instance, that it is very similar to the concept of isonomy "that can be understood as a form of political organisation in which the citizens lived together under conditions of no-rule, without a division between rulers and ruled."[32] But it is new in the important sense that revolutionaries for the first time after centuries have put themselves in a position of using their faculties to make something new. Arendt thus points out that what they felt through the practices of speech-making, decision-making, thinking, and persuasion was an experience of freedom. For Arendt, our modern understanding of revolution as a practice/concept is thus embellished with the idea of a new story that comes into being through the demolition and uprooting of the old and holds with it the promise (or, at least, desire) that freedom as a political way of living will come into being.

Arendt draws a further distinction between revolution and rebellion. To do so, she looks at the history of rebellions and their achievements, focusing particularly on rebellions that took place between medieval and postmedieval periods. The aim, she writes, "of such rebellions was not to challenge authority or the established order of things as such; it was always a matter of exchanging the person who happened to be in authority, be it the exchange of a usurper for the legitimate king or the exchange of a tyrant who had abused his power for a lawful ruler."[33] Unlike revolutions that succeed in transforming the whole sociosymbolic realm and writing a new story, rebellions manage merely to remove from a position of power one ruler and to appoint in his position a new one who appears less tyrannical. Rebellions in this sense fail to be "transformative," to uproot the old or the ancient and to invent in its place a new political system. The difference between rebellions and revolutions does not, however, remain only at the level of what kind of change takes place. Arendt is quick to point out that the role played in rebellions by rebels was also very different:

> . . . the people might be admitted to have the right to decide who should *not* rule them, they certainly were not supposed to determine who *should*, and even less do we ever hear of a right of people to be their own rulers or to appoint persons from their own rank for the business of government. Where it actually happened that men of the people rose from low conditions to the splendour of the public realm, as in the case of the condottieri in the Italian city-states, their admission to public business and power was due to qualities by which they distinguished themselves from the people, by a *virtu* which was all the more praised and admired as it could not be

> accounted for through social origin and birth. Among the rights, the old privileges and liberties of the people, the right to share in government was conspicuously absent. And such a right of self-government is not even fully present in the famous right of representation for the purposes of taxation. In order to rule, one had to be a born ruler, a free-born man in antiquity, a member of the nobility in feudal Europe, and although there were enough words in premodern political language to describe the uprising of subjects against a ruler, there was none which would describe a change so radical that the subjects became rulers themselves.[34]

Rebellion consequently becomes in Arendt's writing an event that does not rewrite history—not only because it does not alter the political structure but, more importantly, because it does not alter the political position of the rebels. The rebel contributes merely to the removal of a ruler but never becomes the ruler. One could say that rebellions construct the rebel as a non-agentic political subject, that is, a figure without political agency. In combination with her two-part standard for revolution itself, this is primarily what allows Arendt to differentiate the concept/practice of revolution from that of rebellion.

I want to pause over briefly, and to contest, this idea of the rebel being a figure without political agency. The contestation arises from Arendt's understanding of revolutions and rebellions developed through constant focus on historical events as the basis for explanations of the meanings of concepts and practices. This is a teleological focus, meaning that Arendt understands what a rebellion or a revolution "does" and therefore "is" by looking at its ends or effects. She reads rebellions and revolutions as complete, closed events. Such reading is problematic for at least three reasons: first, it relies heavily on the achievements or what events do; second, the doing of events is not read beyond linearity and conclusion (achievement); and, third, it fails in understanding the often contingent contribution of the subject (i.e., the rebel) to the event, and the event is therefore somehow disembodied, alienated from the subject. It is the latter point that becomes especially problematic in Arendt's writing. Her approach to rebellion fails to evaluate significantly the contribution that the rebels make in removing a ruler from power or reshaping discourse about authority itself; rather, she evaluates their contribution primarily in terms of what they have not achieved—namely power for themselves. This might be acceptable if one is interested, as Arendt is partially, in separating the concept/practice of revolution from rebellion. Yet it is problematic if one is interested in understanding the rebel or rebellion as a political concept/practice. What Arendt does is to disenfranchise the practices in which the rebels are engaging from the arena of political transformation. This theoretical step disenfranchises the rebel twice: he is not only insignificant politically because he never achieves public political power but also because his political agency is only understood in terms of an end—and hence without a cause. In Judith Butler's words, Arendt fails to understand that:

> Agency exceeds the power by which it is enabled. One might say that the purposes of power are not always the purposes of agency. To the extent that the latter diverge from the former, agency is the assumption of a purpose unintended by power, one that could not have been derived logically or historically, that operates in a relation of contingency and reversal to the power that makes it possible, to which it nevertheless belongs. This is, as it were, the ambivalent sense of agency, constrained by no teleological necessity.[35]

Arendt's conception of the rebel as an ultimately powerless figure constructs power as an external entity that can be possessed. Once power is set up as something external that can be possessed, the rebel—in Arendt's historical sense—is seen as one that does not possess political power and henceforth agency, political agency. But this construction fails to comprehend that agency operates in a nonteleological way and resists the very power that brings her into being. Butler's analysis of agency shows that while subjects might be subordinated (and feel the pain of subordination) and might in everyday terms be understood as powerless, they still possess political agency. This political agency enables subjects to resist subordination, to resist being identified as victims of power. Instead, the resistance to subordination communicates that subjects desire to be disidentified from the position of victims and be identified with subjects that talk through their actions about making a different world from the one that already exists. It is in this sense that I would like to talk of political agency "as that that resists the power that brings it into being by projecting a desired political world" (one that disidentifies with the identification).[36]

Can I Read a Rebel? and Can I Read a Rebel with a Cause?

Arendt's reading of rebellions and the rebel, I argued above, fails to allow the rebel possession of political agency that comes through his or her resistance to power. Arendt's reading also fails to address how political agency operates and what it demands. My suggestion is that we understand the figure of the rebel and his acts as demands for recognition of his political agency and ultimately his political citizenship. It is through this definition of rebellion that I propose to read Ray's film, *Rebel Without a Cause*. In doing so I will focus on the figure of Jim Stark, the film's protagonist and nominal "rebel"[37] and his actions, in two specific scenes.

The first scene takes place in the juvenile division of the police station. This is the encounter between Jim Stark and Ray, a sympathetic police officer, who distances Jim from his parents and his grandmother, who have arrived to pick him up after he is arrested for being drunk and disorderly. The action follows a scene in which Jim's father tries to apologize to the police officer for his son's behavior and expresses puzzlement at that behavior, remarking that the young man's actions are unjustifiable since he has been given everything by his family. When Jim breaks down upon hearing this, Ray removes him from the room. The officer then tries to get at the cause of Jim's discontent. It is here that Jim (James Dean) addresses the matter of rebellion and political agency. Jim looks through a looking hole, sees his family (mother, father, and grandmother) arguing, and wishes aloud that his dad had

> the guts to knock Mom cold once; then maybe she'd be happy and then she'd stop picking on him, because they make mush out of him. I tell you one thing, I don't ever want to be like him. How can a guy grow up in a circus like that? . . . Boy, if, I had one day when I didn't have to be all confused, and didn't have to feel that I was ashamed of everything. . . . If I felt that I belonged someplace, you know, then . . .

Jim expresses through his words and his pained eyes that he does not belong there, in "a circus like that." The word "circus" conveys both his distaste and disapproval of his family; as a metaphor, the word "circus" can be taken to transmit a confused state of family affairs and to expose his perception of the failure of his family to deliver what were supposed to be the satisfying gender and middle-class values of post-World War II America. His family clearly fails in being united and warm. Any form of family respectability disappears amid their everyday fights and is instead translated into the act of keeping up appearances for the sake of the public. His family's gender relations are also a sham. His mother is portrayed as being in control of his father. Jim's desire for his dad to have the "guts to knock Mom cold once" registers further his anger with his family gender relations. If we were to apply Arendt's historical analysis of rebellions to this private rebellion, expressed by Jim's actions and words, we would construe Jim's actions as ones driven by his despair; in a related, criminological sense, he would be read to be acting either as a delinquent not satisfied with his material provisions or refusing the status quo and conventional authority. Put differently, Jim would be read as being disempowered by the failed institution of family. All these explanations, however, lack attention to how Jim's individual agency is produced through this scene. Jim's critical reflections of his family speak volumes about his condition of subordination and his "delinquent" status. Jim's actions and words could be read as practices of resisting the "circus"—that is, his family's failure—and registering his demand to be recognized not as a victim of his familial or social environment but as an individual searching to find somewhere else to belong. His wish to feel that he belonged somewhere else is paradigmatic of this. Through his actions he is transmitting a desire to be recognized as an individual who belongs in a space not necessarily defined by the values of middle-class respectability, family and gender relations, and the American way of life. He also demands an inversion of his own family gender relations by calling upon his father to become a strong masculine figure able to resist his mother's demands and control. Jim's rebellion thus presses for a change in his family relations *and* the recognition of his own individuality and opinion about those relations. In this way, despite the ready critique evident in Jim Stark's yearning to belong somewhere else outside the "circus" of the mid-1950s suburban middle-class family, the film finally recuperates the institution of the family.

The second scene substantiates this reading of the film as one of reconciliation and regeneration, rather than dismissal or rejection, of the institution of the family. After Plato is shot by the police, we see Jim suffer, feeling both guilt and an inability to comprehend his friend's seemingly senseless death. Jim had attempted to negotiate with the police and resolve Plato's surrender peacefully. This attempt to negotiate brings Jim closer to his father: he identifies or, at least, comes close to identifying with his father. In fact, after witnessing Jim's efforts, the father assures his son, for the first time, that they will face things together. After asking his father to help him, Jim hugs him. Jim finds himself here at the moment and site of reconciliation, no longer demanding answers from his father. Having confronted the law and failed to prevent Plato's death, no answer to the questions he previously posed could seemingly relieve the pain. Jim's open wound brings him down to his knees, asking for help from his father, the very figure from whom he had demanded answers and transformation. The act also asks the film's viewer to reconsider Jim and whether this wound has suddenly made him recognize who he is and whether he has given up or forgotten his political dream of rebellion.

His father seems to answer those questions in unequivocal terms: "Look, Jim. You can depend on me. Trust me. Whatever comes, we'll, we'll fix it together. I swear it. Now Jim, stand up. I'll stand up with you. I'll try to be strong as you want me to be. Come on."

Rebels in Arendt never choose a ruler. The rebel's contribution is only in replacing one ruler with another. The rebel himself gains no power—here, Jim has failed and fallen to his knees and cried and asked for help. Jim's father speaks to him. He answers partially his son's wound. He answers partially to what his rebel son wants and dreams of—as a family member and as a political citizen. His father puts down the façade of respectability, of middle-class values, of not standing up to his mother and for once dreams with his son.

Conclusion: Citizenship and Private Rebellion

Political citizenship has traditionally been read as a possession of public institutions. T. H. Marshall's *Citizenship and Social Class* argued in 1950 that citizenship is a possession of the State, which in return cares for the welfare and rights of its citizens.[38] Marshall also argued that state citizenship brings together and binds members of a State. More recently, cultural theorists such as Lauren Berlant have transformed the terrain of discourses surrounding citizenship.[39] Berlant's critique of U.S. citizenship during the Reagan era demonstrates that the idea of a public political arena has been transformed into an "intimate public" sphere. Our contemporary idea of citizenship is, she claims, measured against our private acts. By analyzing Ray's *Rebel Without a Cause* through a critical reflection of Arendt's understanding of revolution and rebellion, my assertion is that youth rebellions traditionally understood as delinquent acts or politically insignificant in fact hide within them a potent political message. Private and individual acts of rebellion might not be revolutionary, might not transform the sociosymbolic order that is being challenged; they carry within them, however, a demand that an individual's critical opinion and demands should be recognized. This demand for individual recognition resists the power relations that bring an individual into being and give rise to an articulation of political citizenship different from what one is experiencing. Jim Stark's words and actions articulate his demand for a familial environment that does not hide behind the façade of middle-class or consumer values, and also the recognition that he is an individual as well as a family member. The end of the film does not necessarily address all his demands: he does not find that other space where he feels he belongs. But his family "circus" does change in such a way as to become closer to his ideal place. No matter how apolitical (or distant from politics) they may appear, private rebellions demonstrate the parameters through which public values and morals can be transformed. At the time of rebellion against particular values, it is likely that neither a complete rejection nor complete transformation will take place. The hope and potential of the rebel, though, is that a future sociopolitical arena could bear the fruits of greater recognition of, and effects on, individual and private rebellion.

Notes

This chapter is a modified version of "Rebel without a cause?" from *Law's Moving Image*, ed. Leslie J. Moran, Emma Sandon, Elena Loizidou, and Ian Christie (London: Cavendish, 2004), 45–60.

1. There are explicit historical linkages between Camus's book, Arendt, and Ray's film. Arendt had read Camus's book and had sent him warm congratulations for his book. Camus had deep respect for Arendt's work. He never read *On Revolution*, which was first published in 1963, three years after Camus's death. Ray on the other hand had read *The Rebel* in 1954, when the book was first published in English and was deeply influenced by it. It is well documented that Camus's work helped convince the director to keep the word "rebel" in the title of the film; for more on this see Eisenschitz.

2. Pountain and Robins (19).

3. See, for example, Mouffe; Berlant (1997); and Brown.

4. Arguably in the same genre are *The Wild One* (Laslo Benedek, 1953), *On the Waterfront* (Elia Kazan, 1954), and *West Side Story* (Robert Wise, Jerome Robbins, 1961).

5. Berlant (1998, 119).

6. We find out early in the film that in their previous living habitat Jim messed a kid up that called him a chicken.

7. The film is full of images of confrontations between Jim and Judy and their respective parents.

8. Pountain and Robins (70).

9. Brogan (604).

10. Brogan (605).

11. Brogan, (605–6).

12. Hurley (2).

13. Hurley (2).

14. Hurley (5).

15. Hurley (6).

16. Hurley (6–12).

17. Hurley (274).

18. Hurley (278).

19. Hurley (291). For an alternative feminist reading of the suburban housewife, see Friedan.

20. Hurley (290–99).

21. Shaw and McKay. For a general discussion of crime and causes of crime, see Henry and Milovanovic.

22. Merton.
23. Cohen.
24. Arendt (28).
25. Arendt (29).
26. Arendt (29).
27. Arendt (29).
28. Arendt (32).
29. Arendt (32).
30. Arendt (32).
31. Arendt (32).
32. Arendt (30).
33. Arendt (40).
34. Arendt (40–41).
35. Butler (15).
36. Berlant (2000, 42–43).
37. See Dyer (esp. 52–54) on Hollywood's use of charismatic actors such as James Dean in playing rebellious characters. Dyer offers a sociological and semiotic analysis of stardom. In relation to the type of the rebel, he argues that one should question the rebelliousness of such types in Hollywood films. In *Rebel Without a Cause*, Dyer argues that Dean is not a rebel, for his character recuperates the institutional family values. He also suggests that the life and death of stars such as James Dean is used by Hollywood to lure the audience into perceiving the character of the film is rebellious. He also warns us of the ways by which the type of the character is used to dominate other types of characters, such as women, homosexuals and blacks. One might suggest that this occurs in *Rebel Without a Cause* in which the masculine young rebel, Jim Stark, played by James Dean, has authority over the female character, Judy, played by Natalie Wood.
38. Marshall.
39. Berlant (1997).

Works Cited

Arendt, Hannah. *On Revolution*. London: Penguin Books, 1990. Originally published in 1963.

Berlant, Lauren. "The Subject of True Feelings: Pain, Privacy, and Politics." In *Transformations: Thinking through Feminisms*. London: Routledge, 2000.

———. "Collegiality, Crisis, and Cultural Studies." *Profession* (1998).

———. *The Queen of America Goes to Washington City: Essays on Sex and Citizenship*. Durham and London: Duke University Press, 1997.

Brogan, Hugh. *The Pelican History of the United States of America*. London: Penguin Books, 1986.

Brown, Wendy. *States of Injury*. Princeton: Princeton University Press, 1995.

Butler, Judith. *The Psychic Life of Power: Essays in Subjection*. Berkeley: University of California Press, 1997.

Camus, Albert. *The Rebel*. London: Penguin Books, 2000. Originally published in 1951.

Cohen, Albert K. *Delinquent Boys: The Culture of the Gang*. Glencoe, IL: Free Press, 1955.

Eisenschitz, Bernard. *Nicholas Ray: An American Journey*, trans. by Tom Milne. London: Faber and Faber, 1993.

Friedan, Betty. *The Feminine Mystique*. New York: Dell, 1984. Originally published in 1963.

Henry, Stuart and Dragan Milovanovic. *Constitutive Criminology: Beyond Postmodernism*. London: Sage, 1996.

Hurley, Andrew. *Diners, Bowling Alleys, and Trailer Parks: Chasing the American Dream in Postwar Consumer Culture*. New York: Basic Books, 2001.

Marshall, Thomas H. *Citizenship and Social Class*. Cambridge: Cambridge University Press, 1950.

Merton, Robert K. "Social Structure and Anomie." *American Sociological Review* 3 (1938): 672–82.

Mouffe, Chantal. "Democratic Citizenship and the Political Community." In *Dimensions of Radical Democracy: Pluralism, Citizenship, Community*. New York: Verso, 1992.

Pountain, Dick and David Robins. *Cool Rules: An Anatomy of an Attitude*. London: Reaction Books, 2000.

Shaw, Clifford R. and Henry D. McKay. *Juvenile Delinquency and Urban Areas: A Study of Delinquents in Relation to Differential Characteristics of Local Communities in American Cities*. Chicago: University of Chicago Press, 1942.

Original theatrical poster for *Rebel Without a Cause*. *(Courtesy of Photofest)*

10

James C. McKelly

Youth Cinema and the Culture of Rebellion

Heathers and the *Rebel* Archetype

Writing from an Italian prison during the Mussolini regime, the socialist cultural critic Antonio Gramsci articulated an idea that would profoundly influence the social, psychiatric, and literary theory of the second half of the twentieth century. In his *Prison Notebooks*, Gramsci identifies "hegemony" as a kind of pervasive cultural consensus regarding a particular set of social values, which in turn privileges, promotes, and protects itself through the establishment of analogous political, cultural, and social structures.[1] According to Gramsci, because of the permeating quality of its consensus, true hegemony need never assert itself through violence; rather, it secures its ascendancy by representing itself as a "natural" order. In so doing, it presents as "natural" an arbitrary and constructed sociopolitical hierarchy for culture and a particular socioeconomic and psychological "identity" for the subject existing within that culture. Through hegemony, ideology is naturalized as history, beauty, order, "common sense," and, on the level of psychology, sanity and maturity.

This naturalization, this latent and vaguely pleasurable dissemination of dominant ideology throughout the social, is accomplished through the agency of culture itself, in all of its formations. In his 1957 work *Mythologies*, Roland Barthes identifies as "mythic" any cultural artifact that in its structure, style, narrative, or thematic implication serves to effect such a naturalization.[2] In this sense, film exerts a profoundly mythological function, contributing to the symbolic order images of the values and behaviors endorsed through hegemony, and facilitating frame by frame the self-identification of the subject within that order.

In one of the myriad ironies of commodity culture, however, film has also functioned as a vehicle by means of which cultural alterity and counter-hegemonic dissent—in short, rebellion—have achieved "projection." As is manifestly evident in the critical discourse, it is a moot point whether the capitalist symbolic order "always already" contains such images of delinquency merely by virtue of the fact that they find representation and commodification in it, or whether it yields to the subversive power of these projections of difference, which carve out for rebellion new symbolic space free of the oblique insinuations of hegemony.

What is not a question of debate is that these mythologies of rebellion symbolically situate the delinquent subject within what Jean-François Lyotard has termed the "*grands recits*,"[3] the hegemonic metanarratives of knowledge, morality, aesthetics, and social progress that wheel above our culture like the constellations of the night sky—those eternal, predictable, "natural," clockwork metonyms of divine order, according to whose positions we orient ourselves, navigate our chaos, measure our "progress," tell our time, chart our destination, and foretell our destiny. During the first planetarium scene in Nicholas Ray's *Rebel Without a Cause* (1955), Jim Stark (James Dean) and his classmates watch these constellations explode and hear humankind's fleeting presence in the universe declared "an episode of little consequence." This simulacrum of apocalypse provides a first cinematic image of youth culture's introduction to what Lyotard identifies as the postmodern condition, and what Douglas Coupland has since termed "life after God"[4]: the legitimating certitude of these *grands recits* of meaning and order has been torched; in the subsequent crisis in value, institutions conventionally viewed as vehicles of social and psychological stability—church, state, school, family—have been disclosed as irrelevant, insufficient, and delusory. With this scene the film presents itself as an archetypic mythology in Barthes's sense of the term—an inaugural cinematic artifact of a postmodern culture of rebellion, which anticipates a radical moral, relational, and psychological disorientation for youth culture, and investigates the forms of responsivity with which youth culture might both express and negotiate this condition.

The diegetic structure of *Rebel* is built around an inquiry into the possible meanings of the figure "honor" in the symbolic order of a culture suffused with cowardice, apathy, denial, self-interest, pragmatism, and hypocrisy. Jim is the precariously situated protagonist trying to Do The Right Thing in facing the twofold moral challenge issued to him in the idiom of a twofold self-destructive threat—physical and social. At its outset the film configures Buzz Gunderson (Corey Allen), the catalyst of both dimensions of this challenge, as an unproblematically assaultive nemesis driven by testosterone and ruthless insecurity. However, at Miller's Bluff, where Jim responds to the first part of the challenge to his "honor" by meeting Buzz in the suicidal "chickie run," the film makes clear in a famous exchange the affinity between these two delinquents: at the edge of the precipice, Buzz admits, "I like you." Jim pauses, and asks, "Then why do we do this?" Buzz replies, "We gotta do something!" Their shared self-destructive risk is a way of cultivating "honor" despite the boredom and morally enervating affluence of their environment. Ray here makes it apparent that even in his role as nemesis Buzz is, like Jim, Judy (Natalie Wood), and Plato (Sal Mineo), a victim of hegemony, driven by self-destructive frustration, sent hurtling toward the literal edge of culture. His fate at the bluff foregrounds the concrete danger of a contrived attempt to construct value on the margins. In Buzz's own words, "It's a crazy game, man!"

Buzz's death precipitates the second, more exacting, dimension of Jim's moral challenge regarding "honor." The Millertown Bluff scene functions as the apogee of the film's depiction of the physical and psychological consequences of marginalization at the hands of hegemony: death or exclusion. The moment just after the crash, in which Jim extends his hand to Judy and pulls her back from the edge, marks a turning point in the film's thematic interest. If the first half of *Rebel* concerns itself with examining the lacerating contradictions that hegemony visits upon youth through the agency of parents—the key indication of which is Jim's oft-imitated howl, "You're tearing me apart!"—the second half of the film chronicles Jim's decision to return to the conventional order, but on his own terms. He wants to accept responsibility for his role in the violence the social order has precipitated—"For once in my life I want to do something right!" he says—but also to insist on the culpability of hegemonic consensus in the tragedy: "We are all involved!" The scene in the abandoned mansion, wherein Jim, Judy, and Plato "play house," represents the imaginative exploration of both the hypocrisies and possibilities of conventional order; Jim's leaving the scene of Plato's death *in a police car with his parents* vividly represents his inclusion in that order.

There is an ambiguity in this reconciliation with hegemony effected by Ray. On the one hand, it confirms Jon Lewis's assertion in *Road to*

Romance and Ruin that *Rebel* is "a very conservative film"[5] exemplifying a "thinly veiled search for authority"[6] that permeates American youth culture. When Jim enters that police car, he capitulates to a dominant order responsible, directly in the case of Plato and indirectly in the case of Buzz, for the deaths of these two fellow outsiders. From this perspective, the film constitutes an opera of tragic, coercive rehabilitation. On the other hand, the final reconciliation enacts the assertion that "rebellion," that volatile combination of exclusion and dissent, can introduce itself as a new term in the symbolic order without compromising its critique of that order. In short, Jim's reconciliation with hegemony makes a rebel "honor" possible by virtue of its own authority, unimpaired by psychosis, alienation, or a romanticized futility. "Honor" becomes more than just "a crazy game."

But no matter how you read the ambiguity at play in its protagonist's movement toward moral orientation, it is ironic that the film very unironically addresses its postmodern issues in a naïve, straightforward, unambiguously "modern" idiom. The film presents itself as remedial, therapeutic, and redemptive; its title notwithstanding, *Rebel Without a Cause* identifies causes, explains symptoms, and implies cures. This is what gives the film its earnest, somewhat clumsy "sociological" tone, something Ray inherited from his mentor Elia Kazan. We see evidence of it in the film's comically oedipal family portraits: Jim's mother (Ann Doran) screaming, "You want to kill your own father!"; Plato lamenting to Jim, "If only *you'd* been my dad!"; and Judy telling her emotionally repressed father (William Hopper), "I didn't *want* to stop [kissing you]!" The film's assumptions are grounded in the Enlightenment-fueled, social-realist moral and aesthetic imagination: though there is a complex problem, yet it is empirically identifiable; the sociologically adventurous artist can suss it out (here we see the significance of Ray's naming his insightful Juvenile Officer "Ray"); and, most importantly, a socially attentive, stylistically realist art can (1) accurately represent it and (2) transmit its enlightening and salvific message to culture. Although the film anticipates the thematization of the postmodern, one can see in many of its generic progeny—*Rumble Fish* (1983), *River's Edge* (1987), and *Heathers* (1988) all come to mind—its stylistic expression of this condition remains locked in the grammar of modernity.

Michael Lehman's *Heathers* tropes on the postmodern culture of rebellion as defined by the *Rebel* archetype, in so many ways that a comparison is inevitable. There are the more superficial associations: the story's antagonist (Christian Slater) is named "J. D.," short for Jason Dean (that the full name conflates America's favorite rebel with America's favorite hockey-masked, cleaver-wielding, machete-brandishing, chainsaw-swinging, pitchfork-poking, speargun-toting, murderous adolescent psychotic is a significance not to be overlooked); like Jim Stark, J. D. has just transferred to a new school from out of state, and has a history of social disruption and subsequent dislocation ("seven schools in seven states and the only thing in common is my locker combination"); his entrance provokes the jealous, aggressive attention of the alpha males of the school's ruling clique and the romantic attention of one of its leading women, he reciprocally engaging both forms of attention; and he and the leading woman together participate directly in the "crazy game" that leads to the death of the clique's big cheese and catalyzes the narrative drama of the film.

Other associations lead to telling distinctions. As with *Rebel*, the diegetic structure of *Heathers* is built around an inquiry into the possible meanings of a particular figure of moral orientation in the symbolic order of a culture suffused with cowardice, apathy, denial, self-interest, pragmatism, and hypocrisy. As we have seen, in *Rebel* that figure is "honor" informed, adversarially, by a conscience desiring social inclusion; in *Heathers*, it is "honor" as well—but an honor informed, consonantly, by a conscience desiring social justice, and linked, due to the protagonist's prominent position in the dominant order, to a form of *ex*clusion.

This difference is signalled by *Heathers*' inversion of *Rebel*'s narrative point of view. We experience *Rebel* almost exclusively from the perspective of Jim Stark, a male outsider seeking affiliation; our witness of the effects of his agency vis-à-vis the social is unmediated. In this way, the film coerces our sympathetic identification. *Heathers* on the other hand problematizes the agency of J. D., its explicitly Starkesque outsider, by virtue of its introspective, first-person voice-over narration by Veronica Sawyer (Winona Ryder), a female insider who seeks not affiliation but difference. Veronica's narration mediates our experience of J. D., disrupting our naïve identification and forcing us, to borrow Slavoj Žižek's expression, to "look awry"[7] at his influence. Furthermore, if we understand J. D. as a Harley-humping synecdoche of the Rebel genre *in toto*, the hermeneutic distance implied in Veronica's narration interrogates not only the central figure of that genre, but the genre itself. *Heathers*' Veronica is *Rebel*'s Judy empowered by ascesis and the narrative authority with which to express it; Veronica is Judy with a monocle and a pen, reconfiguring for us the significances comprised by the culture of rebellion as represented by the conventions of the Rebel genre.

Heathers accelerates the *Rebel* archetype in other ways as well. Like Jim, Veronica is a precariously situated protagonist trying to Do The Right Thing in facing a twofold moral challenge issued to her in the idiom of a twofold self-destructive threat. The first part of Veronica's challenge results from her realization that as a member of the Heathers clique, she is contributing to the establishment of cruelty as the self-destructive social currency of Westerburg High. "I am allowed an understanding that [others] have chosen to ignore," she says. "I must stop Heather." As we have noticed, in *Rebel*, Jim's challenge is conditioned by the desire to belong, on his own terms, to a hegemonic order from which he is exiled: "For once in my life I want to do something right." The Gunderson nemesis is just as marginalized by hegemony as Jim is. In *Heathers*, Veronica's challenge is conditioned by a desire to extricate herself from a hegemonic order in which she is not only included, but privileged with executive influence. And unlike Buzz, the Heathers nemesis is not victimized by hegemony; it constitutes hegemony.

Indeed, from the first line of Veronica's narration—"Heather told me she teaches real life"—the Heathers embody hegemony's naturalization of a particular set of social locations as "real life." The Orwellian imperative of the clique's kingpin, Heather Chandler (Kim Walker)—"Don't think"—neatly summarizes the importance to the dominant order of the inertia of consensus over the possibility of an activist, counter-hegemonic critique. And her elegantly succinct précis of her ascendancy—"They all want me as a friend or a fuck"—demonstrates the degree to which that ascendancy is insinuated into the psychology of the subject, which desires intercourse with the dominant despite the coercive character of that relation. Ironically, hegemony thrives on the complicit desire of the subject. To paraphrase J. D. late in the film, "People are going to look at the ashes of Westerburg and say, it self-destructed not because society corrupted the school, but because the school was society!" Therefore, for Veronica, "doing something right" doesn't just mean taking a firm moral stance; it means attempting to subvert the dominant order at the risk of utter expulsion. As Heather Chandler puts it, "Transfer to Washington, transfer to Jefferson—no one at Westerburg is going to let you play in their little reindeer games."

Heathers also operates as an uncanny deconstructive critique of the self-congratulatory "sociological" presumptions deployed by the Rebel genre generally, and by *Rebel Without a Cause* in particular. As we have seen, *Rebel* implies that like Jim, Judy, and Plato, Buzz Gunderson is a victim of failed bourgeois social institutions, particularly that of the family, which the film critiques straightforwardly with "modern" analytic certitude. And through its figure of institutional enlightenment, Officer Ray Fremick (Edward Platt), *Rebel* suggests that psychology offers the key to averting this victimization. *Heathers* mocks the very idiom of social-scientific analysis and its grounding in experiential cause-and-effect, parodies the rhetoric of dysfunction, and destabilizes the therapeutic pretense of the socially "redemptive" institution. *Rebel* represents redemption as opera; *Heathers* represents redemption as Oprah.

This Oprahfication is accomplished stylistically through the film's increasingly surrealistic treatment of the institutional response to the non-suicides. Particularly exemplary is the funeral service of Ram Sweeney (Patrick Labyorteaux) and Kurt Kelly (Lance Fenton), during which the two deceased jocks, killed in what J. D. has staged as a "repressed homosexual suicide pact," sport their team helmets and cradle footballs in state. The minister, Father Ripper (Glenn Shadix), an unsavory amalgam of Jim Baker, Jerry Springer, and Wavy Gravy decked out in a tie-dyed cassock, testifies that Jesus is "the righteous dude who can solve your problems." As Kurt's tearful father (Mark Carlton) stands over the casket poignantly fondling his son's funereal football, he addresses the corpse: "I don't care that you really were some . . . pansy. You're my own flesh and blood, and well, you made me proud." In the best trash-TV tradition, he then weepily declares to the congregation, "My son is a homosexual. I love my dead gay son!" Ms. Flemming (Penelope Milford), the psychobabbling baby boomer put in charge of Westerburg High's official response, sublimates self-destruction into evidence of authenticity, extolling the "pathetic beauty" of Heather Chandler's non-suicide as "an example of the profound sensitivity of the human animal," and turning the grieving process into a big-top custom-pitched for the media circus she cultivates. "Whether or not to commit suicide is one of the most important decisions a teenager can make," she intones. Profoundly self-annihilating psychosis is not only naturalized, but celebrated, as one of the normative conditions of adolescent development.

The second aspect of Veronica's challenge comes with the realization that J. D., the revolutionary principle that originally had empowered her own anger—which gave, as she writes in her diary, her "teen-angst bullshit . . . a body-count"—has become as enchanted with violent, deceptive coercion as the Heathers had been with hegemonic coercion-as-consensus. "Chaos is great!" he says. "We scared people into not being assholes." *Heathers* brings Veronica face to face not only with her physical complicity in the murders, but also with her psychological complicity—her retributive anger, self-justifying and suppressed, the amoral unleashing of which J. D. functions as the symbolic avatar. The denouement of *Rebel*—Jim's attempt to protect Plato, the innocent traumatized by the effects of hegemony—is represented as an act of mediation with an element of physical risk. The denouement of *Heathers* is represented as a ruthless confrontation in which not only the fate of the innocent is at stake—shots of students cheering at the pep rally are intercut with those of the struggle—but also both the physical and psychological fate of Veronica herself. Earlier she had called J. D. on his Starkesque pretense: "Rebel? You think you're a rebel? You're not a rebel! You're fucking psychotic!" He replies, "You say to-may-to, I say to-mah-to!" At the end of Jim's story, he emerges unscathed save by the deaths of two of his culturally delinquent peers. The Rebel is embraced by a dominant order the hypocritical agents of which—his parents, the police—have understood their failures. At the end of her story, Veronica, on the edge of her own Millertown Bluff between rebellion and psychosis, is responsible for pulling herself back, for forcing the amoral manifestation of her revolutionary anger to self-destruct, and for living with the several deaths for which she is, in a certain psychological sense, directly culpable.

As with Jim Stark's reconciliation with hegemony, there is an ambiguity in Veronica Sawyer's final declaration that "there's a new sheriff in town" as she assumes the Heathers' scarlet mantle—or, rather, the scarlet "scrunchie"—of power. Is the film another instance of Jon Lewis's "search for authority" thesis—meet the new boss, same as the old boss—or is it a myth of morally informed revolution resulting in psychological as well as material liberation? Whatever the case, *Heathers*' expression of a postmodern culture of rebellion serves to liberate the Rebel genre from the grammar of modernity as naturalized by the *Rebel* archetype. In constructing the images and language of this new idiom, Veronica and *Heathers* make the myth of rebellion, of which Jimmy Dean/Jim Stark is the dominant star, burn again.

Notes

1. See Gramsci.
2. Barthes (129–49).
3. Lyotard.
4. Coupland.
5. Lewis (30).
6. Lewis (37).
7. Žižek (9–12).

Works Cited

Barthes, Roland. *Mythologies*, trans. by Annette Lavers. New York: Hill and Wang, 1972.

Coupland, Douglas. *Life After God*. New York: Pocket Books, 1994.

Gramsci, Antonio. *The Prison Notebooks*. New York: Columbia University Press, 1991.

Lewis, Jon. *The Road to Romance and Ruin*. New York: Routledge, 1992.

Lyotard, Jean-François. *The Postmodern Condition: A Report on Knowledge*. Minneapolis: University of Minnesota Press, 1984.

Žižek, Slavoj. *Looking Awry: An Introduction to Jacques Lacan Through Popular Culture*. Cambridge: October Books, 1991.

11

Timothy Shary

The Stark Screen Teen

Echoes of James Dean in Recent Young *Rebel* Roles

Jim Stark was not the first teenage *Rebel* in American cinema, although this chapter will argue that he was the most influential. Youth rebellion was a white-hot topic in 1955 when *Rebel Without a Cause* hit American theaters, and Warner Bros. was only trying to capitalize on the agitated adolescent image that had been promoted in recent years by smaller studios in films such as *City Across the River* (1949) and *Teenage Devil Dolls* (1952), as well as James Dean's previous turn in *East of Eden* (1954).[1] Despite what appeared to be just another entry in a burgeoning teensploitation trend, *Rebel* distinguished itself for a variety of reasons. Its production values were noticeably sophisticated thanks to the creative talents of director Nicholas Ray and his crew; it spoke about the current teen tensions in sincere tones rather than didactic monologues; it witnessed an automatically profound marketing campaign due to the death of its star just days before its release. And it was the resulting veneration of Dean as an icon of young cool and his performance in *Rebel* that embodied that image that made the film such an indelible symbol of youth trying to discover themselves and declare their identity within the prosperous torments of the postwar world. As John Kreidl would claim, "*Rebel*'s success was directly a result of the audience's perception of the film as a statement made by James Dean who was seen, not only as the spokesman for the film, but for his entire generation."[2]

Consider the elements of Jim's character (and how difficult it's become to distinguish Stark from Dean) that resonated with youth at the time, and that remain common to contemporary youth. His upwardly mobile, middle-class parents struggle to understand his inarticulate needs, but his mother is so concerned with the family's social status that she'd rather move away than confront their problems, and his father is so browbeaten by Mom that he's effectively emasculated (a domestic crisis born from postwar fears of women's liberation). Jim does not want to run, and he tenuously hangs on to what he perceives as masculine obligations: he abhors being perceived as cowardly, and reluctantly fights to show his virility, while he quickly assimilates to a father role with Plato (Sal Mineo) and a husband role with Judy (Natalie Wood). And even over the course of the few days (really about thirty hours) in which the story unfolds, Jim exhibits the bipolar swings of a young man unsure of his direction in life, getting drunk one night and slugging down milk the next day, turning to a local cop for guidance even though he knows the legal system can't help him, and racing against Buzz (Corey Allen) in the death-defying duel not out of aggression but because "ya gotta do something." Jim bears all the hallmarks of teen angst that would be filtered through angry young male roles of the following generations, and it was Dean's rendering of these symptoms with such exquisitely conflicted anxiety that gave successive actors the paradigm to follow.

Dean's employment of the "method" has typically been cited as the source of his distinctive acting, and his approach certainly informed the affected performances of the young Warren Beatty and Jack Nicholson in the 1960s. Dean appeared to show real pain on screen, whether he was pounding a desk in an emotional outburst or simply trying to tell his father to act like a man, and his "soulful stare and agonized gestures projected the image of a son either unwilling or unable to accommodate society's expectation of male adulthood," as Thomas Schatz observed.[3] Since he displayed a spectrum of emotions from explosive to subtle, Dean was able to portray Jim as far more complex than the sinister students in *Blackboard Jungle* or the depraved delinquents of *Teenage Crime Wave* (both of which also appeared in 1955).[4]

That range of feeling and the enigmatic image it yielded would be another certain factor in changing the representation of teens after *Rebel*, even though Hollywood would curiously steer clear of adolescent performers by the late 1960s and early 1970s, opting instead to examine the more conspicuous upheavals among college-aged characters.

Still, at least on a formal level, Dean's influence could be detected within the frustrations of Ben (Dustin Hoffman) in *The Graduate* (1967) and Wyatt (Peter Fonda) in *Easy Rider* (1969), as well as in the attitudes and appearances of nostalgic *Rebel*s in *American Graffiti* (1973) and *Grease* (1978). In the later film, John Travolta openly negotiated his character's swings between nice guy and bad boy, but his previous performance in *Saturday Night Fever* (1977) was more significant evidence of the Dean influence. Even though Tony appears more confident because he is better dressed than Jim Stark ever was, inside he is twisted by the expectations of his family, his search for moral order, and doubts about his own authority. Tony became the icon of late 1970s youth style precisely because he did offer such a contrast between surface beauty and inner malaise, at a time when the country gleefully joined in the fads of disco and designer jeans (and designer drugs) to chase away the bitter taste of the Vietnam/Watergate era.

And by the end of the 1970s, the Hollywood industry was also changing its direction. The era of the blockbuster was clearly emerging, and the studios soon learned that the success of high-profit films like *Star Wars* (1977) and *Superman* (1978) were contingent upon drawing a large youth audience, a lesson that was driven home by the publicized failure of adult-oriented *Heaven's Gate* in 1980.[5] Yet by 1980, the studios had further discovered that small youth films could generate handsome earnings as well, which was already being demonstrated within the subgenre of youth horror films such as *Halloween* and *Friday the 13th* and would soon find additional realization in the wave of teen sex comedies that arose in the early 1980s. Clearly, the 1980s marked a departure for American cinema, as the studios came to rely on youth audiences (especially those frequenting the shopping mall multiplexes) more than ever before, and tailored their movies to teens accordingly, releasing a heavy load of teen films through the middle of the decade.

This is what makes the durability and influence of Dean's seminal *Rebel* performance so remarkable, because, as I will hereby demonstrate, his style has been maintained most loyally within *Rebel* characters of the past generation, who have simply modified their approach as they've evolved through the changing times. And by Dean's style, I refer to his fashion (Jim's red nylon jacket was emblematic of his fiery manner and yet middle-class capacity), emotion (the highs and lows, pains and pleasures), and actions (Jim learns to stand his ground despite the forces that resist him). Some actors of the past twenty years (Matt Dillon, Sean Penn, Johnny Depp, Leonardo DiCaprio) appeared to emulate some of Jim/

Dean's characteristics throughout their early careers, yet a survey of diverse performances across teen subgenres reveals the lingering influence of the Dean style and the Stark persona.

The paradigmatic *Rebel* role of John Bender (Judd Nelson) in *The Breakfast Club* (1985) represents a foundational moment at the apex of 1980s teen cinema. Bender (who is almost never called by his first name) instigates nearly all of the action between his detention hall classmates, pushing them to discuss who and why they are, and thereby never effectively masking his curiosity and vulnerability with the delinquent image he projects. As with Jim Stark and company, Bender and his cohort have their failed parents to blame for most of their problems, although by 1985, teens were even more self-aware and articulate about their crises. Bender becomes not only an authoritative father figure to his four diverse peers, he becomes their therapist, asking them how they deal with their messed-up families, and drawing out of them their deeper insecurities, leading to a cathartic group session where all five of them bond over their years of teen frustration.

Bender has elevated the gesticulating pain of Jim to a more potentially violent realm. Where Jim tried to resist fighting, Bender seeks it out, targeting the two most visible threats to his masculine authority, the school principal and the athletic Andy (Emilio Estevez). When both of these men show that they'd not only fight but likely hurt Bender, he turns his rage against nearby objects, pounding desks, throwing books, kicking stairs. Bender's class status is integrally linked to his rage and his role in the school: writer-director John Hughes makes a direct connection between Bender's poverty (marked by his worn clothes) and his aggression, which stems from living under abusive parents and the popularity regime of wealthier kids at school. Where Jim and his peers endured the expansion of the postwar bourgeoisie, Bender's group becomes a testament to Reaganomics and the stratification of American class roles in the 1980s. Like Jim, Bender is literally crying out for attention, to be unburdened by the responsibilities that he has taken on at such a young age, to be liberated from the torment he takes in and turns back on everyone around him.

Yet the film offers a strange resolution for Bender's conflicts: after he ironically woos the prom queen Claire (Molly Ringwald), she gives him one of her diamond earrings, which he sticks in his own ear. This gesture may signify his "payment" for relieving her of her conceited arrogance (or virginity), and it also implicitly suggests a dual shift in Bender's image after the revelatory detention experience, for he is now both richer and more feminine. The earring thus becomes a symbol of Bender's social softening while retaining a rebellious quality for the delinquent who will not reform. Bender's image closes the film, his hand thrust into the air in ambiguous triumph, and unlike Jim's familial reunification after suffering the loss of his surrogate son Plato, Bender is the one student in *The Breakfast Club* who does not return to his parents but rather sets off on his own. In that way, the film suggests that youth rebellion by the mid-1980s had jettisoned the reform of family from its agenda and set out on a newly independent course.

This suggestion is made even more profound in the far darker comedy *Heathers* in 1989. The film appeared after the box office appeal of American teen films in the 1980s had subsided, and was well positioned to skewer the traditions and attitudes of youth culture from the previous generation. There are really two *Rebel*s here, Veronica (Winona Ryder), who joins and later defects from the titular group of condescending elitists, and Jason Dean (Christian Slater), who goes by the shortened name J. D., reminding us that he is not only a juvenile delinquent, but that James Dean is his inspiration. While Veronica negotiates the intricacies of popularity with her ruling clique, J. D. remains confidently removed from the school's social scene, lurking about in his long coat and threatening aggressive jocks with a fake gun. Then the fragile balance of the school's caste system begins to falter when the accepted Veronica becomes attracted to the outcast J. D., following a number of parallels to *Rebel Without a Cause:* J. D. is the new kid in town who has been moved from school to school, although as was typical in 1980s youth films, his parents are long since separated; Veronica is part of the popular crowd but not-so-secretly longs for the lesser pressure of being just another student; both Veronica and J. D. have ineffective fathers who act more juvenile than their children; and as both become attracted to each other, popular kids start to die.

Yet unlike the chosen "chickie run" in *Rebel* that leads to Buzz's death, the students in *Heathers* begin dying at the hands of Veronica and J. D., who poison one of the Heathers in a prank that J. D. allows to turn lethal. Veronica feels remorse, but J. D. continues on his campaign to rid the school of its cool snobs, moving next to a prank that results in the death of two football players. Veronica and J. D. cover the murders by framing them as suicides, in the second case as a repressed gay affair gone wrong, revealing the far more menacing rebellion that they are staging by using the misguided sympathies and the latent homophobia of locals against themselves. Then, in the perverse logic of school power, suicide itself becomes aligned with the popular crowd, until a legitimately unhappy pariah tries to kill herself and is ridiculed for failing to emulate the truly accepted class leaders. This is what makes *Heathers* a turning point in youth cinema, for where most films after *Rebel* had taken youth unrest seriously, by 1989 teenagers had witnessed so much blatant manipulation of their images in the media that even the depiction of an issue as serious as suicide had become ironic. And by staging suicide with ironic humor, *Heathers* suggests that teens truly have vitiated their means of rebellion, leaving only homicide as a form of protest.

Granted, this message is carried out within the film's farcical tone, and reaches its most absurd realization when J. D. plans to blow up the entire school, only to be caught and cornered by Veronica, who saves the community and becomes "the new sheriff in town," in spite of her previous contempt for popular authority. Veronica thereby emerges as a new *Rebel* leader, one who will accept the unaccepted students, a fantasy of altruism far more improbable than the psychotic J. D.'s failed effort at mass murder. The move toward murder as teen rebellion in *Heathers* nonetheless remains significant, even though some past screen teens had become killers, because throughout the early 1990s the ultimate culmination of teen rebellion in many films becomes killing one's oppressors. In the days of *Rebel*, the teen threat was couched in warnings about the disintegration of family values and social order, which were restored before the end of *Rebel* and far more outrageous movies like *Untamed Youth* (1957) and *High School Confidential* (1958). By the end of the 1980s, American families and society had lost the illusion of order, and teens had gained the air of cynicism about these institutions that *Heathers* so vividly celebrated.

The fine line between cynicism and hope would provide much of the tension in the next conspicuous cycle of teen films that emerged in the early 1990s, the African American crime drama. Few films had featured black teenage protagonists before the 1990s, but in 1991, movies like *Up Against the Wall* and *Straight Out of Brooklyn* garnered some attention for their fresh and harrowing portraits of black youth caught up in troubling urban milieux, their lives complicated by crime and class struggle. Then *Boyz N the Hood* brought the most visibility to this emerging cycle later that year, introducing in Tre (Cuba Gooding Jr.) a strong-willed yet sensitive *Rebel* formed to fit the Jim Stark mold. Of course, race was essentially an elided issue in *Rebel* (the relationship between Plato and his caretaker offers some tacit statements), yet in *Boyz*, Tre is aware from a young age that he is growing up in a society that views black youth like him as a minority and a threat. This confrontation with racism infuses Tre with a sense of struggle and determination, as does his relationship with his didactic father, who espouses his ethics of responsibility and morality to his son.

Like Jim Stark, Tre labors to balance his longing to belong with his sense of righteousness, yet he enjoys the benefits of a stronger father who actively talks with him. And while the conflict of conformity that Jim encountered in *Rebel* has been maintained in all subsequent teen *Rebel* depictions, Tre is better able to distinguish between the value of solidarity with his friends and the dangers of following the pack. As a child, Tre sees his friend Doughboy (Ice Cube) imprisoned for murder, and after his release, Tre renews their friendship without emulating Doughboy's violent bravado. Tre is pulled in another direction by his girlfriend Brandi (Nia Long), who encourages him to leave Los Angeles and come to college with her, thereby offering a geographical, intellectual, and familial shift from the tensions of his current environment. This aspect is what gives *Boyz* (and similar films that followed, such as *Juice* and *Menace II Society*) a significant alteration from the *Rebel* mentality, for where Jim was looking for communal stability as a outlet for the failings of his family, Tre knows that he will always encounter racial conflict in America, and his true rebellion would be in breaking out of his supportive but troubled community. Jim and his ilk were effectively spoiled by postwar excesses, whereas Tre is at the other end of the class spectrum, and *Boyz* suggests that the financial and legal systems that have held down African Americans must be challenged at the personal and communal level, among both whites and blacks.

In the film's disturbing climax, Doughboy and his friends invite Tre to join them in killing a group of teens who murdered Doughboy's brother, but Tre's conscience does not let him join in the mayhem. This move once again demonstrates the unexpected sagacity of *Rebel* characters, who tend to turn away from revenge, and even though director John Singleton elected to show the climactic shootings in thrilling detail, Tre's resistance is a far more radical act than murder, for he is indeed breaking the absorbing cycle of violence that the film claims is otherwise destroying the African American community. Jim actually felt remorse over the death of his rival Buzz, but he turned to the police and his family in dealing with the crisis, which *Rebel* shows as an ultimately ineffective decision since it eventually leads to the death of Plato. Tre has seen the lechery of the local police and has had enough of his pushy father, and once again by standing on his own, allied but not conforming with his friends, acceptable to but not compromised by society, the *Rebel* achieves his most fulfilling role.

This role was crucial in appealing to young African American audiences in the early 1990s, although the output of *Boyz*-style crime dramas ended in 1995 after *Clockers*. This did not mean the end of teen *Rebel*s, of course, nor did it signal a lack of social concern on the part of filmmakers. In 1997, the independent feature *Hurricane Streets* featured another delinquent directly descended from the Jim Stark tradition, Marcus (Brendan Sexton III), a fifteen year old who runs with a small gang of mixed-race friends committing petty crimes like shoplifting or more serious crimes, such as smoking dope at that time, a felony. Marcus has already seen his family dissolve; his mother is in prison for killing his violent father and thus the gang provides his sense of familial belonging.

At first Marcus shows a clear resistance to escalating their thievery, even though his friends desire higher stakes, but then he meets Melena (Isidra Vega), a young Latina with whom he develops a gradual romance. Melena gives Marcus a sense of order and direction similar to Jim's Judy and the girlfriends of other *Rebel* incarnations, yet she also becomes his motivation for his ultimate acts of crime and escape, since he witnesses her father abusing her and plans a house robbery to raise money for them to run away.

Following the lineage of *Rebel* and the more recent examples from *Boyz*, the film depicts the impoverished but proud Marcus as a warrior against the supposedly reliable institutions that have failed him: family, friends, and schooling have only brought him torment. Where Jim ultimately turned back to the family and social fold, 1990s *Rebel*s continued to turn away from it. Curiously, unlike the moral decision Tre makes at the end of *Boyz*, Marcus's criminal plan of robbery and running is presented as not only rational but even somewhat warranted, and yet the deeper intent of his action is not dissimilar from Tre's: Marcus and Melena are trying to overcome the violent traditions of their parents and their culture. His vague sense of justice is nonetheless problematized when his gang accidentally kills Melena's father and he calmly handles the situation by disposing of the body. This shows his sense of purpose is intact, yet it leaves open a rather morally loose ending, for Marcus commits yet another robbery before joining Melena on a train out of town, not telling her that her father is dead. The final scenes do suggest that the other boys will be arrested for their crimes, yet the shrewd Marcus can rather happily flee on his good intentions. *Hurricane Streets* revises the teen *Rebel* for the end of the century when no force other than romance is worth defending for teenage boys who have seen their darkest cynicism realized around them.

This mythology blossoms to its fullest in *American Beauty* (1999) in the character of Ricky (Wes Bentley), a quietly distraught high schooler who lives under the schizophrenia of his fascist father and catatonic mother, building a secret empire of drug-running finances to make his escape. Ricky thus engages in a criminal outlet, yet a deeper passion arises through his constant videotaping of the world around him, and especially his neighbor Jane (Thora Birch), a sullen girl whose parents' dysfunction, not unlike Jim Stark's, arises from the mother's excessive control of the father. The film connects Ricky to Jim in various ways as well: he's the new kid who has just moved into town after beating a kid at his previous school, he finds his romantic partner in a sympathetic neighbor, and he is a visual throwback to Jim's era with his outdated and bland clothes. Ricky takes his disinterest in social acceptance to a new level, however, showing none of the need for friends that Jim and other *Rebels* typically exhibit. Ricky's rebellion is rather narcissistic, absorbed as he is in building capital, staying stoned, and deceiving his father. (Indeed, the film suggests that the parents of these children are engaged in dangerous levels of self-deception and delusion.)

Ricky quickly recognizes in Jane a kindred spirit longing to be free of parental tyranny, and shares with her his footage of a plastic bag blowing in the wind, an image that obviously symbolizes his (and many teens') position, aimlessly circling a small but contained area and always threatening to take off. In terms of narrative significance, this scene echoes the planetarium in *Rebel*, where Jim (and more so Plato) saw their temporality and smallness realized before their eyes. Here, the realization for Ricky is not about vulnerability but abundance; his supposed pain arises from not being able to handle the excess of "beauty in the world," and his videotapes have become a way of trying to contain his blithe appreciation of life. Yet perhaps the most intriguing aspect of *American Beauty* is the degree to which it takes its sarcastic commentary, for Ricky and Jane are so earnest in their angst that they become parodic. Teen *Rebels* of the past were able to convincingly writhe with the emotion of entrapment, but Ricky has become a confident zombie, numbed by the inanities and insanities of his parents' culture.

At the turn of the century, Ricky represents the teen *Rebel* lulled into a schizophrenia brought on by so many years of repression and frustration. Expressions of mere anger and doubt are no longer effective in giving *Rebels* an outlet for their pain, and even crime has been rendered passé. Rather, true teen rebellion has become even more internal, dependent on maintaining a drug-induced state of harmony and a drug-financed means of escape, which Ricky makes clear when he proposes to Jane that they run away and live off of his dope money. Alas, Ricky's repressed gay father elects to kill Jane's openly pedophilic father at that moment, sending the young couple's future into doubt, although presumably eliminating two of the sources of their discontent. In a voiceover, Jane's father tells us the snide moral to the story that we need to appreciate the beauty of boredom such as we all endure thereby suggesting the ultimate mode of anti-rebellion, for in the film's view, all means of literal escape from bourgeois boredom are futile, and the best one can hope for are a few moments of happiness within the monotony of life.

As cinematic teen rebels enter the twenty-first century, they are faced with rather daunting prospects for liberation. Their very means of self-identification and resistance have been so excessively depicted and commodified that simply acting against the norm is a commercial (and thus conformist) practice. Anger, crime, drugs, cars, and even romance have been neutralized from their previous potency. Where Jim Stark struggled to articulate his confusion about gender roles and social order, teen rebels of the past generation have moved from articulation to confrontation to disconnection. Jim found solace in family restoration; recent rebels have all but abandoned family for the sake of survival. Indeed, the films profiled here suggest that the rebel cannot return to the family at all, nor for that matter to any friends beyond his girlfriend, who may herself become an obstacle.[6]

The depiction of teen rebels nonetheless continues to evolve from the paradigm that Jims Stark and Dean developed in the 1950s, when many youth must have felt that the cause of their rebellion was ambiguous at best. Jim began the process of identifying teen angst, giving it an image and an etiology, and demonstrating the costs that would inevitably come for future generations of distraught teens. Current teens have by now exhausted the variously defined reasons for their *Rebel*lion, and since they have moved through so many comprehensive ways of enacting it, they no longer have an effective outlet for their angst. Perhaps youths today are again ready for a revolutionary depiction of their situation such as *Rebel Without a Cause* offered in 1955, if indeed today's teenagers can be convinced that there are any causes worthy of their rebellion.

Notes

1. Thomas Doherty explores the emergence of the delinquent and other trends in teen films of the 1950s. See also Mark Thomas McGee and R. J. Robertson.

2. Kreidl (149).

3. Schatz (239).

4. Kreidl traces the influence of *Rebel* to "two whole subgenres of imitation films: the wild youth film and the crazy mixed-up youth film," placing *Crime in the Streets* (1956) and *Juvenile Jungle* (1958) in the first category and *Hot Rod Girl* (1956) and *Dragstrip Riot* (1958) in the latter (153–54).

5. David Cook advances this argument more thoroughly (944–47).

6. This chapter focuses strictly on male rebels in the Stark/Dean mold; see my study of recent teenage girl *Rebel*s.

Works Cited

Cook, David. "The American Film Industry in the Age of 'Kidpix.' " In *History of Narrative Film*, third edition. New York: Norton, 1996.

Doherty, Thomas. *Teenagers and Teenpics: The Juvenilization of American Movies in the 1950s.* Boston: Unwin Hyman, 1988.

Kreidl, John. *Nicholas Ray.* Boston: Twayne, 1977.

McGee, Thomas and R. J. Robertson. *The J.D. Films: Juvenile Delinquency in the Movies.* Jefferson, NC: McFarland, 1982.

Schatz, Thomas. *Hollywood Genres: Formula, Filmmaking, and the Studio System.* New York: McGraw-Hill, 1981.

Shary, Timothy. "Angry Young Women: The Emergence of the 'Tough Girl' Image in American Teen Films." *Post Script* 19(2), 2000.

Jim (James Dean) and members of Buzz's gang look over Miller's Bluff after the fateful chickie run. *(Courtesy of Photofest)*

12

CLAUDIA SPRINGER

In the Shadow of *Rebel Without a Cause*

The Postcolonial Rebel

IN THE YEARS SINCE JAMES DEAN'S death and rebirth as an icon, his rebel figure's arc of influence has reached far and wide. Hollywood's domination of worldwide film distribution, maintained with the assistance of the U.S. State Department, has guaranteed that its products receive the widest possible exposure. American films join American fast food, American television, and American pop music in their relentless international dispersion. Although there are good reasons to condemn American popular culture's assault on the world, the situation is complex and contradictory. For many young people internationally, pop culture from the United States, no matter how tainted by commercial interests, can be experienced as meaningful. Rather than function as passive consumers of hegemonic American culture, global youths often integrate American cultural products into their own traditions and practices to create new hybrid forms.[1] These composite texts frequently make their way back around the globe, influencing production in the cultural capitals. Considering this "international exchange of commodities," Kwame

Anthony Appiah writes that "[i]f there is a lesson in the broad shape of this circulation of cultures, it is surely that we are all already contaminated by each other."[2]

Young people internationally have identified with James Dean's embodiment of disaffection in *Rebel Without a Cause*, and its influence can be seen in texts from diverse cultures. Dean provided a stylistic paradigm—an archetypal posture—for representing alienation. As film scholar Jon Lewis writes, "It is safe to say that after 1955, youth's resort to a kind of mannered anomie—on screen and on the streets—was patterned after James Dean's performance in *Rebel Without a Cause*."[3] Dean became an iconographic fixture around the world, and although most people are unfamiliar with the details of his life, they instantly recognize the contours of the moody, angst-ridden rebel figure he helped inaugurate. The rebel icon achieved an independent existence that could accommodate all sorts of permutations. Its presence internationally is on the one hand evidence of American cultural hegemony. On the other hand, there are endless possibilities for appropriation. James Dean iconography can be turned back against the American interests that produced it, and, as with any ambiguous icon, its meaning is up for grabs.

At the time of the rebel icon's appearance in the fifties, colonial subjects around the world were energized by dreams of independence and the desire to create nations based on nonexploitive principles. Those dreams and desires carried them through the arduous years of wars for independence. When it came, independence was joyously celebrated, but subsequent years brought disillusionment when some of the early leaders who were beacons of hope, such as Patrice Lumumba in the Congo, were assassinated by political opponents, and subsequent leaders were characterized by corruption and profiteering. Countries with great potential have been consigned to poverty by their rulers and by the trade policies of a globalized world that favor the United States and Europe. Many Third World countries have been transformed into sweatshop factories for the production of the First World's luxury items, with workers earning pennies per hour and often laboring in unsafe conditions under armed guard. These postcolonial realities have replaced the obvious colonial enemy of the past with much more diffuse and anonymous enemies. Resistance without a specific target is difficult and can feel futile.

Two films that appropriate James Dean-style rebel iconography in order to interrogate its relevance to the postcolonial world are *Touki-Bouki*, a 1973 Senegalese film directed by Djibril Diop Mambety, and *La Haine* ("Hate"), a 1995 French film directed by Mathieu Kassovitz. Both films revolve around the powerful attraction of American-style rebel iconography to postcolonial subjects. They are concerned with young people estranged from their communities and struggling to define themselves differently from the norm. In both films, young rebels resist the roles thrust on them and move to the margins of their cultures in an attempt to create their own identities. Their attempts, however, are characterized by confusion as they are consistently caught up in historical, political, and cultural currents they do not fully comprehend. Like Jim Stark in *Rebel Without a Cause*, they chafe against their powerlessness in the face of entrenched institutional authority. Jim's disgust with hypocritical adults was paradigmatically expressed by James Dean's contemptuous slouch. Compelling and easily copied, Dean's stance is picked up by the young rebels in *Touki-Bouki* and *La Haine*. But the postcolonial world is not a sunny southern California suburb. The mid-twentieth-century white middle-class American context of *Rebel Without a Cause* is not entirely germane to young people's turbulent postcolonial predicaments. Jim Stark finds himself deprived of a meaningful existence by the vapid homogeneity of a fifties American suburb. The protagonists of *Touki-Bouki* and *La Haine* also feel deprived, but the causes are rooted in colonial erasure of their cultures' histories and in postcolonial perpetuation of Eurocentric ideology. *Touki-Bouki* and *La Haine* reveal the futility of mimicking the rebel icon, which offers a seductive pose but fails to produce any actual political change.

Touki-Bouki was the first feature film made by director Djibril Diop Mambety (1945–1998), who was twenty-eight years old when the film was released in 1973. Mambety grew up in the small town of Colobane near the Senegalese capital of Dakar, the son of a Muslim cleric, and studied theater in Dakar before turning to film. He was reportedly expelled from acting school because of his rebellious lack of discipline.[4] *Touki-Bouki* was highly acclaimed, winning the Special Jury Award at the Moscow Film Festival and the International Critics Award at Cannes.[5] It is a stunningly powerful film about alienated Senegalese youth in which Mambety's piercing gaze "destroys the possibility of illusion."[6]

Like many African films, *Touki-Bouki* is concerned with postcolonial tensions between African traditions and Western influences. It takes place in the early 1970s in the West African country of Senegal, which had achieved independence from France in 1960. Its interest in the destructive legacies of colonialism links it to the extremely influential book *The Wretched of the Earth*, written by the psychologist Frantz Fanon in 1961. Fanon worked in an Algerian hospital during the French-Algerian war, and in *The Wretched of the Earth* he describes the process of African decolonization and the dangers facing newly independent African nations suffering from the aftermath of colonial devastation. Fanon's analysis of neocolonial identification with the former colonial power is especially relevant to *Touki-Bouki*. Fanon writes:

> During the period of unrest that precedes independence, certain native elements, intellectuals, and traders, who live in the midst of that imported bourgeoisie, try to identify themselves with it. A permanent wish for identification with the bourgeois representatives of the mother country is to be found among the native intellectuals and merchants. This native bourgeoisie, which has adopted unreservedly and with enthusiasm the ways of thinking characteristic of the mother country, which has become wonderfully detached from its own thought and has based its consciousness upon foundations which are typically foreign, will realize, with its mouth watering, that it lacks something essential to a bourgeoisie: money.[7]

In *Touki-Bouki*, postcolonial tensions crystallize in Mory (Magaye Niang), a young man torn between conflicting desires for an African identity and Western trappings of wealth and power. Mory is not an intellectual nor a merchant, but he desperately wants to distinguish himself from his fellow Senegalese. Fanon refers to the national bourgeoisie's "contemptuous attitude toward the mass of the people,"[8] and Mory illustrates the attitude perfectly with his venomous words, "You street-sweeping niggers, you city nigger. I'm not one of you." Mory is guided by a Eurocentric belief that freedom and happiness lie outside of Africa in Europe, where fame and fortune await his arrival.

Mory is a former shepherd who lives in rural Senegal on the outskirts of Dakar but emulates the lifestyle of an American motorcycle rebel and dreams of escaping Senegal for Paris. His youthful anger, directed at authority figures and the monotony of village life, is expressed in a culturally hybrid style: he roars through the countryside on a Western motorcycle, but it is decorated with African ornaments—steer horns mounted on the handlebars and a Dogon cross, a Malian fertility symbol, on the back.[9] The film follows the misadventures of Mory and his university-student girlfriend Anta (Mareme Niang) as they tear through the countryside on Mory's motorcycle, trying through various bungled schemes to steal enough money to book passage to Paris on an ocean liner. In Dakar, the two finally commit robbery successfully and, dressed in expensive stolen Western clothes, start to board a ship bound for Paris. Mory, however, hesitates on the boarding ramp, and, after exchanging a long and silent gaze with Anta, runs back into the city. Anta embarks by herself on the journey to France.

Significantly, Mory and Anta choose to be hyenas by adopting the James Dean stance in defiance of their elders and traditional village life. *Touki-Bouki* means "the hyenas' journey" in Wolof. Nwachukwu Frank Ukadike writes that "In West African oral tradition, this animal (symbolic of 'trickery and social marginality'), [is] notoriously known for its greed and mischievousness, and for its repulsive, nasty smell."[10] Francoise Pfaff asserts that "the animal is used by Mambety in his story, which again opposes nonconventional individuals to the established mores and laws of society."[11] As hyenas, Mory and Anta are outsiders on the perimeter of their culture. They are disdainful of the tiresome routines of village life, and they reject adults' expectations of them. As a result, adults assail them with criticism. Although the language and cultural context are different from *Rebel Without a Cause*, the tone of adult admonishment sounds similar. In *Rebel*, Jim squirms in agony while his mother, father, and grandmother bicker over him at the police station where he has been brought in for public drunkenness late one night. In *Touki-Bouki*, Anta's mother and another woman shout at her that she doesn't respect tradition. Anta responds, "To hell with the traditions!" As she dashes off, her irate mother calls after her, "You'll wind up emptying chamber pots. And your university won't change that. . . . I'm ashamed for you. You and that Mory. What's he riding today? A motorbike or an ox? And that university where you lose all respect. God will punish you someday." Mory, too, is denounced by a woman known as the sorceress who brandishes a bloody knife she has been using to skin a slaughtered goat and shouts at Anta that Mory is a "bum, parasite, and good-for-nothing." Mory and Anta are malcontents in the tradition of Jim Stark, who renounces his parents' anxious, conformist suburban mentality. Likewise, Mory and Anta reject the older villagers' conformity and limited perspectives.

Djibril Diop Mambety discussed his interest in "marginalized people" in an interview:

> I believe that they do more for the evolution of a community than the conformists. Marginalized people bring a community into contact with a wider world. The characters of *Touki-Bouki* are interesting to me because their dreams are not those of ordinary people. Anta and Mory do not dream of building castles in Africa; they dream of finding some sort of Atlantis overseas. Following their dream permitted me to follow my own dreams, and my way of escaping those dreams was to laugh at them. Mory and Anta's dreams made them feel like foreigners in their own country. So they were marginalized people, in that respect.[12]

Mambety values marginalized people for contributing unconventional dreams of alternative lives. Jim Stark in *Rebel* is remembered most vividly for his rejection of his parents' values, but he also briefly carves out an alternative existence with Judy and Plato in an abandoned mansion.

While the ersatz nuclear family they create is not a radical departure from the suburban domesticity they despise, it substitutes empathy and compassion for their parents' emotional paralysis and indifference. Their dream life comes under attack by teenage bullies and misguided police, and it is destroyed when Plato is shot and killed. In *Touki-Bouki* Mory and Anta pursue a more ambitious dream of escape, one that has been handed down to them by the insidious ideology of Eurocentrism. Their dream of fulfillment in France is based on a Eurocentric disdain of all things African and a belief in European superiority. While Jim Stark dreams innocently of a sincere and responsive family when he rejects the status quo, Mory and Anta dream of wealth and power in a postcolonial context that deprives them of their innocence.

Touki-Bouki is Mambety's indictment of Senegal's postcolonial dependence on France. In the film, the French presence is everywhere in Senegal, in the economic infrastructure as well as in the dreams of Senegalese youths. Mory builds an elaborate fantasy about striking it rich in France. He tells Anta, "It's an easy hustle. All we need is a bit of ready cash, throw it around, tip the right guys, play it like we're loaded, hang out where the money is. France, here we come. Paris, the gateway to paradise, and when we come back, they'll call me Mr. Mory." The film comments on his desires with Josephine Baker singing "Paris, Paris, Paris; it's paradise on Earth" nondiegetically (in French) as Mory speeds along on his motorcycle. A level of irony is added by the fact that Josephine Baker's fame in Paris was not based solely on her considerable dancing and singing talents, but was inextricably caught up with her presentation as a "savage" black woman who had to dress in "jungle" attire onstage despite having grown up in East St. Louis, Missouri. Baker's praise for Paris as the gateway to paradise in the song may be fueling Mory's fantasy of French glory, but it should also function to warn him about the reality of French racism.

Instead, Mory's neocolonial dream takes over the diegesis. In an extended fantasy sequence, he and Anta are driven through Dakar in a motorcade, coyly waving at the huge cheering crowds lining the streets, celebrating their triumphant return from France. The fantasy sequence occurs after Mory and Anta have stolen money and clothes, and Mory has stripped naked in the back seat of a stolen chauffeur-driven convertible. The stolen car is an American flag on wheels; it is painted with the red, white, and blue stars and stripes, evoking the American Dream of individual wealth and power that has invaded Mory's consciousness. Mory stands nude, arms outstretched, driven through the dusty countryside, crosscut with shots of cheering crowds in his fantasy. The fantasy becomes more elaborate, with Mory and Anta dressed in fashionable Western clothes receiving the adulation of their wildly enthusiastic fans in Dakar and then arriving at their village, where villagers dance and sing their praise. The sorceress who earlier cursed Mory for owing her money now leads the celebratory singing and dancing. Mory smugly hands her a large wad of cash.

Mory is destined for disillusionment, just as Jim Stark's haven from adult interference is destroyed. *Touki-Bouki* foreshadows Mory's disenchantment with a recurring analogy between him and cattle being led to their deaths in a slaughterhouse. Ironically, the film's cattle motif recalls Jim Stark's brazen "moo" in the planetarium when the constellation Taurus is displayed. Jim, however, lives in a sanitized suburb, far-removed from Mory's dusty environment where humans and cattle live in close proximity. The opening credit sequence of *Touki-Bouki* makes the analogy between Mory's shattered dreams and slaughtered cattle with a shepherd boy riding a steer and leading a herd of cattle across the dusty land to their slaughterhouse deaths. After the cattle arrive at the slaughterhouse and we see one of them killed in an unflinching long take, the shepherd (who might be Mory as a child) returns alone, slowly and methodically riding his steer accompanied by the nondiegetic sound of a traditional African flute. The loud roaring sound of a motorcycle intrudes on the shot, joining the flute in a jarring clash. A shock cut suddenly places the viewer with Mory speeding through a village on the motorcycle adorned with cattle horns, while shouting and cheering children run alongside him. The camera tracks quickly, capturing the motorcycle's exhilarating speed while its raucous engine fills the soundtrack.

Like the cattle, Mory also sets a course across the countryside without understanding that he is drawing closer to his destruction, although what awaits Mory is not literal death but rather the death of his dream. When he finally reaches the Dakar harbor and the ship bound for Paris, seemingly fulfilling the first step in his dream, he is confronted by the disdain of white racist Europeans for Africans. A sequence of shots onboard a luxury yacht presents fashionably dressed, rich white Europeans, young and old, lounging about, loudly condemning Senegal as intellectually barren. A white man opines that "African art is a joke made up by journalists in need of copy," and the Senegalese are put down as "big children" who "have no heart." Meanwhile black men carry heavy baggage onto the ship, doubled over from the weight of their cargo and the insults they endure. When Mory encounters French racism at the harbor, he confronts the experience of being unwillingly excluded.

Mory's neocolonial fantasy thus crashes against the reality of racism when he reaches the ship, the symbol of transit between Senegal and France. His decision to flee from the ship back into Dakar is nonverbal, represented only visually, and relies for meaning on a complex juxtaposition of sounds and images. Shots of Mory running from the ship are crosscut with the barren white ship's deck, where Anta looks lost and alone, often decentered in the static shots, overwhelmed by the cold impersonal ship that represents white European power. The confident physicality she has exhibited up until that point has been replaced by small hesitant gestures, and she nervously clutches her suitcase like a lifeline. The shots of Mory are in sharp contrast; the camera tracks rapidly as he runs headlong through the streets. His body seems to be flinging itself back into his familiar surroundings, away from the ship's threatened oblivion. Loud, jarring, dissonant music and shouts fill the soundtrack, while the shots of Mory and Anta are crosscut with cattle being put to death in the slaughterhouse. Mory's flight from the ship is a figurative rejection of servitude to France: the former colonial power. Although the film's open ending does not provide Mory with a solution to his conflicting desires, he has escaped Anta's shipboard confinement and its implications of loss of self.

Postcolonial divisiveness permeates the film. In one powerful sequence, Mory and Anta have stopped in an outdoor stadium where a wrestling match is about to take place. An announcer informs the gathering crowd that this athletic event is part of a long partnership between France and Senegal, and that the proceeds will be used to purchase a memorial honoring General de Gaulle. Mory and Anta, motivated by the dream of obtaining French wealth, steal a large wooden box outside the stadium, hoping that it contains the match's proceeds. Their theft on the one hand signifies a return of misappropriated African wealth to two Africans—Mory and Anta—but, on the other hand, they intend to spend it on their own pursuit of French luxuries. As it turns out, Mory has chosen the wrong box, one containing a skull and amulet, the fetishes of one of the wrestling contestants. The two boxes that Mory chooses between represent two related concepts: one contains a huge cache of money destined to commemorate Senegalese subservience to France; the other contains a skull, a literal signifier of Senegalese death as a result of the destructive legacy of French colonial power.

Touki-Bouki is effective in capturing the conflicts and ambiguities running through postcolonial Senegalese society. Early in the film we see shots of Anta, wearing Western trousers and shirt, studying at an outdoor desk in the vast impoverished shantytown outside of Dakar where she lives while dozens of other women in traditional robes scrub clothes in buckets of water and line up for their water rations. There is a sharp contrast between the westernized Anta studying and the traditionally garbed women performing manual labor. The contrast between the old and the new becomes heightened soon after when Anta disrupts her mother's traditional ways and is harshly scolded as a result. Anta's mother is dressed in a traditional robe and sits at her small vegetable stand waiting for customers. When one arrives, Anta's mother complains that her son hasn't written to her from Paris for a long time. Her customer commiserates: "Ah, France! Nothing good comes of it. White women and clap. Ask our marabouts to bring your son back." Anta's mother hastens to explain that her son went to Paris to study. The customer has filled her basket and tells Anta's mother, "Put it on my tab. I'll pay when my husband returns." Just then Anta arrives, grabs the produce from the woman and says, "My ass! You pay now. We want a TV too." It is at this point that the two women shout at Anta that she doesn't respect tradition and she exclaims, "To hell with the traditions!" The scene concisely illustrates the clash of traditional communal values with new western-inspired individualism. For Anta's mother, empathy for her customer outweighs the economic imperative, and their shared understanding is part of the flexible give-and-take of village life. Instead of trying to understand her mother's perspective, Anta flees with Mory, but at the end it appears that her energetic spirit is about to be broken by the crushing weight of French racism.

Touki-Bouki represents Mory and Anta's restlessness stylistically as well as in its narrative. The film eschews the realist aesthetic of *Rebel Without a Cause* in favor of elliptical editing and a disruptive visual style that some critics have labeled avant-garde. In both its characterizations and its stylistic discontinuities, *Touki-Bouki* resembles Godard's *Breathless* (1959): Mory is a drifter and petty thief who is full of dreams but is consistently ineffectual, not unlike Michel in *Breathless*, and both young men team up with women students drawn to their nonconformity. Godard's Michel, a generic hybrid, owes some of his traits to James Dean. The route from Dean to Michel to Mory follows rebel iconography's trajectory from Hollywood to France to Senegal, each culture inflecting it with its own particular context. While *Rebel Without a Cause* served as an inspiration for films about disaffected young people, it did not inspire stylistic imitation by Godard or Mambety. By 1959, when Godard made *Breathless*, Nicholas Ray's overwrought melodramatic Hollywood aesthetic seemed ill-suited to convey a young rebel's unsettled edginess, and the same was true for Mambety in 1973.

There is disagreement among critics about whether *Touki-Bouki*'s experimental style derives from Western modernism or reflects an African sensibility that captures the fractured inconsistency of postcolonial African life. Nwachukwu Frank Ukadike characterizes the two opposing views: ". . . while non-African critics have read the film as an avant-gardist manipulation of reality, an Africanist analysis would attempt a reconfigurative reading that synthesizes the narrative components and reads the images as representing an indictment of contemporary African life-styles and sociopolitical situations in disarray."[13] Ella Shohat and Robert Stam point out that techniques Westerners typically perceive as their own avant-garde tradition often have antecedents in the artistic practices of the Third World. They write that "one cannot assume . . . that 'avant-garde' always means 'White' and 'European,' or that Third World art, as Jameson sometimes seems to imply, is always realist or premodernis."[14] Ghanaian-British director John Akomfrah states that *Touki-Bouki* is

> not technically an avant-garde film, if by avant-garde people mean that it's trying to do something weird. It is more a portrait of African urban reality which is profoundly suffused with the tempering of that reality. Everybody knows about the restlessness that you see in towns and cities, in Accra and Lagos. This is one of the few films which actually captures that to-ing and fro-ing—not only through storytelling but also through a narrative parody of that movement. It's very graceful.[15]

What is interesting about the debate over *Touki-Bouki* is that cultural dislocation governs every aspect of the film, from its plot to its style to its critical reception. Mambety made cultural hybridity the inescapable center of his film. When asked by N. Frank Ukadike where *Touki-Bouki*'s jarring and discontinuous style comes from, Mambety responded that "it's the way I dream" and that "cinema must be reinvented, reinvented each time, and whoever ventures into cinema also has a share in its reinvention."[16] For Mambety, *Touki-Bouki* is a personal film that expresses his particular vision in a manner that he felt was necessary to tell the story of Mory and Anta's fractured lives.

The motorcycle's exhilarating speed and the James Dean-style rebel stance are powerfully seductive for Mory and Anta, and also for another rebel who turns their quest upside down, replacing their fantasy of opulence with its opposite. He is a young white man who lives in a large baobab tree, wearing animal skins and long hair and carrying a Stone Age-style ax. He steals Mory's motorcycle from Anta, who runs in terror from this crazed wild man who has presumably fled European values in pursuit of a back-to-nature fantasy. The motorcycle acts as a shared symbol of rebellion for these very different rebels, but the rebel stance it confers fails as effective political action. Mambety indicates as much early in the film when he portrays the allure of the motorcycle as essentially sexual. When Anta makes love to Mory alongside his motorcycle, we don't see Mory; instead, we see close-ups of Anta's hand clutching the Dogon cross on the back of the motorcycle. By excluding Mory from the shots of lovemaking, Mambety makes the motorcycle Anta's lover, and, like Kenneth Anger in his film *Scorpio Rising* (1964), reveals the sexual energy invested in the rebel's motorcycle by its love-struck enthusiasts. At the end of the film, the motorcycle has been destroyed by the white wild man in an accident that has left him badly injured, with one observer commenting, "From the baobab tree to a motorcycle. Now there's a jump that can kill you." Anta has set sail for France, and Mory is alone.

What undermines Mory and Anta's quest is that they choose to express their marginalization by rejecting Africa and dreaming of luxuries associated with France. They have chosen to distance themselves from traditional villagers but have not found a viable alternative. Political activism is ruled out when they are excluded by students involved in political organizing. Early in the film Mory arrives at the university on his motorcycle to meet Anta, and his path is blocked by a group of young male students riding in the back of a pickup truck. They shout at him, "Think this is a circus?" and accuse him of being responsible for Anta's arriving late at their meetings. One of them mutters that women just want to be screwed. They attack Mory, dragging him from his motorcycle with a rope as if he were a steer and tying him up on the back of the truck where he stands with outstretched arms as if crucified. His humiliation is crosscut with the slaughter of a goat, heightening the sense of his status as a sacrificial victim. These students, the film indicates, may think of themselves as politically progressive, but their disdain for the working-class Mory and their misogynistic dismissal of Anta mark them as retrograde elitists and render their political efforts futile.

Mory and Anta, like hyenas, and like Michel in *Breathless*, respond to their situation by preying on people. Mory descends on Charlie, a rich gay Senegalese man who fancies him. While the stereotypically effeminate and simpering Charlie waits for Mory in the bath, Mory steals all of his clothing and flees. In the meantime, Anta has lifted another guest's wallet. They steal Charlie's car (the one painted like an American flag) and light out for the travel agency to book passage to France. The film's evocation of gay desire hearkens back to *Rebel Without a Cause*. Plato's adoration of Jim is decidedly homoerotic, and Jim is nonjudgmental as he accepts Plato's friendship. The homoerotic implications were more explicit in the film's original script, causing the Production Code Administration to require several cuts.[17] Contemporary knowledge of Sal Mineo's gay sexuality and James Dean's bisexuality lend their scenes together a poignant sexual frisson. *Touki-Bouki* falls back on a buffoonish gay caricature, but includes a self-reflexive joke when Charlie phones the police department to report the theft and speaks to an officer whom he reminds of their previous sexual encounter. The officer's name is Mambety.

Mory and Anta are momentarily elated by the robbery, but their dream cannot sustain them, and they are left with less than they had. Each one is alone at the end of the film: Anta decentered and displaced onboard the sterile white ship, and Mory running away in panic without a goal. Mambety leaves us with two lost souls and an open ending; their future is uncertain. A flashback to Mory and Anta after they have made love, stretched out beside the motorcycle on a cliff overlooking the sparkling sea, is a brief reminder of a moment of harmony, one that emphasizes the beauty of Africa without fantasies of fame and fortune overseas.

Interestingly, Mambety himself remained curious about his protagonists' fates, especially Anta's, and revisited them nineteen years later when he made his second feature film, *Hyenas* (1992). According to Mambety, "I began to make *Hyenas* when I realized I absolutely had to find one of the characters in *Touki-Bouki*."[18] Elsewhere he explains, "In *Hyenas* the two characters from *Touki-Bouki* reappear: the girl who leaves to cross the Atlantic and the boy who stays on the continent as if he has betrayed her."[19] *Hyenas* was Mambety's last feature-length film. He died of lung cancer in 1998 at age fifty-three.

The 1995 French film *La Haine* ("Hate"), directed by Mathieu Kassovitz, could be seen as an alternative vision of what might have happened to Mory and Anta, or, more accurately, to their children, had they sailed to Paris together. Mory dreamt of French riches and of the glamour promised by Josephine Baker's lyrics, but in *La Haine* the lives of dispersed postcolonial subjects in France are anything but glamorous. As the title suggests, *La Haine*, which won the award for Best Director at the 1995 Cannes Film Festival, is shot through with rage at the continued existence of French racism and institutionalized injustice.

Made forty years after *Rebel Without a Cause* and twenty-two years after *Touki-Bouki*, *La Haine* is evidence that Jim Stark's adolescent fury is still relevant. Transposed into completely different contexts, Jim's smoldering anger is a powerful model for the frustration felt by young people growing up in societies marked by hypocrisy. Jim represents the clarity with which young people can see their society's faults, especially the lies told by official discourses about the existence of equal opportunities for all of its citizens. *Rebel Without a Cause* resonates through the decades and across the globe because it transcends its particular setting to provide a template for social criticism infused with the strong emotions of adolescence.

La Haine concerns three young men who live in an HLM *(habitation à loyer modéré)*, a low-income housing project, outside Paris. Each of the three friends represents an immigrant group: Sayid (Saïd Taghmaoui) is of Arab descent, Vinz (Vincent Cassel) is Jewish, and Hubert's (Hubert Koundé) origins are African. *La Haine* revolves around the violence and frustration of everyday life in an HLM, where immigrants encounter constant hardships that include their vilification by the police, the media, and the French political right wing. As Kevin Elstob writes in a review of the film, ". . . *Hate* covers much terrain. It interweaves root causes of social and political unrest in France today: immigration, racism, exclusion, poverty, crime, and violence."[20]

What Mory and Anta in *Touki-Bouki* did not realize is that one of the legacies of French colonialism is a strong French right-wing hatred of immigrants from the former colonies. The issue of immigration has generated enormous tension in France and has revealed the depths of right-wing racism in the virulently xenophobic rejection of immigrants and their descendents. Ironically, the official French policy of transforming colonial subjects through education into French citizens never resulted in widespread acceptance of those new French citizens in France. According to Alec G. Hargreaves and Mark McKinney,

> . . . tensions are nowhere more acute than in relation to minorities originating in ex-colonies who have now settled in France. French-speaking to a very large extent, yet culturally distinct in other ways and still marked by exclusionary memories of the colonial period, these minorities defy the political logic of francophonie by being residents and in many cases citizens of France while appearing to many among the majority population to belong elsewhere.[21]

Hostility is not directed solely at the immigrants themselves, but also at their descendents. As Hargreaves and McKinney write, "These aspects of the neo-colonial gaze affect second- and third-generation Maghrebis [North Africans] as much as their immigrant forebears."[22] There have of course been a few immigrants who have been treated as dignitaries in France. One such dignitary, Leopold Senghor, the first president of Senegal after it gained its independence from France in 1960, who held office until 1980, retired from politics to Normandy with his French wife, was elected to the Académie Française, and on his ninetieth birthday was honored by French President Jacques Chirac.[23] Hargreaves and McKinney observe, however, that

> [t]he majority of France's post-colonial minorities are to be found in more humble milieux, foremost among which are the *banlieues* (literally, "suburbs"), which in the 1990s have become a byword for

> socially disadvantaged peripheral areas of French cities containing relatively dense concentrations of minority ethnic groups.[24]

Mory and Anta, unlike their countryman Leopold Senghor, might easily have ended up in an HLM, and if they had had children, those children might have grown up in the milieu depicted by Mathieu Kassovitz in *La Haine*.

Vinz, Hubert, and Sayid are like angry descendents of Jim Stark stuck in a suburban wasteland and contemptuous of conformist drones. They wear tight jeans and leather jackets and swagger like the juvenile delinquents who caused a nationwide panic in the United States in the 1950s and inspired the script for *Rebel Without a Cause*. But Jim Stark's cozy middle-class suburb is a far cry from an impoverished HLM. And unlike the confused policeman's shot that kills Plato, the violence in *La Haine* is part of a consistent pattern of police brutality directed against minority racial and ethnic groups relegated to the desolate margins of the city. The three friends in *La Haine* are fully aware of their outsider status, and it is their shared sense of entrapment in a rigid class system that allows their friendship to transcend the conflicts that divide their ethnic and racial groups. When they get annoyed with each other, they often hurl racial and ethnic epithets, but the insults are used loosely and also metaphorically, so that even the Jewish Vinz asserts that he doesn't want to be "the next Arab iced by the pigs." These are rebel outsiders whose lives are in jeopardy every day. The film centers on two themes that both echo with aspects of *Rebel Without a Cause*. First, there is the nature of the police force and its relationship to discontented young people. Second, there is the problem of where alienated youths can turn for meaningful guidance. Jim in *Rebel* wants desperately to be guided by his spineless father. The three young men in *La Haine* do not expect much from their families. Instead, ironically, they turn to pop culture and the media, to texts such as *Rebel Without a Cause*, for their life lessons.

The three young men's bleak lives are conveyed in *La Haine*'s stark and gritty black-and-white cinematography and in their aimless drift through twenty-four hours, which is given structure with intertitles that interrupt the narrative to announce the time of day. The narrative begins at 10:38 in the morning and ends at 6:01 the following morning. But the structure imposed by references to the precise time of day is misleading, for it doesn't correspond to structure in the young men's lives. There are several moments in the film when an intertitle interrupts a scene, only to return to the same scene and virtually the same shot. Nothing has changed. But *La Haine* is not only a film about bored, restless kids without purpose in their lives, for these young men are caught up in fierce social conflicts and political battles. The dilemma they face is how to respond effectively, how to be authentic rebels when the rebel stance packaged by the media is hopelessly incapable of providing clarity or producing results.

The film's main theme is the question of how to respond to violence. It is introduced in the prologue when, accompanied by a black screen, a male voiceover asks, "Heard about the guy who fell off a skyscraper? On his way down past each floor he kept saying to reassure himself: 'so far so good.' " The black screen dissolves to a long shot in color of the earth in space, and the voiceover continues: "How you fall doesn't matter. It's how you land." At this point, a molotov cocktail falls to earth from space, and the planet explodes. The film edits to a black-and-white shot of an exploding car and then the unfolding confrontation between protesting young people and riot police. A television newscast reports that the riots, in which young people attacked a police station in the Muguet projects, began two days ago in response to alleged police brutality. A local teenager was severely beaten under questioning and the police officer responsible was suspended. The victim, Abdel Ichaha, is hospitalized in critical condition.

The planet earth, destroyed in the prologue by the molotov cocktail, is a motif in the film, appearing on billboard advertisements accompanied by the words, "The world is yours" (*Le monde est à vous*). This phrase is a reference to the 1932 gangster film *Scarface*, in which the rise and fall of kingpin Tony "Scarface" Camonte is underscored by a neon sign with the same phrase. When Tony is at the height of his power, surrounded by wealth and luxuries, the world is indeed his, but at the end of the film, the same phrase is cruelly ironic as Tony's world has crashed around him and he is killed by the police. In *La Haine*, the phrase is never anything but ironic, since the three young men never experience a rise to success. To them, the phrase is a cruel taunt, causing one, Hubert, to squeeze his eyes shut in an agonized grimace when he reads it, and another, Sayid, to spray paint the word "*vous*" to read "*nous*," meaning "The world is ours." By the end, it is clear that the world is anything but theirs.

The idle young men in the HLM have been left behind by the system; they have no hope of employment or escape from poverty. Gangsta rap music surrounds them, venting their frustration and providing them with a contemporary version of the classic gangster tales like *Scarface*. *La Haine* illustrates three different styles of resistance to the system: Sayid is an opportunist and hustler who tries to turn situations to his advantage; Vinz tries to turn the violence of the system against it, becoming brutal in response to brutality; and Hubert desperately wants to escape and seeks a conciliatory stance that will end the self-perpetuating cycle of death. Sadly, the social forces they oppose prove too powerful for any of their strategies, and two of them are destroyed at the end of the film. Sayid, the opportunist, survives, but only through happenstance; clearly, he could be the next victim.

The teasing, bantering name-calling indulged in by the three friends contrasts with the virulent racism they encounter elsewhere. Most horrifically, Hubert and Sayid are tortured by a cop who has tied them to chairs in an interrogation room and beats and insults them. Before bringing them in, he proves himself no different from the criminals he is supposed to stop; he finds cocaine on Sayid and says "Good stuff, I'm keeping it" and launches into a monologue on the merits of different kinds of cocaine. At the police station, he tells Hubert, whose arms and legs are bound, to pick something up with his feet "like your people do back home." The torturer tells another cop, "They're great with their feet." Sayid is called an "Arab sonofabitch" by the same cop. Jim Stark's gentle treatment in the police station in *Rebel* could not be farther from this viciousness. Jim has a heart-to-heart talk with Ray, an avuncular police officer who encourages him to punch a desk to let off steam and invites him to come back any time. Hubert and Sayid are tortured. The cop in *La Haine* is a racist and psychotic sadist, but the question posed by the film is whether he is an anomaly who has found an officially sanctioned niche to practice his violence or whether his brutal racism is instead a manifestation of the French power structure it is his job to protect and maintain.

There is some ambiguity early in the film about whether the police are all corrupt thugs. A police lieutenant intervenes after the three friends get in a scuffle with police guarding the hospital room of their comatose friend, Abdel, the victim of police brutality. They are not allowed to see Abdel, and Sayid is arrested for his persistence. When the lieutenant tells Hubert and Vinz that the police are protecting Abdel, Hubert asks, "Who protects us from you?" Even after the lieutenant arranges for Sayid's immediate release, the three friends remain guarded with him, and Vinz responds with disgusted rage when Hubert and Sayid agree to shake the lieutenant's hand. This cop appears to be concerned about their welfare, but the three friends reject his good will. The film refuses to adopt the rhetoric of institutional benevolence displayed in *Rebel* when the kindly officer establishes a bond with Jim, breaking through his hostility with calm and sympathetic firmness. In *La Haine*, even Hubert's moderate stance—his rejection of acts of violent retribution against the police—is only an acknowledgment of the overwhelming power of the police force, not a belief in the possibility of police altruism.

In a pivotal scene that takes place in a public restroom, the friends, primarily Hubert and Vinz, argue about the appropriate response to police brutality. Vinz at this point has possession of a policeman's gun and has declared that he will shoot a cop if their friend Abdel dies. Their conversation begins as Hubert and Vinz relieve themselves. Hubert says that "Wanting to kill a cop is jackshit." Vinz responds that he didn't say that, only that if Abdel dies, he'll kill a cop. He continues that without his gun back there (they just escaped from a pursuing cop when Vinz drew his gun and prepared to shoot, but Hubert, a boxer, punched the cop to prevent the shooting and allow them to flee) they would've been history, "or my name's not Rodney King." Hubert answers, "It's not the same thing." Vinz then accuses Hubert and Sayid of doing nothing to change things even though "we live in rat holes." He repeats that if Abdel dies, he'll kill a cop "so they know we don't turn the other cheek now!" Sayid interjects: "Wow! What a speech. Half Moses, half Mickey Mouse." Hubert says, "Forget it Vinz, you're out of your league." He points out that if Abdel dies, they lose a friend; but if Vinz kills a cop, cops don't all go away, adding, "You're just one guy. You can't blow them all away." Vinz asks, "Who made you a preacher? You know what's right and wrong?" Hubert responds that "in school we learned that hate breeds hate." Vinz answers, "I didn't go to school; I'm from the street. Know what it taught me? Turn the other cheek, you're dead, mothafucka!"

The film's tragic irony is that after a series of events propel Vinz to reject his vengeful stance, a new situation suddenly invalidates both of their positions and destroys them. First, a television news report announces that Abdel has died from his injuries. Sayid and Hubert abandon Vinz, with Sayid saying, "You want to kill a pig, go ahead. But you're on your own. We're outta here." Shortly after, a group of racist skinheads attacks Sayid and Hubert, but Vinz appears with his gun. All the skinheads but one scatter, and Vinz holds the remaining one at gunpoint, shouting to Hubert, "You think I'm all talk? Watch! Try and stop me!" Sayid does try to stop him, but Hubert takes the opposite approach, sarcastically urging Vinz on: "Go ahead and do it. Do your good deed! The only good skinhead is a dead skinhead: shoot him! . . . Do it for Abdel." After an agonizingly long pause, Vinz is unable to shoot the trembling skinhead. The prospect of shooting an unprotected human being at close range leaves Vinz shaking and gagging.

After Vinz's change of heart, events quickly come to a crashing end. The three friends catch the first morning train out of Paris to their housing project. Back home in bright daylight, they part in the courtyard, yawning after their night in the streets. Before he leaves, though, Vinz gives his gun to Hubert, signaling that cop-killing is no longer his goal. Vinz and Sayid walk away, only to have a police car careen to a stop beside them and two policemen jump out and grab them. The cops hurl insults at them and one cop points his gun directly at Vinz's head, taunting him and pretending to shoot. The gun suddenly fires, and the cop stares in surprise as Vinz slumps, dead, to the ground. Vinz has died as a result of a cop's cruel, careless bravado. Hubert has meanwhile run over to join his friends, and when Vinz is shot, pulls the gun Vinz had just relinquished to him and points it at the cop who fired the shot. The cop simultaneously trains his gun on Hubert. The cop and Hubert hold guns at each other's heads in an anguished stand-off that symbolizes the destructive futility of the larger confrontation between the police and angry youths. The voiceover from the opening of the film returns with the lines, "It's about a society falling. On the way down, it keeps telling itself, 'so far so good, so far so good, so far so good.' How you fall doesn't matter." The camera zooms into a close-up of Sayid's horrified face. As he shuts his eyes in a helpless grimace, there is an offscreen gunshot. The screen goes black as the narrator finishes, "It's how you land."

The film doesn't reveal who was shot, Hubert or the cop, but, clearly, Hubert is doomed either way. In a split-second decision, Hubert has sacrificed his life out of loyalty to his friend Vinz and out of unspeakable outrage. The film thus ends with an ironic and tragic twist that renders futile Hubert's avoidance of violent confrontation. Avoidance is pointless, the film suggests, because state-sanctioned police violence seeks out young minority men condemned as troublemakers. Up until the end, the film could be read as endorsing Hubert's pacifist stance, but that is no longer possible—or at the very least it is problematic—after the cop blows away Vinz.

Hubert, Sayid, and Vinz cast about for an effective response to state-sponsored violence, but their reference points are banal and trap them in incomprehension and paralysis. The "truths" to which the three friends turn time and time again all derive from pop culture, which is incapable of providing adequate role models or solutions. It cannot even pose the right questions. The pop culture references in the film are mostly, but not exclusively, from American films and TV programs. As Kevin Elstob writes,

> Today's suburban Parisian youth thrive on Anglo-American rap, reggae, and rock music, incorporate American and African fashion into their dress code, and spray-paint New York style graffiti on walls and bridges. At the same time, the immigrants among them are expected to assimilate in a country where 15 percent of voters back the National Front, the extreme right-wing political party whose xenophobic, reactionary platform advocates, among other things, repatriating all immigrants.[25]

The three friends in *La Haine* turn to pop culture to fashion their rebel personae, gazing into mirrors to practice the style they have chosen. James Dean's rebel icon is only one of their influences. In his mirror, Vinz practices drawing a gun and mimics the notorious lines of Robert DeNiro's character Travis Bickle in *Taxi Driver*: "You talkin' to me?! You talkin' to me?!" Like Travis Bickle, Vinz's head is shaved and he is bare-chested. Vinz chooses vigilante violence more because his idol Bickle resorts to violence than because Vinz understands the ramifications of his choice.

Vinz is not the only one who invents himself in the mirror. In his mirror, Sayid makes faces and says, "I'm Senor Duck: I fucka you, I fucka her, I fucka him. . . ." He then asks Vinz to give him a haircut so he can get lucky with a girl that night. When Vinz butchers his hair, Sayid is furious, and Vinz tries to placate him by saying, "It's the style in New York. The killer cut. So stop whining." New York is their cultural mecca. Later, walking through the Parisian streets at night, they engage in an impassioned debate about the merits of American cartoon characters.

> Vinz: Coyote's a bad motherfucker. Roadrunner's a pussy. Pick between Tweetie and Sylvester.
>
> Sayid: . . . I say Sylvester's the real gangsta.
>
> Vinz: . . . I say Tweetie's the baddest. He always wins.
>
> Hubert: Sylvester fucks Tweetie and you! . . . Anyway, Sylvester's a black brother.

Their experiences are all filtered through pop culture. It envelopes their lives, providing touchstones that are sometimes ridiculous (while botching an attempt to hotwire and steal a car, one asks the others, "How'd they do it on TV?" as they try to remember MacGyver's technique) and sometimes poignant, as when Hubert says that he identifies with Sylvester as a black brother.

Mass media imagery and iconography constitute a large aspect of the young men's shared experience in *La Haine*, but they are left without representational models equal to the complexity of their circumstances. Neither James Dean nor Travis Bickle nor the full roster of American cartoon characters can teach them how to effectively oppose racism, unemployment, poverty, or police brutality. *La Haine* shows that HLM dwellers are not just passive consumers of pop culture, but their appropriations of it have only limited effectiveness. As Hargreaves and McKinney write,

> . . . the markers—graffiti, music, dancing, dress codes, etc.—through which young *banlieusards* (literally, "suburb dwellers") seek to

> reterritorialize the anonymous public housing projects in which they are corralled are saturated with references to global networks of multiethnic youth culture in which they participate daily through the mass media.[26]

Kevin Elstob describes a significant scene in the film when the peacefulness of a quiet afternoon is shattered by a young disc jockey. With two enormous speakers placed in the window of his fifth- or sixth-story apartment, he mixes and samples Edith Piaf singing "Je ne regrette rien" ("I have no regrets") and "Police," a powerful anthem by the French rap group Supreme NTM—sung in French with a chorus that includes the English line "Fuck the police."[27] The sampled music succeeds in providing a heightened sense of community among disaffected young people, and it loudly announces their rage and sense of alienation, but it cannot provide a solution to the young men's dilemma of how to respond to police brutality.

The film leaves ambiguous whether pop culture is entirely a paralyzing trap for the young men or whether it also gives them a symbolic sense of strength. Traps are everywhere in the film's mise-en-scène with its emphasis on circular courtyards, walls, locked doors, narrow corridors, claustrophobic rooms, and tunnels. Perhaps pop culture is as much a trap as the physical environment that prevents these young men from escaping oppression. However ineffective American pop culture is in the film, *La Haine* acknowledges that it is an undeniable aspect of young French people's lives; the film does not endorse its control by the French state. A feature of French right-wing ideology is the desire to protect the French language from "corruption" by English phrases. It was in this spirit that French President "Chirac's administration was . . . fighting a hopeless rearguard action against the ever-widening inroads made by the English language and American popular culture into the everyday cultural practices of the French."[28] Hargreaves and McKinney point out that

> [t]he latest innovation in this unequal struggle consisted of revised quotas, introduced at the beginning of 1996, requiring radio stations to prioritize "French" songs over those in other languages. One of the ironies of these and earlier quotas has been to facilitate the emergence of rap as a major force on the contemporary music scene in France. Short of new songs meeting the official quota criteria, broadcasters have filled their vacant air time with rap recordings by minority ethnic *banlieusards* featuring French-language vocals adapted from black American models.[29]

The French state's efforts to preserve an ideal of French purity are ludicrous given the hybrid nature of lived experience, certainly in postcolonial times, but even long before. Cross-cultural borrowings have a history that predates even the European "age of exploration." The notion of national purity is a mythic one:

> Few, if any, individuals are entirely mono-cultural. Although they may not always realize it, most people participate—whether as producers, consumers or intermediaries—in a variety of cultural communities. To the extent that a sense of identity is derived from such communities, multiple identities are the norm, rather than exceptional features of personal experience. The proliferation of ever more sophisticated communication networks implies, moreover, a constant challenge to simplistic notions of neat demarcation lines between "national" cultures. To a greater or lesser degree, all cultures are engaged in a constant process of renewal, which is driven in part by borrowings from elsewhere.[30]

One way in which pop culture's rebel stance shapes the young friends in *La Haine* is to validate their machismo. The confused vulnerability of James Dean in his three films has been abandoned by these young men in favor of swaggering male heterosexuality. Women in the film are primarily sex objects, and the young men treat them with a mixture of predatory fascination and disdain. The three friends' bonds are tight but lack the homoerotic overtones of Jim Stark and Plato in *Rebel Without a Cause*. No matter how persecuted the young men in *La Haine* feel, they gain a sense of power from being men, but always at the expense of women.

La Haine broadens its context from the nuclear family of *Rebel Without a Cause* to encompass vital political issues. The problems faced by Vinz, Hubert, and Sayid are more critical than those faced by Jim Stark in *Rebel*, who only had to contend with a dysfunctional family and high school bullies. *Rebel* leads us to believe that the police shot Plato out of helpless ignorance, not viciousness. *La Haine* shows us a consistent pattern of police violence against young residents of HLMs. The film refuses to engage in vilifying the young men's families for their problems and it avoids *Rebel*'s armchair psychology. The three friends in *La Haine* would have little to gain from reconciliation with their fathers; their problems are much larger and more profound.

The film in fact pokes fun at its own status as a rebel film with characters who shrug in clichéd despair at the state of kids today. In one scene, the three friends have been thrown out of an opening at an upscale Parisian art gallery for causing a disturbance. At the door, Hubert shouts back into the gallery, "Go suck cocks in hell." The gallery director turns to the elegant patrons and shrugs, saying, "Troubled youth!" Ironically, Sayid falls back on the same cliché after he berates his younger sister for skipping school and hanging out with her friends in the projects. "Kids these days!" he mutters in an exasperated tone. In yet another twist on the cliché, Vinz is chastised by his grandmother who thinks he is responsible for burning down the school. She predicts the trajectory of his bad behavior: "You'll start that way and then you'll skip temple." Rather than condemn the grandmother for misunderstanding Vinz, the film and Vinz himself treat her with gentle amusement. *La Haine* is intelligently self-conscious about the conventions of rebel films and enlists them ironically. It acknowledges that audiences expect to see certain conventions in films about teenagers, but refuses to reduce the young men's circumstances to fit the conventional molds.

Rebel Without a Cause launched its charismatic young hero into the world where he is still a model for alienated adolescents. And alienation is an understandable response to the conflicts and tensions of the postcolonial world. In the James Dean-style rebel icon, disaffected postcolonial youths find the archetypal outsider, still exerting a powerful influence after half a century. While acknowledging the appeal of the rebel stance, *Touki-Bouki* and *La Haine* also challenge its ability to provide an effective position from which to oppose injustice. Eurocentrism, racism, poverty, and police brutality are crushing adversaries. The rebel icon is no match for their devastating exclusivism and violence.

Notes

1. This process is captured in *Ça Twiste à Popenguine*, a 1993 Senegalese film directed by Moussa Sene Absa, in which Senegalese youth in 1964 adopt the names and styles of French pop stars and American R & B performers in the context of life in a small Senegalese fishing village where the reign of strict Christian and Islamic elders and the rigid schooling in French language and history are experienced as stifling.
2. Appiah (119, 124).
3. Lewis (20).
4. Sklar (41).
5. Mambety (1999, 1).
6. Sklar (42).
7. Fanon (178).
8. Fanon (179).
9. Ukadike (221).
10. Ukadike (176).
11. Quoted in Ukadike (176).
12. Mambety (1999, 2–3).

13. Ukadike (173).
14. Shohat and Stam (294).
15. Akomfrah (38).
16. Mambety (1999, 3).
17. Alexander (209–10).
18. Sklar (42).
19. Mambety (1995, 38).
20. Elstob (45).
21. Hargreaves and McKinney (4).
22. Hargreaves and McKinney (19).
23. Hargreaves and McKinney (12).
24. Hargreaves and McKinney (12).
25. Elstob (44).
26. Hargreaves and McKinney (26).
27. Elstob (45).
28. Hargreaves and McKinney (13).
29. Hargreaves and McKinney (13).
30. Hargreaves and McKinney (11).

Works Cited

Akomfrah, John. "Dream Aloud: John Akomfrah, the Ghanian-British Director, on the Exhilaration of African Cinemas," (interview by June Givanni). *Sight and Sound* 5.9 (September 1995): 37–39.

Alexander, Paul. *Boulevard of Broken Dreams: The Life, Times, and Legend of James Dean*. New York: Viking, 1994.

Appiah, Kwame Anthony. "The Postcolonial and the Postmodern." In Bill Ashcroft, Gareth Griffiths, Helen Tiffin, eds. *The Post-Colonial Studies Reader*. London: Routledge, 1995.

Elstob, Kevin. "Review of *Hate* ('La Haine')." *Film Quarterly* 51.2 (winter 1997–98): 44–49.

Fanon, Frantz. *The Wretched of the Earth*. New York: Grove Press, 1963.

Hargreaves, Alec G. and Mark McKinney. "Introduction: The Post-Colonial Problematic in Contemporary France." In Alec G. Hargreaves and Mark McKinney, eds., *Post-Colonial Cultures in France*. London: Routledge, 1997.

"In Memoriam: Djibril Diop Mambety." *Library of African Cinema 2000* (California Newsreel catalog of film and video): 13.

Lewis, Jon. *The Road to Romance and Ruin: Teen Films and Youth Culture*. New York: Routledge, 1992.

Mambety, Djibril Diop. "African Convesations: An Interview with Djibril Diop Mambety," (interview with June Givanni). *Sight and Sound* 5.9 (September 1995): 30–31.

———. "The Hyena's Last Laugh: A Conversation with Djibril Diop Mambety," an interview by Nwachukwu Frank Ukadike. California Newsreel Library of African Cinema online, www.newsreel.org/articles/mambety.htm, originally published in *Transition 78* 8.2 (Durham and London: Duke University Press, 1999): 136–53.

Shohat, Ella and Robert Stam. *Unthinking Eurocentrism: Multiculturalism and the Media.* New York: Routledge, 1994.

Sklar, Robert. "Anarchic Visions." *Film Comment* 36.3 (May–June 2000): 40–43.

Ukadike, Nwachukwu Frank. *Black African Cinema*. Berkeley: University of California Press, 1994.

Cast and Production Credits

Cast (in credits order)

James Dean .... Jim Stark
Natalie Wood.................................... Judy
Sal Mineo .... John "Plato" Crawford
Jim Backus .... Frank Stark
Ann Doran .... Mrs. Stark
Corey Allen .... Buzz Gunderson
William Hopper .... Judy's father
Rochelle Hudson .... Judy's mother
Dennis Hopper .... Goon
Edward Platt .... Ray Fremick
Steffi Sidney.. Mil
Marietta Canty............................... Plato's Nurse
Virginia Brissac .... Mrs. Stark
Beverly Long .... Helen
Ian Wolfe .... Dr. Minton (lecturer at planetarium)
Frank Mazzola .... Crunch
Robert Foulk .... Gene
Jack Simmons....................................... Cookie
Tom Bernard .... Harry
Nick Adams .... Chick
Jack Grinnage .... Moose
Clifford Morris .... Cliff

Rest of cast listed alphabetically

Dorothy Abbott............................ Nurse (uncredited)
Jimmy Baird .... Beau (Judy's little brother) (uncredited)
Paul Birch .... Police Chief (uncredited)

Paul Bryar .... Desk sergeant #2 (uncredited)
Louise Lane .... Policewoman (uncredited)
Nelson Leigh .... Desk sergeant #1 (uncredited)
David McMahon .... Crunch's father (uncredited)
Peter Miller .... Hoodlum (uncredited)
Bruce Noonan .... Monitor admonishing Plato (uncredited)
House Peters Jr. .... Officer at police station (uncredited)
Stephanie Pond-Smith .... Girl (uncredited)
Nicholas Ray .... Man in last shot (uncredited)
Gus Schilling .... Attendant (uncredited)
Almira Sessions .... Old lady teacher (uncredited)
Dick Wessel .... Planetarium guide (uncredited)
Robert Williams .... Ed (Moose's father) (uncredited)

Production Credits
Directed by
Nicholas Ray

Writing Credits
Nicholas Ray (story)
Irving Shulman (adaptation)
Stewart Stern (screenplay)

Produced by
David Weisbart

Original Music by
Leonard Rosenman

Cinematography by
Ernest Haller

Film Editing by
William H. Ziegler (as William Ziegler)

Production Design by
Malcolm C. Bert (uncredited)

Art Direction by
Malcolm C. Bert (as Malcolm Bert)

Set Decoration by
William Wallace

Costume Design by
Moss Mabry

Makeup Department
Gordon Bau . . . . Makeup Artist

Second Unit Director or Assistant Director
Don Alvarado. . . . . Assistant Director (as Don Page)
Robert Farfan. . . . . Assistant Director

Sound Department
Stanley Jones . . . . Sound

Stunts
Rodney Amateau . . . . Stunt Double (uncredited)
Ron Burke . . . . Stunts (uncredited)

Other Crew
Dennis Stock . . . . Dialogue Supervisor
Frank Mazzola . . . . Technical Advisor (uncredited)
Floyd McCarty . . . . Still Photographer (uncredited)

Selected Bibliography

Alexander, Paul. *Boulevard of Broken Dreams: The Life, Times and Legend of James Dean*. New York: Viking, 1994.

Andrew, Geoff. *The Films of Nicholas Ray: The Poet of Nightfall*, second ed. London: BFI, 2004.

Biskind, Peter. *Seeing Is Believing: How Hollywood Taught Us to Stop Worrying and Love the Fifties*. New York: Pantheon, 1983.

Briley, Ron. "Hollywood and the Rebel Image in the 1950s." *Social Education* 61.6 (October 1997): 352–58.

Byars, Jackie. *All That Hollywood Allows: Re-Reading Gender in 1950s Melodrama*. Chapel Hill: University of North Carolina Press, 1992.

Considine, David M. *The Cinema of Adolescence*. Jefferson, NC: McFarland, 1985.

Dalton, David. *James Dean: American Icon*. New York: St. Martin's Press, 1984.

DeAngelis, Michael. *Gay Fandom and Crossover Stardom: James Dean, Mel Gibson, and Keanu Reeves*. Durham, NC: Duke University Press, 2001.

Doherty, Thomas. *Teenagers and Teenpics: The Juvenilization of American Movies in the 1950s*, revised and expanded ed. Philadelphia: Temple University Press, 2002.

Dyer, Richard. "Don't Look Now: The Male Pin-Up." In "*Screen*," *The Sexual Subject: A "Screen" Reader in Sexuality*. London: Routledge, 1992.

Eisenschitz, Bernard. *Nicholas Ray: An American Journey*, trans. Tom Milne. London: Faber and Faber, 1993. Originally published in 1990.

Elsaesser, Thomas. "Nicholas Ray (Part 1)." *Brighton Film Review* 19 (April 1970).

Gilbert, James. *A Cycle of Outrage: America's Reaction to the Juvenile Delinquent in the 1950s*. New York: Oxford University Press, 1986.

Kreidl, John Francis. *Nicholas Ray*. Boston: Twayne, 1977.

Lewis, Jon. *The Road to Romance and Ruin: Teen Films and Youth Culture*. New York: Routledge, 1992.

Lindner, Robert. *Rebel Without A Cause: The Hypnoanalysis of a Criminal Psychopath*. New York: Grune & Stratton, 1944.

May, Elaine Tyler. *Homeward Bound: American Families in the Cold War Era*. New York: Basic Books, 1988.

McCann, Graham. *Rebel Males: Clift, Brando and Dean.* New Brunswick: Rutgers University Press, 1991.

McGee, Mark Thomas, and R. J. Robertson. *The J.D. Films: Juvenile Delinquency in the Movies.* Jefferson, NC: McFarland, 1982.

Morin, Edgar. *The Stars*, trans. Richard Howard. London: William Morrow, 1972. Originally published in 1960.

Neale, Steve. "Masculinity as Spectacle." *"Screen," The Sexual Subject: A "Screen" Reader in Sexuality.* London: Routledge, 1992.

"Nicholas Ray: le lyrisme." *Etudes Cinématographiques* 8–9 (second edition trimester, 1961).

Perkins, V. F. "The Cinema of Nicholas Ray." *Movie* 9 (May 1963).

Pettigrew, Terence. *Raising Hell: The Rebel in the Movies.* New York: St. Martin's Press, 1986.

Rathgeb, Douglas L. *The Making of Rebel Without a Cause*, foreword. Stewart Stern. Jefferson, NC: McFarland, 2004.

Ray, Nicholas. *I Was Interrupted: Nicholas Ray on Making Movies*, ed. and intro. by Susan Ray. Berkeley: University of California Press, 1993.

———. "Story into Script." *Sight and Sound* (Autumn 1956): 70–74.

Roffman, Peter, and Jim Purdy. *The Hollywood Social Problem Film: Madness, Despair, and Politics from the Depression to the Fifties.* Bloomington: Indiana University Press, 1981.

Rosenbaum, Jonathan. "Circle of Pain: The Cinema of Nicholas Ray." *Movies as Politics.* Berkeley: University of California Press, 1997.

———. "Looking for Nicholas Ray." *American Film* VII. 3 (December 1981).

Shulman, Irving. *Children of the Dark.* New York: Holt, Rinehart, and Winston, 1956.

Simmons, Jerold. "The Censoring of *Rebel Without a Cause.*" *Journal of Popular Film and Television* 23.2 (Summer 1995): 56–63.

Spoto, Donald. *Rebel: The Life and Legend of James Dean.* New York: Harper Collins, 1996.

Wagner, Jean. *Nicholas Ray.* Paris: Rivages/Cinema, 1987.

Contributors

Daniel Biltereyst (PhD 1993, Brussels University) is a professor in film, television, and cultural media studies at the Department of Communication Studies, Gent University, Belgium, where he leads the Working Group in Film and TV Studies. His work on film and television as central fora for public debate, controversy, and censorship has appeared in journals such as *Media, Culture & Society*, and *European Journal of Cultural Studies* and readers such as *Cinema of the Low Countries* and *Understanding Reality TV*. More information can be found at www.psw.rug.ac.be/comwet/wgfilmtv.

Mick Broderick teaches Media Analysis at Murdoch University, Perth and is Associate Director of the Centre for Millennial Studies at the University of Sydney. He is author of *Nuclear Movies* and *Hibakusha Cinema: Hiroshima, Nagasaki and the Nuclear Image in Japanese Film.*

Jon Lewis is a professor of English at Oregon State with five books to his credit, including *Hollywood v. Hard Core: How the Struggle over Censorship Saved the Modern Film Industry* and *The End of Cinema as We Know It: American Film in the Nineties*. In 2003, Lewis was named Editor of *Cinema Journal*.

Elena Loizidou is a lecturer in Law at Birkbeck Law School, University of London. She researches and publishes in the areas of criminal law and criminal justice, gender and sexuality, and law and cultural representations. Loizidou is a coeditor of *Law's Moving Image* and is currently completing a book on Judith Butler and Critical Legal Theory.

James C. McKelly is Associate Professor of English at Auburn University. He specializes in twentieth-century American cultural studies, film studies, and modernism, and has published his work in *Screen*, *African American Review*, and *Profession*. He is currently working on a series of articles theorizing contemporary American cinema.

Jon Mitchell has taught at UCD, Trinity College Dublin, and NUI Maynooth for the last three years. He also previously taught the American history module at the University of Wales, Lampeter (2000–2001). He was educated at the University of Glamorgan, Pontypridd (BA 1997), and the University of Wales, Swansea (PhD 2002). His research interests include masculinity and American identity in mid-twentieth-century American fiction, and Millennialist influences upon American culture, both from a new Americanist perspective. Mitchell's article on "Policing 'The Last Barrier of Civilization': Secular Millennialism and the 'Salvation' of Anglo-America" will be included in the forthcoming edition of the *Irish Journal of American Studies.*

Murray Pomerance is Chair and Professor in the Department of Sociology at Ryerson University. He is the author of *An Eye for Hitchcock*, *Johnny Depp Starts Here*, and *Magia d'Amore*, and the editor of *American Cinema of the 1950s: Themes and Variations* and *BAD: Infamy, Darkness, Evil, and Slime on Screen*, both published by the State University of New York Press.

Nicholas Ray (1911–1979) wrote the original story for, and directed, *Rebel Without a Cause.*

Timothy Shary is the director of the Screen Studies program at Clark University in Worcester, Massachusetts. He is the author of *Generation Multiplex: The Image of Youth in Contemporary American Cinema* and is completing two new books on teen film history.

J. David Slocum is Associate Dean of the Graduate School of Arts and Science at New York University, where he teaches Cinema Studies and Art & Public Policy. He is the editor of *Violence and American Cinema* and *Terrorism, Media, Liberation*, and the author of the forthcoming *Cinema and the Civilizing Process: Violence and American Movies, 1894–1964.*

Claudia Springer is a professor in the English Department and Film Studies Program at Rhode Island College, where she also directs the Graduate Program in Media Studies. She is the author of the book, *Electronic Eros: Bodies and Desire in the Postindustrial Age.*

Susan White is Associate Professor of English at the University of Arizona, where she is an award-winning teacher. Her research interests focus on genre and intersections between film and literature, and she is the author of numerous essays in film history. She also serves as the Film Editor of *Arizona Quarterly*.

George M. Wilson is Professor of Philosophy at the University of California, Davis. His main areas of research are philosophy of language, theory of action, and aesthetics (film and literary theory). He is the author of *Narration in Light: Studies in Cinematic Point of View* and *The Intentionality of Human Action*. Recent articles include studies of reference and pronominal descriptions, semantic realism and Kripke's Wittgenstein, and film narration. He has held a fellowship at the National Humanities Center and has been a visiting professor at Princeton, Harvard, and the University of Padua.

Index

www.ingramcontent.com/pod-product-compliance
Lightning Source LLC
LaVergne TN
LVHW042322150826
845780LV00023B/73
9780791466469